What Happened on the Cross

What Happened on the Cross

Forgiveness Not Punishment

Nick Peros

Foreword by Cyril Guérette

WIPF & STOCK · Eugene, Oregon

WHAT HAPPENED ON THE CROSS
Forgiveness Not Punishment

Copyright © 2020 Nick Peros. All rights reserved. Except for brief quotations in critical publications or reviews, no part of this book may be reproduced in any manner without prior written permission from the publisher. Write: Permissions, Wipf and Stock Publishers, 199 W. 8th Ave., Suite 3, Eugene, OR 97401.

Wipf & Stock
An Imprint of Wipf and Stock Publishers
199 W. 8th Ave., Suite 3
Eugene, OR 97401

www.wipfandstock.com

PAPERBACK ISBN: 978-1-7252-6369-7
HARDCOVER ISBN: 978-1-7252-6363-5
EBOOK ISBN: 978-1-7252-6364-2

Manufactured in the U.S.A.   08/06/20

Scripture quotations marked (NIV) are taken from the Holy Bible, New International Version®, NIV®. Copyright © 1973, 1978, 1984, 2011 by Biblica, Inc.™ Used by permission of Zondervan. All rights reserved worldwide. www.zondervan.com. The "NIV" and "New International Version" are trademarks registered in the United States Patent and Trademark Office by Biblica, Inc.™

Scripture marked (NKJV) taken from the New King James Version®. Copyright © 1982 by Thomas Nelson. Used by permission. All rights reserved.

Scripture quotations marked (NASB) taken from the New American Standard Bible® (NASB), Copyright © 1960, 1962, 1963, 1968, 1971, 1972, 1973, 1975, 1977, 1995 by The Lockman Foundation. Used by permission. www.Lockman.org

Scripture quotations marked (NLT) are taken from the Holy Bible, New Living Translation, copyright ©1996, 2004, 2015 by Tyndale House Foundation. Used by permission of Tyndale House Publishers, a Division of Tyndale House Ministries, Carol Stream, IL 60188. All rights reserved.

Scripture quotations marked (NIrV) are taken from the Holy Bible, New International Reader's Version®, NIrV® Copyright © 1995, 1996, 1998, 2014 by Biblica, Inc.™ Used by permission of Zondervan. All rights reserved worldwide. www.zondervan.com. The "NIrV" and "New International Reader's Version" are trademarks registered in the United States Patent and Trademark Office by Biblica, Inc.™

Scripture quotations marked (RSV) are from the Revised Standard Version of the Bible, copyright © 1946, 1952, and 1971 National Council of the Churches of Christ in the United States of America. Used by permission. All rights reserved worldwide.

Scripture quotations marked (TLB) are taken from The Living Bible copyright © 1971. Used by permission of Tyndale House Publishers, a Division of Tyndale House Ministries, Carol Stream, IL 60188. All rights reserved.

Scripture quotations marked (CJB) taken from the Complete Jewish Bible by David H. Stern. Copyright © 1998. All rights reserved. Used by permission of Messianic Jewish Publishers, 6120 Day Long Lane, Clarksville, MD 21029. www.messianicjewish.net.

Scriptures marked (YLT) taken from Young's Literal Translation, public domain; Scriptures marked (ASV) taken from American Standard Version, public domain; Scriptures marked (Geneva Bible) taken from Geneva Bible, public domain.

Contents

Foreword by Cyril Guérette | vii
Introduction | ix

PART I: THE BEGINNING | 1

1. Creation | 3
2. Darkness—The Curse of God | 21
3. Angels | 34
4. Description of Lucifer/Satan | 43
5. The Angelic Rebellion | 53
6. The Restoration | 79
7. The Creation of Man | 87
8. Eden and the Testing of Man | 101
9. The Temptation and Fall of Man | 116
10. The Aftermath of the Fall | 130
11. God's Unfolding Plan—Sacrifice and the High Priest | 160

PART II: THE CROSS | 183

12. God the Son | 185
13. The Incarnation | 203
14. The Second Man, the Last Adam, the High Priest | 213
15. The Temptation in the Desert | 226
16. The Crucifixion | 235
17. The Realm of the Dead | 276
18. The Resurrection | 287
19. It is Finished | 310

Foreword

WHAT HAPPENED ON THE Cross addresses a topic that remains a thriving public debate in contemporary academic and pastoral theology: the nature of the work of salvation accomplished by Jesus on the cross. This conversation strikes at the heart of what it means to be Christian, and it is a source of the upheaval of faith for many of the upcoming generation. The question is as simple as it is profound: How can God have punished his Son for the sins of every person on earth and still have been just? In this work, Nick Peros takes a fresh look at the questions involved and offers a Bible-centered, comprehensive approach to the topic of how our salvation was accomplished at Calvary.

One of the most intriguing aspects of *What Happened on the Cross* is it does truly offer a new and refreshing paradigm for seeing the nature of salvation, which is a significant accomplishment in its own right. Whatever theory of atonement you may hold to currently, you can expect to be genuinely challenged by Peros's presentation as he grapples with an enormous amount of biblical literature from both the Hebrew Scriptures and the New Testament.

The current debate today largely centers around a Reformed view of penal substitution which has been standard to most Evangelical preaching for centuries, and which is now being challenged by evolving questions and a strong resurgence of the *Christus Victor* view popular with a growing Anabaptist theological school of thought. Peros challenges both views, arguing you can't ignore the need for the blood of Jesus in the biblical account of atonement, but it doesn't represent divine punishment. The *Christus Victor* view often leaves those conducting close study of the word of God trying to understand the special emphasis put on Jesus' blood in its pages. Likewise, the penal substitution view presses those of us who are adherents with troubling questions about divine child abuse.

Peros is careful to allow a bulk of Scripture to speak as he builds his case, and in doing so creates a nuance that is engaging. This work stands out amongst many modern writings on the subject as it does not interact with modern theologians by name but instead belongs to an older form of systematic theology that brings it closer to biblical theology. By painting a picture of the theological theme of salvation all the way from the creation to Revelation, the author builds an argument for a unique view of the physicality or the reality of sin, and the need for an incarnate God to finally wash away our sins permanently.

The author's theological acumen becomes apparent despite not using the traditional academic style. The project is harkening back to times when a writer went about building a case for a theological doctrine from the Scriptures themselves, not relying on other theologians and thinkers to create a case. Peros has built a fresh picture of redemption spanning from Genesis to Revelation; a systematic theology that adheres to the authority of the Bible. With almost 750 Scripture verses used to support the argument, the reader becomes aware this work is predicated upon a firm foundation. The author speaks quite strongly at times, more certainly than many of us in professional theological academia are used to, but this passion for the truth is what drove him to discover new connections and present a bold and original picture of salvation.

As this is a theological hot-button topic, the timing of this work for publication couldn't have been better. Peros's presentation of key themes helps any reader get a better understanding of the Scriptures involved in the current atonement theory debate and will be enjoyed for its unique perspective by people on both sides or those confused who are looking for a good guide. As a theologian, I recommend *What Happened on the Cross* for its faithfulness to Scripture and novel philosophical insight, and as a pastor, I can recommend it as a conversation partner to help the average Christian think through the complexities of an important topic—our salvation in Jesus.

Dr. Cyril Guérette (PhD, MPhil, BTh)
Assistant Professor of Biblical Studies and Theology,
Tyndale University College
Lead Pastor, Groundswell Church (www.thegroundswellchurch.com)

Introduction

THE INCARNATION, CRUCIFIXION, AND resurrection of Jesus Christ are the central events of human history. Two thousand years ago, Jesus Christ was conceived and born of a virgin, the Son of God—God incarnate—married forever to human flesh. At age thirty, Jesus began his public work, living a sinless life, and revealing himself as the Messiah. At age thirty-three, he was crucified under Pontius Pilate, giving himself as a sacrifice upon the cross for the sins of humanity. He died upon the cross, and three days later, he rose from the dead—the living and resurrected Lord, who by his death and resurrection provided salvation for all humanity.

The resurrection of Jesus Christ is the proof Jesus accomplished on the cross what he had set out to accomplish, namely, the salvation of all humanity and the redemption of all creation. But what exactly took place on the cross that allowed for this to be accomplished? What was happening on the cross that resulted in salvation for all? *How* was this salvation accomplished?

During the Reformation a new idea was proposed which described how salvation was accomplished on the cross. Over the years, this view has taken a firm hold of many Christians' understanding of what happened on the cross. This new view is described as "penal substitution" and is an extension of the "substitution" ideas of Anselm, the eleventh-century Archbishop of Canterbury.

In this view, all human beings are required to be punished for their sins, but Jesus Christ hung on the cross in place of you and me in order to bear the punishment for our sins. Further, while Jesus hung on the cross, having been crucified in place of every man and woman who has ever lived or will ever live, God the Father divinely punished Jesus, instead of us, for all the sins we have ever committed or will ever commit. In so doing, God the Father poured out his divine wrath upon Jesus Christ, instead of upon us, so as to satisfy his divine justice—which, according to the theory of penal substitution, is the requirement of God's law. Penal substitution holds that, in being punished for all of the sins of humanity, Jesus Christ satisfied the full requirement of God's law.

The key element behind this view is God's justice is tied to his divine law—if God's law is broken or transgressed, then the law demands punishment. Only by punishing transgression can God maintain his perfect justice.

The punishment referred to in this view is not the physical punishment inflicted upon Jesus Christ by human hands, but rather a divine punishment poured out upon Jesus Christ by God the Father. This divine punishment is described as the wrath of God, and is in addition to the physical punishment suffered by Jesus through his flogging and crucifixion at the hands of the Romans.

According to the penal substitution view, this divine punishment was owed by us, to God, for committing sin and transgressing his law. In this view, we, humanity, owe a debt to God. As a result of Jesus taking our punishment upon himself on the cross, being punished for us on our behalf while on the cross, the requirement of God's law was satisfied, and the penalty, or debt, exacted by God's law has been paid for on behalf of all humanity. As a result, we no longer need to pay any penalty for our sins. By believing in Jesus Christ, we partake in what he accomplished for us on the cross, partake of him bearing the punishment for each of our sins, and, as a result, our sins are now no longer counted against us and there is no longer any punishment remaining for our sins. As a result, we can now have a right relationship with God.

The problem with the penal substitution view is it is completely unbiblical and has no scriptural support. There is not a single verse in Scripture that connects a sacrifice for sin with punishment—the very concept of a sin sacrifice being the recipient of punishment does not exist in the Bible. There is not a single verse in Scripture that says God poured out his wrath upon *any* Old Testament sacrifice for sins, nor upon Jesus Christ while he hung upon the cross. There is not a single verse in Scripture that says Jesus Christ was punished by the Father for our sins; there is not a single verse in Scripture that says Jesus Christ was our substitute upon the cross; there is not a single verse in Scripture that says Jesus Christ paid any penalty upon the cross.

Introduction xi

The Bible never says our sins have been *paid* for, rather, we are told repeatedly and specifically that, because of what Jesus Christ did on the cross, our sins have been *forgiven*—not paid for, not punished, but forgiven. Jesus himself offers a precise understanding of what he means by forgiveness in the parable of the unmerciful servant found in Matthew 18.

> "Then Peter came to Jesus and asked, 'Lord, how many times shall I forgive my brother or sister who sins against me? Up to seven times?' Jesus answered, 'I tell you, not seven times, but seventy-seven times. Therefore, the kingdom of Heaven is like a king who wanted to settle accounts with his servants. As he began the settlement, a man who owed him ten thousand bags of gold was brought to him. Since he was not able to pay, the master ordered that he and his wife and his children and all that he had be sold to repay the debt. At this the servant fell on his knees before him. 'Be patient with me,' he begged, 'and I will pay back everything.' The servant's master took pity on him, canceled the debt and let him go." (Matt 18:21–26 NIV)

This parable shows clearly what Jesus means by forgiveness. In this parable, a servant owed his master a very great deal of money. The master at first demanded payment, whereupon the servant, who could not in any way pay such a large debt, begged for more time, promising he would pay the master back. The master, seeing this, was moved by mercy and forgave the entire debt. This does not mean the master found someone else who would pay that servant's debt on the servant's behalf, but rather, the debt was completely and fully *canceled*—it was completely *forgiven*, left unpaid, never to be paid, so that no debt remained. This is how Jesus illustrates forgiveness.

According to Jesus's illustration of what it means to forgive—and in this case what it means specifically to forgive a debt—forgiveness means to let the offense go, to cancel it, to truly forgive it so it remains forever *unpaid*. It does not mean the debt is paid for by some other party on behalf of the debtor. In this same way, the Bible teaches us that God has *forgiven* our sins:

> "All the prophets testify about him that everyone who believes in him receives forgiveness of sins through his name." (Acts 10:43 NIV)

"In him we have redemption through his blood, the forgiveness of sins, in accordance with the riches of God's grace." (Eph 1:7 NIV)

"... in whom we have redemption, the forgiveness of sins." (Col 1:14 NIV)

"I am writing to you, dear children, because your sins have been *forgiven* on account of his name." (1 John 2:12 NIV)

The Bible tells us repeatedly that because of what Jesus Christ did on the cross, our sins have been *forgiven*. According to Jesus's own illustration of what it means to forgive, to have our sins forgiven means our sins have been *canceled*—they have been let go, to remain forever unpaid. If our sins had instead been *paid for* by Jesus Christ on the cross by way of him being punished for our sins on our behalf, then our sins have never been forgiven, nor canceled, but rather paid for. It is impossible to have sins be both *paid for* and *forgiven*—these two things are contradictory.

If, on the cross, Jesus was not punished for our sins, and did not pay any penalty for our sins, how then could our sins be forgiven? Where is the justice in that? The Bible never refers to Jesus Christ as "the Lamb of God who pays for the sin of the world," rather, he is described as "the Lamb of God who takes away the sin of the world" (John 1:29 NKJV). By his sacrifice on the cross, Jesus Christ did not *pay* any penalty for our sins, rather, he *took our sin away*. This is how salvation was accomplished.

But what does it mean to take our sin away? How was that done, and how is it just? If our sins have never been punished, doesn't that mean God is not just? How we understand what happened on the cross speaks directly to how we understand the character and nature of God. What kind of God is he? Is he a God who demands satisfaction, punishment, and vengeance, or is he a God of love, mercy, and forgiveness? In fact, Jesus taking our sin away is a magnificent witness to God's supreme and perfect justice, founded in his great and infinite love.

The foundation upon which we are to understand what happened on the cross—of how and why our salvation was accomplished—is to understand that Jesus Christ is the Second Adam. In fact, this is the true grace of God, that there even was a Second Adam (referred to in the Bible as the Last Adam because, even though Jesus Christ is the Second Adam, he is also the Last Adam, since after Jesus Christ there will never be another Adam. In this book the term "Second Adam" will be used interchangeably with the "Last Adam").

In order to understand the nature and work of the Second Adam—to ultimately understand what happened on the cross—we must first understand the nature of the First Adam, the father of humanity, and the fall of man. In order to fully understand the First Adam and the fall of man, we must also understand creation, the angelic rebellion, and the origin of sin—we must understand the beginning.

PART I

The Beginning

1

Creation

In the beginning, God created the Heavens and the earth.
(Gen 1:1 NIV)

God is Creator

THE BIBLE TELLS US God is the creator, he is the maker of all things, and nothing exists apart from him. The Bible tells us this creation happened "in the beginning."

The Beginning

What is "the beginning?" The beginning is defined as the initial creation of time and space. Too often, we think of time and space as some sort of preexisting, eternal elements—but they are not. Until God created time and space, they did not exist. Time and space are in fact the physical fabric of creation, they are the canvas upon which the rest of creation was made. Time and space were created by God first, before he created anything else.

Time had a Beginning

Second Timothy 1:9 testifies to the fact that time had a beginning when it tells us: ". . . This grace was given us in Christ Jesus before the beginning of time" (NIV). We are told here that time had a "beginning." We, as creatures of time and space, cannot comprehend the concept of the creation of time, nor do we even have the language to speak of such a thing since all of our language, as well as our nature, is completely subject to time. Yet, it remains true that time is as much a created thing as is the moon or a rock. When 2 Timothy 1:9 talks about "the beginning of time," this is, in fact, the same "beginning" as outlined in Genesis 1:1. The creation of time is "the beginning."

Time and Space: The Fabric of Creation

Existing hand in hand with time is space. Time and space are united elements, the one is inextricably tied in its nature to the other. Time is as much the nature of space as space is the nature of time, and together they act as the fabric of God's creation.

The term "fabric of creation" means the physical foundation upon which all the rest of creation would be constructed. This concept of the fabric of creation, the foundation upon which all creation was to be laid, is affirmed throughout Scripture:

> He stretches out the Heavens like a canopy, and spreads them out like a tent to live in (Isa 40:22 NIV).

> The Lord wraps himself in light as with a garment; he stretches out the Heavens like a tent (Ps 104:2 NIV).

> The Lord your Maker, who stretches out the Heavens and who lays the foundations of the earth (Isa 51:13 NIV).

In each of these verses, as well as in many others, God's creative act is described as a "stretch[ing]" out of the heavens—these are the heavens of Genesis 1.1—with those heavens being spread out like a "tent" or a "canopy." These are words and images of fabric and material. All the heavens exist only within and upon the foundation of time and space, so as God "stretches" out the heavens, and "spreads" them out like a tent, it is implicit that includes the foundational fabric upon which the heavens are laid, and that foundational fabric is the fabric of time and space.

The Fabric of Creation Created First

Since time and space are the foundational fabric of creation, they were created before the heavens and the earth that were to be laid upon that fabric, and therefore the creation of time and space constitutes the beginning. In Genesis 1:1, the "beginning" *precedes* the creation of the heavens and the earth. Since "the beginning" precedes the creation of the heavens and the earth, and since the creation of time and space constitutes "the beginning", this again affirms that time and space was created first, and then, as stated in Genesis 1:1, the heavens and the earth were created next.

Time and space, as the foundational fabric of creation, are themselves wholly physical and, as such, define the physicality of God's creation. All of God's creation as created in Genesis 1.1, including all the heavens, is constructed upon the foundation of time and space and, as such, is therefore just as physical as is time and space. The entirety of God's creation is a physical creation.

The Heavens

In Genesis 1:1, after the "beginning," after the creation of time and space, God then created the heavens. Why is the word "heavens" plural? If we contrast Genesis 1:1 with Revelation 21:1, we see a slight difference:

> In the beginning God created the heavens and the earth. (Gen 1:1 NIV)

> Then I saw a new heaven and a new earth, for the first heaven and the first earth had passed away, and there was no longer any sea. (Rev 21:1 NIV)

In Genesis 1:1, God is described as creating the "heavens," while Revelation 21:1 describes a new "heaven." Why is "heavens" in Genesis 1:1 plural while in Revelation 21:1 it is not? What does this difference mean?

The Three Heavens

Genesis 1:1 is an account of the initial act of creation by God, while Revelation 21:1 is not. As a result, Genesis 1:1 is describing a different event than is Revelation 21:1, and the Genesis 1:1 description is a very specific and exact description of the initial creation.

In the Bible, the term "the heavens" is a collective term that refers to three types of heaven. From the perspective of standing on the earth, when we look up, we see the heavens as follows: First, we see the sky that surrounds the earth, which is defined as the first heaven. Second, when we look beyond the earthly sky, we see what we call outer space, where the sun, moon, stars, and galaxies reside, which is the second heaven. Beyond outer space is the place where God has established his throne within his creation, the place which we call Heaven (referred to here as "Heaven" to distinguish it from the other two heavens)—the Bible calls this, the place of God's throne, the third heaven. As a result, the plural term "heavens" referenced in Genesis 1:1 encompasses all three types of heaven, and describes *each* of the three types of heaven as being created in "the beginning."

The Third Heaven

The third heaven, the place where God has established his throne, which we commonly refer to simply as "Heaven," is specifically referred to by Paul as the "third heaven" in 2 Corinthians 12:2, "I know a man in Christ who fourteen years ago was caught up to the third heaven" (NIV). The third heaven, referred to here by Paul, is the same heaven where God has established his throne. Paul's use of the term "third heaven" affirms the Bible's description of three different types of heaven—the earthly sky, outer space, and Heaven—with the three different types of heaven collectively referred to in Genesis 1:1 by the term "the heavens." As a result, when Genesis 1:1 tells us God created the "heavens," this plural term is referring to, and includes, all three aspects of that term: it includes the creation of Heaven, the place where God has established his throne within his creation, and which is the home of God's holy angels; it includes what we call outer space, the place where the sun, moon, stars, and galaxies reside; and it includes the earthly sky, or the atmosphere around the earth. All of this is included in the term "heavens," and it was all created in Genesis 1:1.

The Third Heaven—The Seat of God's Throne

From the perspective of standing on Earth, when we look up at the sky, we see first the earthly sky, the first heaven, and then we see outer space, the second heaven, and then, from our perspective, the third heaven is beyond that. However, from God's perspective, this order is reversed, and when Genesis 1:1 tells us God created the "heavens," God in fact created the heavens in that *reversed* order. What we call the third heaven, the place where God established his throne within the creation, was actually the first of the heavens God created, and what we call the second heaven (outer space) was created second, and what we call the first heaven, the earthly sky, was created third, created in conjunction with the earth.

As a result, after God created time and space—the foundational fabric of creation upon which he would create the entire universe—the next thing God created was Heaven, where God would establish his throne within his creation.

Too often we think of God's Heaven, the place of his throne, as some sort of preexisting, eternal abode of God, that it has always been and that, like God, it is eternal and uncreated. This is not true. Heaven, the place where God decided to temporarily establish his throne, is a created place within creation and is as much a part of God's physical creation as is the sun or the moon. Like all of God's creation, Heaven had a beginning. As a created place, Heaven is also subject to—and was created both within and upon—time and space. In fact, Heaven is just as physical as everything else in creation.

The Physicality of Heaven

Time and space are physical elements, and together they define the nature of God's creation—all of God's creation is *physical*, since all of God's creation is subject to time and space, for the very definition of "physical" means to be subject to time and space. Heaven is a created place within God's creation, created as one of the heavens in Genesis 1:1, in "the beginning" and is therefore subject to time and space. As a created place within time and space, Heaven is just as physical as is all the rest of God's creation, no less physical than Earth, and as a part of God's physical creation Heaven itself has a physical location within the universe.

The Physical Location of Heaven

Hebrews 4:14 testifies to the fact that Heaven has a physical location within God's creation when it tells us of Jesus Christ's ascension to Heaven: "Therefore, since we have a great high priest who has passed through the heavens . . ." (NASB). Hebrews 4:14 describes the ascension of the resurrected Jesus Christ to (the third) heaven, to take his seat at the right hand of God the Father. We are told here that as Jesus ascended to Heaven, he did so by first *passing through the heavens*. Once again, the word "heavens" here is plural. "Heavens" refers to the fact that, in order for Jesus to ascend from Earth to reach the third heaven, the seat of God's throne, Jesus had to first *pass through* the other two heavens, having to pass through the earthly sky (the first heaven), and then the rest of space (the second heaven) before reaching Heaven (the third heaven)—the earthly sky and outer space are the *heavens* through which Jesus Christ passed as he ascended to the third heaven. Just as the first heaven and the second heaven are unquestionably physical, and have measurable locations, and since Jesus had to pass through those two physical heavens in order to reach the third heaven, this tells us the third heaven—Heaven itself—is also just as physical as the other two heavens and, as a result, also has a measurable location in the universe. In fact, based on Hebrews 4:14, we can understand the physical location of Heaven as being just past, or outside, the edge of the universe (that is, just past the second heaven—outer space—since Jesus had to pass through the second heaven in order to reach the third heaven).

In addition, there are numerous verses that further describe the location of Heaven, describing it as being physically beyond, or *above*, the first and the second heavens:

> Be exalted, O God, *above the heavens;* let your glory be over all the earth. (Ps 57:5 NIV)

> The Lord is exalted over all the nations, his glory *above the heavens.* (Ps 113:4 NIV)

> Let them praise the name of the Lord, for his name alone is exalted; his splendor is *above the earth and the heavens.* (Ps 148:13 NIV)

> Such a high priest truly meets our need—one who is holy, blameless, pure, set apart from sinners, exalted *above the heavens.* (Heb 7:26 NIV)

In each of these verses, God's glory and splendor are referred to as being "above the heavens." This is not just a metaphorical statement of exaltation, rather it is an actual description of physical reality. The term "the heavens" here refers again to the first and second heavens, which are the same heavens through which Jesus Christ passed as he ascended to

Heaven to take his seat at the right hand of the Father in Hebrews 4:14. Just as Hebrews 4:14 implicitly tells us the third heaven—the place where God has established his throne—is beyond the first and second heavens through which Jesus ascended, likewise the verses in Psalms further affirm this when they describe God's glory and exaltation as being located "above the *heavens.*" This is a description of physicality, a description of location, and again affirms the third heaven has a physical location in the universe. According to the verses in Psalms, this third heaven is not only located at the edge of the created universe, but is also located in an upward direction, or *above* the earth, beyond the other two heavens (Ps 148:13). All of this testifies to the physicality of the created heaven.

God's Throne Established

Further affirmation that Heaven is a created place—rather than an eternal, uncreated place—is found in the numerous Scriptures that describe God as establishing his throne in Heaven:

> The Lord reigns forever; he has *established his throne* for judgment. (Ps 9:7 NIV)

> *Your throne was established long ago*; you are from all eternity. (Ps 93:2 NIV)

> The Lord has *established his throne in heaven*, and his kingdom rules over all. (Ps 103:19 NIV)

To establish something means to set it up, or to create it, as seen in these alternative examples:

> But I will *establish* my covenant with you. (Gen 6:18 NIV)

> Then David knew that the Lord had *established* him as king over Israel and had exalted his kingdom for the sake of his people Israel. (2 Sam 5:12 NIV)

> These are the decrees, the laws and the regulations that the Lord *established* at Mount Sinai between himself and the Israelites through Moses. (Lev 26:46 NIV)

To establish something means to bring it into being, which means that until a thing is established, it does not exist. The various Scriptures quoted above all affirm this truth. For example, in Genesis 6:18, God establishes, or "brings into being," his covenant with Noah to never again destroy the earth with a flood. Prior to God establishing this covenant with Noah, that covenant did not exist. To establish the covenant means to bring it into being.

Likewise, in 2 Samuel 5:12 we are told that David knew his earthly throne was now "established" by God, meaning it was now "brought into being"—put into place, as a certainty to unfold. Until God had established David's throne, David had no throne; to establish his throne is to set it up, or to bring it into being.

In Leviticus 26:26 we are told how God gave his laws and regulations to Israel, and in doing so, he "established" these very laws and regulations. Once again, prior to God establishing his laws and regulations with Israel, those laws and regulations did not exist in Israel. The act of establishing the laws and regulations is what brought those laws and regulations into being in Israel. In every instance throughout the Bible, to establish something means to bring it into being.

Likewise, when Psalms 9:7, 93:2, and 103:19 tell us God has "established" his throne in Heaven, it is telling us God created his throne, or brought it into being in Heaven. This means until God established his throne in Heaven, it did not exist. Heaven was created to be the seat of God's throne within his own creation. The fact the Bible repeatedly tells us God established his throne in Heaven affirms God's throne had a beginning, which likewise implicitly affirms Heaven, as the seat of God's throne, itself had a beginning. That beginning of Heaven is the same "beginning" referred to in Genesis 1:1. Once God created Heaven within the fabric of time and space, he then chose Heaven as the location where he would establish his throne within his own creation.

The establishment of God's throne in Heaven was an important event, for with the establishing of God's throne in the created Heaven, within God's creation, God himself came to fully and physically *inhabit* his own creation.

God Inhabits His Creation

God is certainly greater than time and space since he is the creator of both. However, God is not *outside* of time and space; rather, since "the beginning," God is fully *within* time and space, fully inhabiting both time and space—he is *in* his creation.

A clear analogy to this is found in a man who builds a house. Since the man is the builder of the house, the man is always greater than the house which he has built, for he is the maker of the house. But once the house is finished, the man then goes to live inside the house and inhabits the house. The man is always greater than the house, since he is its maker, but he is now living within the house of his making, inhabiting it. Once he inhabits his house, he is no longer *outside* his house, but within it.

It is exactly the same with God and his creation. God created time and space, as well as the rest of all creation, including Heaven. He created Heaven as the place where he would establish his throne within his creation so he himself would fully and physically *inhabit* his own creation, not remain outside of it. Just like the man who builds a house, God is always greater than his creation, for he is its maker. But just like the man who builds a house and then enters into it to inhabit the house, God has come to dwell within his creation, to inhabit it fully. So it is not true to say God is outside of time and space; rather, he dwells within it. As a result, God is always greater than time and space and is always greater than his whole creation, but he is not outside of it, rather he is *in* it, inhabiting it fully. The establishment of God's throne within the created Heaven is a testimony to the fact that God inhabits his own creation.

The Ascension and Resurrection as Evidence of the Physicality of Heaven

We know the resurrected Jesus Christ is God incarnate, who, ever since his incarnation, is eternally a physical human being with an eternal, resurrected human body of flesh and bone. His incarnation was not temporary—only lasting thirty-three years—but it is eternal; Jesus Christ is incarnate forever. Jesus himself describes his resurrected body: "See my hands and my feet, that it is I myself; touch me and see, for a spirit does not have flesh and bones as you see that I have" (Luke 24:39 NIV). Jesus makes it clear his resurrected body is a *physical*, human body of *flesh and bone*, and not a spiritual body. Throughout the New Testament, the physicality of Jesus Christ is affirmed, clearly telling us he is incarnate God in *human* flesh:

> Every spirit that acknowledges that Jesus Christ has come *in the flesh* is from God. (1 John 4:2 NIV)

> The Word *became flesh* and made his dwelling among us. (John 1:14 NIV)

It is with this same incarnate *physical human body* that Jesus ascended into Heaven in Acts 1:9, to sit at the right hand of the Father (Heb 1:13; 4:14). This resurrected, physical, human Jesus is now sitting at the right hand of the Father, sitting there as a resurrected, physical flesh-and-bone man.

If Heaven, the seat of God's throne, is not a physical place, but rather some sort of spiritual dimension, then the question remains how and where is the physical, resurrected, flesh and bone Jesus sitting? Is he floating in some alternate dimension or in some spiritual state? The Bible does not say Jesus ascended into Heaven to float at the right hand of the Father, rather, we are told the physically resurrected Jesus is actually *sitting* on an actual seat at the right hand of the Father. Since the resurrected Jesus is a physical flesh-and-bone human being, the seat upon which he is sitting must also be a physical seat.

Since the physical Jesus is sitting, in Heaven, upon a physical throne, then upon what is Jesus' physical throne itself sitting? Is his physical throne floating in some cosmic dimension? No, rather, the physical seat itself, the actual throne upon which Jesus is sitting, must rest upon an actual physical platform; this physical platform must itself be sitting upon an actual physical base which, ultimately, is itself sitting upon an actual physical world.

As a result, not only is God's Heaven an actual physical place in the universe, a created place subject to time and space, but Heaven must certainly be a physical world, or what we would describe as a planet, just as is Earth. All of this must be true because the resurrected Jesus Christ is a physical, flesh-and-bone, resurrected human being who is right now sitting in Heaven at the right hand of the Father, upon a physical throne. Heaven itself must be just as physical as is the resurrected Jesus Christ.

The Creation of Angels

After creating time, space, and Heaven, and after establishing his throne in Heaven, God then continued with the rest of his creation by creating the angels. We know the angels were created by God *before* he created the earth, but also *after* he created Heaven. When God created the "heavens and the earth," the angels were created *between* the creation of the heavens and the earth. We know this from Job 38:4–7: "Where were you when I laid *the foundation of the earth*? Tell me, if you have understanding, who set its measurements? Since you know. Or who stretched the line on it? On what were its bases sunk? Or who laid its cornerstone, when the morning stars sang together and all the sons of God shouted for joy" (NIV)? The angels watched God as he laid "the foundation of the earth." What is the foundation of the earth?

Just as the Bible refers to three heavens, it also refers to the earth in three different ways. Throughout the Bible, the earth is referred to by the following terms: "the foundations of the earth," "the earth," and "the world."

The Foundations of the Earth

The term "the foundations of the earth" means the actual physical *planet itself*, which is eternal and everlasting, as seen in Micah 6:2: "Hear, you mountains, the Lord's accusation; listen, you *everlasting foundations of the earth*" (NIV). Further, when Job 38:4–7 tells us of God laying the foundations of the earth, he is describing God's creation of the planet itself. The "foundations of the earth" is the *planet* Earth.

The Earth

The term "the earth" means the physical *surface* of the planet—this is how we are to understand Genesis 9:11: "... Never again will there be a flood to *destroy the earth*" (NIV). In Genesis 9:11, God specifically tells us the flood *destroyed* the earth, but obviously Planet Earth is still here. Is this not a contradiction or an error? No, since the term "the earth" refers only to the *surface* of the planet, not to the planet itself. The flood completely destroyed the *surface* of the planet, but the planet itself, the foundations of the earth, remains eternal, as is clearly affirmed in Micah 6:2 when he writes of the "everlasting foundations of the earth." There is no contradiction between Genesis 9:11 and Micah 6:2—Planet Earth itself is eternal, but the *surface* of the planet can be, has been, and will be destroyed, and when we are told in Genesis 9:11 that the flood destroyed the earth, that is an accurate description, for the flood *did* destroy the *surface* of the earth.

God Created the Earth

When Genesis 1:1 tells us God created "the earth," it is referring specifically to the creation of the *surface* of the earth, but in this case, since it is also at the time of "the beginning," it is implicit that the *foundation* of the earth—that is, the planet itself—is also created at that same time. This is further confirmed in Psalm 102:25, which tells us the *foundations* of the earth were laid, or created, "in the beginning": "*In the beginning* you laid *the foundations of the earth*" (NIV). This "in the beginning" referred to in Psalm 102:25 is the same "in the beginning" as Genesis 1:1. As a result, when Genesis 1:1 tells us God created the earth in the beginning, it includes the creation of the foundations of the earth, the planet itself, upon which the surface of the earth was created. In Genesis 1:1, God created Planet Earth.

The World

The term "the world" refers to all that exists and takes place *upon the surface* of the earth. This refers to all life, people, and civilization. When we are told in John 3:16 that God "so loved the world," the term "the world" is referring to the *people* who inhabit the surface of the earth.

Angels

It is in this context that we approach Job 38:4–7, where we encounter the term the "sons of God." In the Old Testament, the term "sons of God" is always and only used in reference to angelic or heavenly beings, as is made clear in Job 1:6: "Now there was a day when the sons of God came to present themselves before the Lord, and Satan also came among them" (NKJV).

There is no question the "sons of God" of Job 1:6 are angelic beings. These are the same angelic beings referred to in Job 38:4–7, which specifically tells us the sons of God *watched* God as he laid *the foundation of the earth*, that is, the *angels watched God* as he *created Planet Earth* itself.

This creation of Planet Earth occurred in Genesis 1:1, occurring after the creation of the third heaven (heaven) and the second heaven (outer space). Since the angels watched God as he created the earth in Genesis 1:1, we know the angels were created in Genesis 1:1 *before* God created the earth.

Heaven, the Home of Angels

We also know the angels were created *after* God created (the third) heaven, since the Bible tells us specifically that Heaven is the home of angels. Since Heaven is the home of angels, Heaven was certainly created before the angels were created.

> For I tell you that their *angels in heaven* always see the face of my Father in heaven. (Matt 18:10 NIV)

> But about that day or hour no one knows, not even the *angels in heaven*, nor the Son, but only the Father. (Matt 24:36 NIV)

We know from Matthew 18:10 and 24:36 that angels live in Heaven, which is to say Heaven is the home of angels. As a result, we know when God created the angels, he created them in Heaven, their home. When Job 38:4–7 tells us the angels, the sons of God, watched God as he created the earth, we know the angels were *in Heaven* with God as they watched God create the earth. This of course means after God created Heaven, but before God created the earth, God created the angels.

In the sequence of creation, we therefore know that after God created time and space first, he then created Heaven, where he established his throne, and next he created the angels, the sons of God, who watched God as he created the earth, singing and shouting for joy as they witnessed that event. The creation of time and space, of Heaven and of angels, is all included in Genesis 1:1.

Creation of the Earth

After God created time and space, Heaven, and the sons of God (angels), he created the earth, creating first the foundations of the earth, which is the planet itself, and then the surface of the earth upon it.

The Earth was created full and complete in Genesis 1:1, in the beginning, and we are told the creation of the earth was witnessed by all the angels. Genesis 1:1 specifically gives the order of creation as "the heavens" first, and *then* "the earth". This same account of the *order* of creation, the order of "heavens" first and then "the earth," continues throughout the Bible:

> *That you have forgotten the Lord your Maker, Who stretched out the heavens and laid the foundations of the earth.* (Isa 51:13 NASB)

> Thus *the heavens and the earth* were completed in all their vast array. (Gen 2:1 NIV)

> For in six days the Lord made *the heavens and the earth*. (Exod 20:11 NIV)

In these verses, and throughout the Bible, the order of creation is always given as "heavens" first and then "the earth," which is exactly consistent with the order of creation as given in Genesis 1:1.

The Physicality of Angels

God's entire creation is a *physical* creation, which means everything God created was made within and upon the fabric of time and space, and as a result is subject to time and space. This includes both Heaven, where God established his throne, and the angels. Heaven and angels, as created things, are subject to time and space, and are therefore physical.

Often we use words like "spiritual" or "spiritual realm" or "spiritual beings" when talking about angels. Such terms carry with them an implication that angels are somehow not subject to the physical creation, as are we, and are not subject to time and space; this is false. Angels, as created beings, were created within the fabric of time and space and, like us, or the earth, the moon, or Mars, are fully subject to time and space.

What does it mean for an angel to be subject to time and space? Put very simply it means this: if an angel wanted to get from point A to point B, then that angel must physically move through both space and time to get from point A to point B, just as would we.

For example, if an angel was in London and wanted to get to New York City, he would have to travel from London to New York by physically moving across the earth, moving through physical space, in order to get to New York. Furthermore, this travelling through space, across the earth, to go from London to New York, would also involve *time*—as the angel moves from London to New York, there will be the passage of *time*. All of which is to say that, as creatures of time and space, angels are subject to the restrictions of time and space. Just like you and I, an angel can only ever be in any one place at any one time, and to get from one place to another place, an angel must physically move through space and time to get there. The Bible gives us a specific account of exactly such a situation in Daniel 10:12–14:

> Do not be afraid, Daniel. Since the first day that you set your mind to gain understanding and to humble yourself before your God, your words were heard, and I have come in response to them. But the prince of the Persian kingdom resisted me twenty-one days. Then Michael, one of the chief princes, came to help me, because I was detained there with the king of Persia. Now I have come to explain to you what will happen to your people in the future, for the vision concerns a time yet to come. (NIV)

In this passage, Daniel is visited by an angel who was sent by God to explain to Daniel the meaning of a vision God had given him. The angel tells Daniel he, the angel, was sent by God on the first day he, Daniel, was seeking wisdom to understand the vision. We are told in Daniel 10:2 it took that angel twenty-one days to reach Daniel. The angel then tells Daniel he, the angel, was resisted, or held up, by a powerful fallen angel, here described as the Prince of Persia, and that this fallen angel prevented him from getting to Daniel. Next, the angel tells Daniel that one of God's great angels, Michael, here described as one of the chief princes, came to his aid and, implicitly, defeated the fallen angel called the Prince of Persia, at which time Daniel's angel was able to continue and finally come to Daniel. This angel tells Daniel this whole episode took twenty-one days.

This entire account teaches us, and affirms, some very specific qualities about the nature of angels. First, they have to physically move through space to go from point A to point B (in this case, to go from Heaven to Daniel). Second, it shows us as an angel moves through space it also moves through time—in this case, it took twenty-one days for the angel to reach Daniel. Third, it shows us, as an angel moves through space and time to reach his destination, the angel can be held up, or can be met with obstacles on his journey.

In every respect, this account in Daniel clearly shows that angels are creatures of time and space, and as such are subject to it. The definition of being physical is to be subject to time and space. Since angels are very clearly subject to time and space, we know angels are physical beings. An angel may be able, for now, to move through time and space a lot faster than you and I currently can, but they are, no less, still subject to it.

A Different Kind of Physical

Although angels are physical beings, they are a different *kind* of physical than are human beings. You and I are creatures of flesh, bone, soul, and spirit, whereas angels have a different kind of physical nature.

Why, then, would anyone teach that angelic beings, or spirits, are not physical? It is the result of a wrong understanding of what it means to be physical, being the result of a Greek philosophy understanding of physical. The argument, stated in a very basic, colloquial way, would go something like this: "Angels, or spirit beings, are invisible, we can't see them, and they can go through walls, and as a result, they are not physical beings." Again, that argument is based on a wrong understanding of what it means to be physical.

If it is true that something is defined as "spiritual" because it is invisible and can go through walls, then we have to ask about x-rays and gamma rays. Both x-rays and gamma rays are invisible—we cannot see them with our eyes. Also, both x-rays and gamma rays can go through walls, and yet we know for a certainty both gamma rays and x-rays are absolutely physical things, even though they are both invisible and can go through walls.

Yet no one, anywhere, describes x-rays or gamma rays as spiritual entities. Why not? It is because we have discovered ways to measure and observe x-rays and gamma rays and therefore we can, indirectly, see they are a part of the physical creation. They are a part of the physical universe that we, for now, in our current physical state, are not able to perceive without the aid of equipment and machinery, but they are nonetheless physical. Both gamma rays and x-rays are absolutely physical, being fully subject to time and space as are we, but they are part of the physical realm which, for now, without machinery or equipment, we cannot perceive.

Angels are exactly the same kind of thing. Like x-rays and gamma rays, they are invisible to us, and they can do things you and I (for now) cannot—such as go through walls, travel at great speed, and more. But that is only because they are, like x-rays and gamma rays, a different kind of physical than are you and I—no *less* physical than you and I, just a different *kind* of physical. Our physicality is one of flesh, bone, and spirit—that is what defines a human being, whereas angels would have a physicality whose substance is something other than flesh and bone, just as gamma rays and x-rays are a substance that is something other than flesh and bone. This is further affirmed when we consider Heaven is itself a physical place—if the physical Heaven is the abode of angels, then the angels themselves must also be just as physical as Heaven.

For the time being, we cannot perceive that particular physical realm of angels, just as we, for now, cannot perceive the full spectrum of light. Light is, in fact, made up of a whole spectrum of different colors, and it is also a spectrum that includes radio waves and the infrared spectrum. With our eyes, we cannot see radio waves, the color spectrum of light, or the infrared spectrum of light. The reason is currently we are not physically tuned to see those physical spectrums—our perception is limited. For now, we are limited to seeing only white light. We experience the same limitations in regards to the physical realm of angels. For now, we are not currently tuned to see that physical realm of angels. The Bible speaks of these limitations of our perceptions in the following verses:

> For now we see in a mirror, dimly, but then face to face. Now I know in part, but then I shall know just as I also am known. (1 Cor 13:12 NKJV)

> For the things which are seen are temporary, but the things which are not seen are eternal. (2 Cor 4:16 NKJV)

> By faith we understand that the worlds were framed by the word of God, so that the things which are seen were not made of things which are visible. (Heb 11:3 NKJV)

Each of these verses describes things which are seen and things which are unseen, and 1 Corinthians 13:12 specifically tells us that, for now, when we look at the universe, at God's creation, we see it only dimly, unclearly, that is, our perception of it is limited. Together these verses affirm there are whole aspects of God's *physical* creation that, for now, we are just not tuned to perceive. One day, however, that will change and we will be able to perceive what is currently imperceptible to our eyes. This is in fact contained within 1 Corinthians 13:12 when it continues to tell us that, for now, we only know, or perceive, in part, but later we shall perceive, or know, even as we are perceived. All of this affirms that in our full redemption we will see God's physical creation in all of its fullness, including those aspects of God's physical creation that currently are invisible to us, which includes the realm of angels.

The day is coming when we will at last see the physical creation for what it actually is, in all of its fullness. We are given a glimpse of this in 2 Kings 6:1–17, when the prophet Elisha and his scribe were surrounded by an armed force, facing what seemed like certain death. Elisha's scribe was fearful for his life, and then we are told: "And Elisha prayed, 'Open his eyes, Lord, so that he may see.' Then the Lord opened the servant's eyes, and he looked and saw the hills full of horses and chariots of fire all around Elisha" (2 Kgs 6:17 NIV).

When God opened the eyes of Elisha's servant, he saw that he and Elisha were *surrounded* by a great host of mighty, angelic warriors and chariots of fire, ready to do battle on their behalf. That great host of God was always there, but until God opened the eyes of the servant they were invisible to him, he could not perceive them, even though they were physically all around him. The angelic army was the physical reality that surrounded them, but Elisha's servant was not able to see it because it was part of the physical realm that is currently beyond our perception. When Elisha prayed God would "open his eyes," Elisha's servant was given the ability to perceive that aspect of the physical creation that is invisible to us, but which is no less real and no less physical. As a result, we know every aspect of God's creation, including what we call the spiritual realm—Heaven and angels—is a part of God's *physical* creation, being itself physical and subject fully to time and space.

In the beginning God created the heavens and the earth, creating them perfect in every respect, a glorious creation without blemish or fault. Yet, in the very second verse of the Bible, we encounter a creation under a curse.

2

Darkness—The Curse of God

IN GENESIS 1:1, GOD created the heavens and the earth, and they were created perfect and without fault. The earth, from the beginning, was created to be the home of man, and as such it was created beautiful and perfectly habitable for man.

The Uninhabitable Earth

We know the earth was created as a habitable place, for Isaiah 45:18 tells us:

> For this is what the Lord says—
> he who created the heavens,
> he is God;
> he who fashioned and made the earth,
> he founded it;
> he did not create it to be empty,
> but formed it to be inhabited—
> he says:
> 'I am the Lord,
> and there is no other.' (NIV)

We are told in Isaiah 45:18 that God created the earth specifically to be *inhabited*, he did *not* create it to be empty. This means when God created the earth in Genesis 1:1, the earth was created as *habitable*, created as a place upon which *man* could live. However, by Genesis 1:2, something has changed, something drastic has happened, for we read: "The earth was *without form*, and *void*; and *darkness* was on the face of *the deep*. And the Spirit of God was hovering over the face of the waters" (NKJV).

Though the earth was created perfect and habitable in Genesis 1:1, by Genesis 1:2 the earth was formless and empty, covered by a global ocean and wrapped in darkness. We are also told the Holy Spirit was there, hovering over the global ocean. In Genesis 1:2, the earth is utterly *uninhabitable*, completely uninhabitable for man. We know from Isaiah 45:18 that the condition of the earth in Genesis 1:2 is *not* how God had created it.

What happened? What caused the uninhabitable, formless, empty, dark, and flooded condition of the earth we see in Genesis 1:2?:

> I *beheld the earth*, and indeed it was *without form*, and *void*;
> And the heavens, they had *no light*.
> I beheld the mountains, and indeed they trembled,
> And all the hills moved back and forth.
> I beheld, and indeed there was *no man*,
> And all the birds of the heavens had fled.
> I beheld, and indeed the fruitful land was a wilderness,
> And all its cities were broken down
> At the presence of the Lord,
> *By his fierce anger*. (Jer 4:23–26 NKJV)

This prophecy of Jeremiah, like many prophecies, speaks on various levels simultaneously. On the one hand, it is prophesying a desolation to come upon Israel, but on the other hand, it also is harkening back to a time that describes, almost exactly, the earth in Genesis 1:2.

Jeremiah 4:23 tells us the earth was without form and void, that it was empty and had "no light." There was only one time in Earth's history when these conditions existed, and that was in Genesis 1:2—never since that time has the earth been formless or empty or without light. Jeremiah goes on to tell us there was no man and, in fact, no life upon the earth. Again, the only time in Earth's history when these conditions existed was in Genesis 1:2. At that point the prophecy in Jeremiah telescopes forward to the parallel desolation foretold upon Israel.

What is most important here is that as Jeremiah summarizes this condition of the earth, he also tells us what caused the earth to be empty, formless, dark, and lifeless—he tells us these conditions upon the earth were the result of the LORD's "fierce anger."

Based on what we read in Isaiah 45:18, Genesis 1:2, and Jeremiah 4:23–26, as well as many other verses in the Bible, we can conclude the following: in Genesis 1:1, God created the earth as perfect and as fully habitable for man, yet by Genesis 1:2, the earth was a cursed and desolate wasteland, a ruin, made so by God's wrath. The condition of the earth in Genesis 1:2 was *not* how God originally created it in Genesis 1:1. Something happened between Genesis 1:1 and Genesis 1:2 that caused God to curse the earth as well as the entire creation.

How can we say that the earth in Genesis 1:2 is cursed? There are three elements that are present upon the earth in Genesis 1:2 that clearly show the earth in Genesis 1:2 as a cursed Earth. These three elements are darkness, a global ocean, and the presence of the Holy Spirit.

The Curse of Darkness

> God is light; in him there is no darkness at all.—1 John 1:5 (NIV)

Darkness in the Bible is never a good thing—it is always and only ever associated with the enemy or with the curse and wrath of God. Darkness *always* represents the absence of God, the curse of God, and the outpouring of his wrath. There are many verses throughout the Bible that testify to this. Here are a few, with a brief comment following each one.

Darkness Associated with Satan, Evil, or the Enemy

> "To open their eyes and turn them from darkness to light, and from the power of Satan to God, so that they may receive forgiveness of sins and a place among those who are sanctified by faith in me" (Acts 26:18 NIV).

We are told in this passage that when one comes to Christ, they have their eyes opened and they are turning from darkness to light, turning from the power of Satan to God, thereby equating darkness with the power of Satan.

> "For our struggle is not against flesh and blood, but against the rulers, against the powers, against the world forces of this darkness, against the spiritual forces of wickedness in the heavenly places" (Eph 6:12 NASB).

Ephesians 6:12 equates the forces of darkness with the spiritual forces of wickedness.

> "For he rescued us from the domain of darkness, and transferred us to the kingdom of his beloved Son" (Col 1:13 NASB).

Here we are told there is a domain (or kingdom) of darkness, which is in contrast to the kingdom of Jesus Christ.

> "The night is almost gone, and the day is near. Therefore let us lay aside the deeds of darkness and put on the armor of light" (Rom 13:12 NASB).

The deeds of darkness, associated with "the night," are contrasted with the armor of light, which is associated with "the day."

> "Do not be bound together with unbelievers; for what partnership have righteousness and lawlessness, or what fellowship has light with darkness?" (2 Cor 6:14 NASB).

This verse equates unbelievers and lawlessness with darkness.

Darkness Associated with the Curse, Wrath, or Judgment of God

> For if God did not spare angels when they sinned, but cast them into hell [Tartarus] and committed them to pits of darkness, reserved for judgment. (2 Pet 2:4 NASB)

> These are springs without water and mists driven by a storm, for whom the black darkness has been reserved. (2 Pet 2:17 NASB)

Both of these verses tell us a place of darkness is reserved for God's judgment upon evil.

> Then the Lord said to Moses, 'Stretch out your hand toward the sky so that darkness spreads over Egypt—darkness that can be felt.' (Exod 10:21 NIV)

One of God's plagues—or curses—upon Egypt was a plague of darkness.

> Then the king said to the servants, 'Bind him hand and foot, and throw him into the outer darkness; in that place there will be weeping and gnashing of teeth.' (Matt 22:13 NASB)

Darkness is a place of judgment upon evil, and it is not a good place.

> That day will be a day of wrath—a day of distress and anguish, a day of trouble and ruin, a day of darkness and gloom, a day of clouds and blackness. (Zeph 1:15 NIV)

The "day of darkness and gloom" is specifically described here as a day of God's wrath, a day of distress, a day of anguish and trouble.

> I form the light and create darkness, I bring prosperity and create disaster; I, the Lord, do all these things. (Isa 45:7 NIV)

Here, light is equated with prosperity, while darkness is equated with disaster, and God is the one who creates both, which affirms that darkness is a curse of God.

Contrast of Light and Darkness

> God saw that *the light was good,* and he separated the light from the *darkness.* (Gen 1:4 NIV)

At the beginning of Genesis 1, we are told the "light" was "good," and that the (good) light was separated from the darkness. It is implicit in this that, since the light was good, and since the good light was separated from the darkness, then the darkness, by contrast, was bad.

> You are all children of the light and children of the day. We do not belong to the night or to the darkness. (1 Thess 5:5 NIV)

> For you were once darkness, but now you are light in the Lord. Live as children of light. (Eph 5:8 NIV)

In both of these verses, Christians are children of light, not of darkness, and in Ephesians 5:8, Christians are described as actually *being* light.

> Yet when I hoped for good, evil came; when I looked for light, then came darkness. (Job 30:26 NIV)

Here, "good" is equated with "light," while "evil" is equated with "darkness."

> I have come as Light into the world, so that everyone who believes in Me will not remain in darkness. (John 12:46 NASB)

Whoever believes in Jesus Christ has come into the light, and has come out of darkness—again, there is a contrast with light and darkness, where light is good and of God, while darkness is bad and not of God.

> This is the judgment, that the Light has come into the world, and men loved the darkness rather than the Light, for their deeds were evil. (John 3:19 NASB)

In these verses, darkness is again contrasted with light, and the darkness is opposed to the light. It is clear from these verses, as well as many others throughout the Bible, that darkness is never a good thing—it is always associated with evil, the enemy, or the wrath or curse of God. The clearest affirmation of this truth is in 1 John 1:5.

God is Light

> God is light; in him there is no darkness at all. (1 John 1:5 NIV)

This verse is very clear—God himself *is* light; he doesn't just give off light, he *is* light itself, light is part of his divine nature, and in him there is *no darkness*. How then are we to understand Genesis 1:2, "Now the earth was formless and empty, *darkness* was over the surface of the deep, and the Spirit of God was hovering over the waters" (NIV)? How can a God, who himself is light, a God in whom *there is no darkness*, create an Earth that is *surrounded* by and *engulfed* in darkness? In fact, how can a God, who himself is light, a God in whom there is no darkness, create an entire *universe* filled with darkness (just take a look at the night sky)? How is this possible?

It is not possible, because God did *not* create the earth covered in darkness, and neither did he create a universe filled with darkness. The earth as described in Genesis 1:2 is *not* how God created it; rather, by Genesis 1:2, the earth is cursed, a ruined wasteland upon which was poured the wrath of God. The darkness that covers the earth in Genesis 1:2 is the result of God's curse.

Likewise, the universe itself is under God's curse, filled with darkness end to end, thereby also evidencing the wrath of God upon it. This curse of darkness upon the universe is affirmed in Isaiah 50:3, where God tells us he clothed the heavens with darkness: "I clothe the heavens with darkness and make sackcloth its covering" (NIV). To clothe the heavens with darkness means the darkness was applied to the heavens *after* they were created. This verse also continues to tell us God made sackcloth the covering of the heavens. Sackcloth is always used throughout the Bible to represent suffering and hardship, so when we are told God clothed the heavens with darkness, and then equating that with giving the heavens a covering of sackcloth, it clearly denotes the heavens, the universe, is suffering under God's wrath. This suffering of the universe is further evidenced in the following verses from Romans 8:19–22:

> For the creation waits in eager expectation for the children of God to be revealed. For the creation was subjected to frustration, not by its own choice, but by the will of the one who subjected it, in hope that the creation itself will be liberated from its bondage to decay and brought into the freedom and glory of the children of God. We know that the whole creation has been groaning as in the pains of childbirth right up to the present time. (NIV)

This passage in Romans tells us creation itself is currently subject to suffering and is in bondage to decay, waiting eagerly for its liberation. This is the same suffering and bondage of creation as seen in Genesis 1:2, as evidenced by the darkness engulfing the earth, which is the same darkness that also engulfs the entire universe. That entire darkness—the darkness engulfing the earth in Genesis 1:2, and the darkness filling the entire universe—was the result of God's curse upon the earth and upon the entire creation.

Isaiah 45:18 affirms God did not create either the earth or the universe in that cursed condition, rather, they became that way after they were created. This is clearly affirmed across many translations. Here are three different translations of Isaiah 45:18 to illustrate this; regardless of the translation, they all tell us the same thing:

> For this is what the Lord says—he who created the heavens, he is God; he who fashioned and made the earth, he founded it; *he did not create it to be empty,* but *formed it to be inhabited.* (NIV)

> For thus says the LORD, who created the heavens (he is the God who formed the earth and made it, he established it *and did not create it a waste place*, but formed it to be inhabited). (NASB)

> For the Lord is God, and he created the heavens and earth and put everything in place. *He made the world to be lived in, not to be a place of empty chaos.* (NLT)

Across various translations, Isaiah 45:18 clearly tells us God did *not* create the earth as an empty wasteland of chaos. He did *not* create it to be uninhabitable. God created the earth, in Genesis 1:1, as perfect and as habitable for man. The earth *became* a cursed and empty wasteland *afterward*. This truth is also affirmed by the description of the earth in Jeremiah 4:23–27, where the formless emptiness of the earth is connected directly to the wrath of God.

Psalm 97 and Psalm 18—God Surrounded by Darkness

In Psalm 97, we are told the following:

> The Lord reigns, let the earth be glad;
> let the distant shores rejoice.
> *Clouds and thick darkness surround him;*
> *righteousness and justice are the foundation of his throne.*
> *Fire goes before him*
> *and consumes his foes on every side.*
> *his lightning lights up the world;*
> *the earth sees and trembles.*
> *The mountains melt like wax before the Lord,*
> before the Lord of all the earth. (Ps 97:1–5 NIV)

These verses tell us "clouds and thick darkness" surround God. Doesn't this tell us darkness is a natural part of God's very own presence, where he is surrounded by "thick darkness?" Isn't this is a description of God reigning, a description of his glory and therefore something over which the earth should be glad? Does this not then mean that darkness is good? In fact it does not. As we continue to read, the thick darkness which is surrounding God in these verses is completely tied to his wrath and to the destruction of his enemies, as we are told in verses 3–4:

> Fire goes before him
> and *consumes his foes* on every side.
> his lightning lights up the world;
> the earth sees and trembles.

The darkness described in Psalm 97 is related inextricably to the wrath which God pours out upon his foes, a wrath which sees the very earth tremble, and the mountains melt. The darkness of Psalm 97 is inextricably tied in with the wrath, or judgment, of God. We see the same thing in Psalm 18:7–15:

> The earth trembled and quaked,
> and the foundations of the mountains shook;
> they trembled because he was angry.
> Smoke rose from his nostrils;
> consuming fire came from his mouth,
> burning coals blazed out of it.
> He parted the heavens and came down;
> dark clouds were under his feet.
> He mounted the cherubim and flew;
> he soared on the wings of the wind.
> *He made darkness his covering, his canopy around him—*
> *the dark rain clouds of the sky.*
> Out of the *brightness of his presence* clouds advanced,
> with hailstones and bolts of lightning.
> *The Lord thundered from heaven;*
> the voice of the Most High resounded.
> *He shot his arrows and scattered the enemy,*
> with great bolts of lightning he routed them.
> The valleys of the sea were exposed
> and the foundations of the earth laid bare
> at your rebuke, Lord,
> at the blast of breath from your nostrils." (NIV)

We are told here that God makes "darkness his covering, his canopy around him" (v. 11). Once again, if darkness is the result of the wrath or curse of God, then how can God make darkness "his covering?" Does this not mean that darkness is part of the very presence of God himself? No, it does not, for as we continue to read, we are told once again that, in this context of Psalms 18, God "thundered from heaven" and that he "shot his arrows and scattered the enemy." Therefore, as with Psalm 97, the darkness described here as covering the LORD is inextricably connected with God visiting judgment upon the enemy by way of the outpouring of his wrath.

We see then, without exception, throughout the Bible darkness is always and only the result of God's wrath, the result of his curse and of his judgment. As a result, we know this is therefore also certainly true of the darkness that covers the earth in Genesis 1:2. The very fact the earth in Genesis 1:2 was covered in darkness is witness to the fact the earth was cursed.

The Curse of the Global Ocean

In addition to the darkness that is covering the earth in Genesis 1:2, there are two other elements present upon the earth—one of which is the global ocean that completely covers the earth. In the Bible, the sea always represents the judgment of God. One of the primary reasons oceans are a curse upon the earth is they make all the areas they cover completely uninhabitable to man. Also, throughout the Bible, God uses seas and oceans to visit judgment upon peoples as well as upon the earth.

This, of course, is most clearly seen in Genesis 6–7, where God destroyed Earth by means of the flood. The flood, the global ocean, was God's judgment upon the earth. Also, the beast in Revelation 13 arises from the sea, which is to say it rises from a place of judgment (Rev 13:1). Pharaoh's entire army was obliterated by the Red Sea, the judgment of God upon Egypt (Exod 15:4).

Furthermore, the whole concept of salt (which is a prime element of all the oceans and seas) as relating to judgment is also shown in the judgment upon Lot's wife, who, upon fleeing Sodom with her husband Lot and their daughters, disobeyed God and looked back and, as a result, became a pillar of salt (Gen 19:26).

The oceans of the earth are also a further curse in that we cannot drink ocean water. Human beings of course need water to live—without water, we die. Yet if we had a diet of drinking only ocean water, we would die—drinking ocean water would kill us. Even though we need water to live, ocean water is, in effect, a poison to us.

As a result, it is clear throughout the Bible that the seas and oceans are a curse upon the earth, making all the land that they cover completely uninhabitable for man. The oceans and seas are used by God to bring judgment upon the earth, whether at the flood, upon Pharaoh's army, or as the source of the beast of Revelation. All of this evidences that the seas and oceans are a judgment from God, even to this day.

As a result, the global ocean that covers the earth in Genesis 1:2 is therefore a curse upon the earth, an oceanic covering that makes the earth utterly uninhabitable for man, the judgment of God upon the earth. Although God created a perfect Earth in Genesis 1:1, an Earth fully habitable for man (Isa 45:18), as of Genesis 1:2, the earth is under the curse of darkness as well as under the curse of a global ocean and is utterly uninhabitable for man.

Lifting the Curse of Darkness

The curse of darkness and the curse of the oceans in Genesis 1:2 remain today, though they are mitigated by God's mercy and his unfolding redemption, which begins in Genesis 1:3. The Bible, though, tells us ultimately these two elements of God's curse upon the earth—darkness and seas—will finally be lifted and removed when God redeems Earth, so as to make it what it was always intended to be:

> No longer will there be any curse. The throne of God and of the Lamb will be in the city, and his servants will serve him. They will see his face, and his name will be on their foreheads. *There will be no more night.* (Rev 22:3–5 NIV)

> Then I saw a new heaven and a new earth; for the first heaven and the first earth passed away, and *there is no longer any sea.* (Rev 21:1 NIV)

These passages describe the ultimate redemption of the earth. Two key points of that redemption is the lifting of all curses upon the earth (Rev 22:3). This lifting of all curses upon the earth includes specifically the lifting of the curse of darkness (night), as well as the lifting of the curse of seas—the two curses upon the earth present in Genesis 1:2—both of these curses will be finally and fully removed by God upon his redemption of the earth.

As a result, from these various passages which outline the removal of all curses upon the earth, and which specifically include the removal of the curse of darkness and the curse of seas, it is clear the two elements upon the earth in Genesis 1:2—darkness and the global ocean—are elements of God's curse upon the earth.[1]

The Third Element—The Holy Spirit

In addition to the two elements of God's curse that are present upon the earth in Genesis 1:2, the curse of darkness and of the global ocean, there

---

1. In various translations of Genesis 1:2, for the words "Now the earth was formless and void . . ." there is often a small footnote attached to the word "was," with an explanation that the word "was" can also be translated as "became." In fact, that is the correct sense by which to understand Genesis 1:2—God did not create the earth as an empty chaos wasteland, he created it perfect, but it *became* an empty, chaos wasteland, surrounded by darkness and the global flood, all as a result of the curse of God.

is a third element present, and that is the Holy Spirit himself. The Holy Spirit is described in Genesis 1:2 as being present over the earth:

> and the Spirit of God was hovering over the waters. (Gen 1:2)

Why would the Holy Spirit be present upon the earth when the earth is in an accursed state? The Holy Spirit's presence in Genesis 1:2 can be understood via 2 Thessalonians 2:1–8:

> Concerning the coming of our Lord Jesus Christ and our being gathered to him, we ask you, brothers and sisters, not to become easily unsettled or alarmed by the teaching allegedly from us—whether by a prophecy or by word of mouth or by letter—asserting that the day of the Lord has already come. Don't let anyone deceive you in any way, for that day will not come until the rebellion occurs and the man of lawlessness is revealed, the man doomed to destruction. He will oppose and will exalt himself over everything that is called God or is worshiped, so that he sets himself up in God's temple, proclaiming himself to be God. Don't you remember that when I was with you I used to tell you these things? And now you know what is holding him back, so that he may be revealed at the proper time. For the secret power of lawlessness is already at work; but the one who now holds it back will continue to do so till he is taken out of the way. And then the lawless one will be revealed, whom the Lord Jesus will overthrow with the breath of his mouth and destroy by the splendor of his coming. (NIV)

In this passage we are told there will be a man of lawlessness coming upon the earth; this "man of lawlessness" is traditionally understood to be the coming antichrist. We are told something, or some "one," is holding back the man of lawlessness from being revealed (2 Thess 2:6, 7), and that the man of lawlessness will not be revealed until the one who holds him back is taken out of the way.

Who is the one who is holding back the revealing of the man of lawlessness? Many people understand that the one who is holding back the revealing of the man of lawlessness is, in fact, the Holy Spirit. In that capacity, the Holy Spirit is restraining or holding back evil.

It is in this capacity that we are to understand the Holy Spirit's presence upon the earth in Genesis 1:2—he is present upon the accursed Earth because he is restraining, or holding down, great evil, an evil that has been cast down to the earth, a casting down which resulted in both the earth and the creation being cursed.

Darkness—The Curse of God

The Earth in Genesis 1:1 was created perfect, beautiful and fully habitable for man (Isa 45:18), but the earth in Genesis 1:2 is formless and void, utterly uninhabitable, surrounded by darkness, and covered by a global ocean; the earth in Genesis 1:2 is a cursed place. Over it all is the presence of the Holy Spirit, who is there in the capacity as a Restrainer of evil.

Why is the earth in Genesis 1:2 cursed? What was the evil that was cast down upon it which the Holy Spirit was restraining? What caused this? The curse upon the earth in Genesis 1:2, the curse of darkness and of the global ocean, as well as the curse of darkness that is upon the entire universe, was the result of the fall of the angels, the angelic rebellion.

3

Angels

IN THE SEQUENCE OF God's creation, God first created time and space, the fabric of creation. Second, he created heaven, the place where he established the temporary seat of his throne within his own creation. Third, he created the angels, who inhabit and live with God in heaven (Mark 13:32). Fourth, after he created the angels, God continued to create the rest of the heavens (the fullness of space) and the earth, all while the angels watched him, rejoicing as he created the earth (Job 38:4–7).

The Sons of God

The angels were created to inhabit heaven—heaven is their home. They were created to serve. They, like you and I, were created in God's image, since in the Old Testament they are called "the sons of God" (Job 1:6; 2:1; 38:7; Gen 6:1 NKJV). Though they are created in God's image, unlike us, they were not created in his likeness (Gen 1:26).

In the entire time span between Adam and Jesus Christ, no human being is ever called a "son of God." We know very clearly from Luke 3:38 that Adam was the son of God, and we know Jesus Christ is the Son of God. Apart from that, no other human being between Adam and Jesus Christ is ever called a son of God. Also, in the Old Testament, no human being ever calls God "Father."

After Jesus' Resurrection, when a human being believes in Jesus Christ, they become "born again" (1 Pet 1:23), born of the Holy Spirit, and at that point they are born a "son of God" (Rom 8:14, 19; 9:26). As a result, we see then that Adam was the created son of God, Jesus Christ is the begotten Son of God, and Christians are the adopted sons of God (Rom 8:15). These three uses of the term "sons of God" as applied to human beings occurs only in the New Testament. The term "sons of God," when used in the Old Testament, refers solely to the angelic beings of heaven.

The Nature of Angels

As sons of God, angels, like you and I, have bodies and physicality, though theirs is a different kind of physicality than the flesh-and-bone physicality of human beings. As sons of God, they also have will, intelligence, emotion, and personality, and they can choose between good and evil—like us, they are moral beings. Unlike you and I, angels were not born, they were created:

> Praise the Lord!
> Praise the Lord from the heavens;
> Praise him in the heights!
> Praise him, *all his angels*;
> Praise him, all his hosts!
> Praise him, sun and moon;
> Praise him, all you stars of light!
> Praise him, you heavens of heavens,
> And you waters above the heavens!
> Let them praise the name of the Lord,
> *For he commanded and they were created.*
> (Ps 148:1–5 NKJV)

The angels were not created one at a time, but were created en masse as a great host (Ps 148:5), seemingly innumerable:

> But you have come to Mount Zion and to the city of the living God, the heavenly Jerusalem, to an innumerable company of angels. (Heb 12:22 NKJV)

> A fiery stream issued, and came forth from before him. A thousand thousands ministered to him; ten thousand times ten thousand stood before him. (Dan 7:10 NKJV)

> Praise him, all his angels; praise him, all his hosts! (Ps 148:2 NKJV)

Throughout the Bible, the angels always appear only as male, never as female. All angelic beings were created perfect, holy, and good.

Ranks of Angels

Although God created an innumerable number of angelic beings, angels are not all the same, for they differ in terms of rank, power, wisdom, and function. The entire angelic host is ordered as a hierarchy, ranging from the greatest, most powerful, and wisest heavenly beings, to the least powerful. There are a total of nine angelic ranks outlined in the Bible.

The First Angelic Rank—The Cherubim

Cherubim (the plural of cherub) are the greatest and highest angelic rank. These are the most powerful and most intelligent angelic beings, and they are almost always associated with God's throne and with his glory:

> And Hezekiah prayed to the Lord: "Lord, the God of Israel, enthroned between the cherubim." (2 Kgs 19:15 NIV)

> So the people sent to Shiloh, that they might bring from there the ark of the covenant of the Lord of hosts, who dwells *between* the cherubim. (1 Sam 4:4 NIV)

> ... whose name is called by the Name, the Lord of Hosts, who dwells *between* the cherubim. (2 Sam 6:2 NIV; also Ps 80:1; 99:1; Isa 37:16)

Cherubim were also stationed to guard the tree of life in Eden after Adam was driven out of the garden, driven out in an act of love, mercy, and compassion from God (Gen 3:24).

Cherubim were also placed on the ark of the covenant, to cover and to view the mercy seat, where the blood of the sacrifice was sprinkled (Exod 25). Cherubim were also part of the artistic design of the Tabernacle (Exod 36–37). Additionally, both Ezekiel 1:4–28 and 10:1–17 specifically describe God's throne as sitting both *upon* and *between* the Cherubim. The Cherubim have a physical connection to the throne of God.

The Second Angelic Rank—The Seraphim

Seraphim are the second-greatest rank, and their name means "burning ones." Seraphim are mentioned in the Bible only once, in Isaiah 6:1–7. They are described as having six wings and as being above the throne of God.

The Third Angelic Rank—Thrones

Thrones (or Ophanim) are the third-highest rank (Col 1:16)

The Fourth Angelic Rank—Dominions

Dominions are the fourth-highest rank (Col 1:16 NKJV; NASB; Eph 1:21)

The Fifth Angelic Rank—Principalities

Principalities are the fifth-highest rank (Col 1:16 NKJV; Eph 6:12; Rom 8:38 NKJV; Col 2:15 KJV; Eph 1:21 NKJV).

The Sixth Angelic Rank—Powers

Powers are the sixth-highest rank (Col 1:16 NKJV; Eph 6:12; Romans 8:38; Col 2:15 KJV; Eph 1:21 NKJV)

The Seventh Angelic Rank—Rulers

Rulers are the seventh-highest rank (Luke 12:11 NASB; Eph 1:21; Col 1:16; Eph 3:10; 6:2, 12; Titus 3:1 NKJV)

The Eighth Angelic Rank—Authorities

Authorities are the eighth-highest rank (Luke 12:11 NASB; Eph 1:21; Col 1:16; Eph3:10; 6:2; 1 Pet 3:22; Titus 3:1 NKJV)

The Ninth Angelic Rank—Angels

Angels are the ninth-highest rank—these are God's messengers to mankind.

In some rankings of the angelic hierarchy, Seraphim are described as the highest angelic rank, while Cherubim are listed as second. There seems to be no biblical basis to list the Seraphim above the Cherubim. The Cherubim are specifically connected with the very throne of God, with God's throne described as being physically *between* the Cherubim as well as physically sitting *upon* them—there is a physical connection between God's throne and the Cherubim. The Seraphim are described as being above God's throne, in flight above and around it, so while the Seraphim still have a connection to God's throne, it is not the same intimate physical connection the Cherubim are described as having.

In addition, the presence of the Cherubim on the ark of the covenant signifies their intimate connection with God's plan of forgiveness and salvation, and their presence guarding the tree of life, which is a profound task, signifies their position of highest power. Also, Lucifer is described as being of the Cherubim rank (Ezek 28:14). As a result, there is strong reason to list the Cherubim as the highest angelic rank, and the Seraphim as the second-highest rank.

In some listings of the angelic ranks, one of the ranks is listed as Virtues. This is a matter of translation, but the rank of Virtues corresponds to the rank of Dominions, and, as a matter of translation, Virtues is interchangeable with Dominions.

The Ordering of the Lower Angelic Ranks

Cherubim, Seraphim, and thrones are the three highest angelic ranks, and this is agreed upon by virtually all listings of the angelic hierarchy. As a guide as to how we are to rank the lower angelic ranks, we can turn to Colossians 1:16:

> "For by him all things were created that are in heaven and that are on earth, visible and invisible, whether thrones or dominions or principalities or powers. All things were created through him and for him" (NKJV).

In this listing of some of the lower angelic ranks, after thrones, which all rankings agree is the third-highest rank, Paul lists the ranks in order as dominions, principalities, and powers. This gives good reason to list the hierarchy, from thrones downward, as dominions, principalities, and powers, as described in Colossians 1:16. The ranks of rulers and authorities are mentioned numerous times in the New Testament, and always in that same order—rulers and authorities (Eph 3:10; 6:12; Col 1:16). As a result, this gives very good reason to rank rulers and authorities in that order, rulers first, and then authorities. The rank of angel is almost universally acknowledged as the lowest rank and is always listed last. Based on various Scriptures, the nine ranks of angels, listed in order from greatest to lowest, are Cherubim, Seraphim, thrones, dominions, principalities, powers, rulers, authorities, angels.

Archangel

In some listings of the angelic hierarchy, the rank of archangel is included and listed as the eighth-highest rank, just above the rank of angel. The term "archangel" appears in the Bible twice:

> For the Lord himself will descend from heaven with a shout, with the voice of the archangel, and with the trumpet of God. And the dead in Christ will rise first. (1 Thess 4:16 NASB)

> Yet Michael the archangel, in contending with the devil, when he disputed about the body of Moses, dared not bring against him a reviling accusation, but said, 'The Lord rebuke you!' (Jude 9 NKJV)

In both cases, the term "archangel" is used with the prefix "the," denoting someone specific. In 1 Thessalonians we are told it is the voice of *the* archangel, and again in Jude Michael is described as *the* archangel. As a result, it seems the term "archangel" does not refer to a rank of angel, but rather is a title that is applied specifically to only one angel. Based on Jude 9, there is good reason to understand that only Michael has the title or position of archangel.

Angels Named in the Bible

There are only two specific holy angels named in the Bible, and a third fallen heavenly being.

Gabriel

One of the angels named in the Bible is Gabriel: "I am Gabriel, who stands in the presence of God" (Luke 1:19 NASB, also Luke 1:26; also Dan 8:16; 9:20, 21) In Luke, it is the angel Gabriel who is sent to announce to Mary that she will become pregnant and give birth to the Son of God. Nothing else is told us of Gabriel. However, Gabriel himself specifically tells Mary he stands "in the presence of God." As a result of that phrase, some are of the opinion Gabriel is a Cherub, since it is always the Cherubim rank that is associated with the throne of God, and by extension, with the presence of God. It would make sense that God would send an angel of the highest rank to announce the birth of his Son to the woman who will bear him, especially since there was an Enemy that could very well try and thwart that mission of announcement (in a similar thwarting action of the enemy as described in Dan 10:13).

Michael

The other holy angel named in the Bible is Michael, and he is mentioned a number of times:

> Then Michael, one of the chief princes, came to help me, because I was detained there with the king of Persia. (Dan 10:13 NIV)

> However, I will tell you what is inscribed in the writing of truth. Yet there is no one who stands firmly with me against these forces except Michael your prince. (Dan 10:21 NASB)

> At that time Michael, the great prince who protects your people, will arise. There will be a time of distress such as has not happened from the beginning of nations until then. (Dan 12:1 NIV)

> Yet Michael the archangel, in contending with the devil, when he disputed about the body of Moses, dared not bring against him a reviling accusation ... (Jude 9 NKJV)

> Then war broke out in heaven. Michael and his angels fought against the dragon, and the dragon and his angels fought back. But he was not strong enough, and they lost their place in heaven. (Rev 12:7–8 NIV)

The descriptions of Michael show him to be a powerful angel, with great responsibilities.

In Daniel 10:2–13, we are told Daniel was visited by an angel who was sent to explain the vision of God given to Daniel. The angel also tells Daniel he, the angel, was sent to Daniel on the first day he, Daniel, set himself to understand the vision, which we are told in Daniel 10:2 was three weeks prior to that. This angel then tells Daniel that as he, the angel, was traveling to reach Daniel, he was "withstood" by a fallen angel, described as a "prince of the kingdom of Persia" (Dan 10:13), who withstood the holy angel for twenty-one days. At that time, Michael came to his aid and defeated the fallen angel who was withstanding Daniel's messenger. In the description given by the holy messenger angel, he describes Michael as "one of the chief princes" (Dan 10:13). This signifies that Michael, as a "chief prince," is an angel of high rank.

We are also told Michael is "the great prince who protects your people" (Dan 12:1), with Michael again being described as "your prince" (Dan 10:21). In both cases, Michael is described as being the special protector of the nation of Judah, the Jews, Daniel's people, and most likely, by extension, of all Israel, in which regard he is also referred to specifically in Daniel 12:1 as "the great prince." Also, the term "*the* great prince," rather than "*a* great prince" seems to signify Michael is perhaps of a unique rank and position in heaven. This is also further supported by the description of Michael as "*the* archangel" (Jude 9).

We are told in Revelation 12:7–8 that "war broke out in heaven, and that Michael and his angels fought against the dragon, and the dragon and his angels fought back. But he was not strong enough, and they lost their place in heaven." This is a clear description that Michael was involved in the casting out of Lucifer and the rebel angels from heaven. Also, we are told here it was "Michael and *his* angels," which seems to signify Michael has authority over other angels, and is certainly an authority over the heavenly host, or the angelic heavenly army, being in effect a General of the heavenly armies. Also, in Jude 9, we are told Michael personally disputed with Satan and defeated him.

Taken together, these descriptions of Michael show him to be an angel of the highest rank, almost certainly of the Cherubim rank, described as "the great prince," as "the archangel," as Protector of Israel and Judah, as the leader of the heavenly armies, and as being personally involved in defeating Satan.

Lucifer/Satan

There is one other angelic name mentioned in the Bible—Lucifer. It is mentioned in Isaiah 14:12. "How you are fallen from heaven, O Lucifer, son of the morning! How you are cut down to the ground, you who weakened the nations!" (NKJV). A number of modern translations do not translate the name "Lucifer" here; rather, they translate it as follows: "How you have fallen from heaven, *morning star*, son of the dawn! You have been cast down to the earth, you who once laid low the nations!" (NIV).

In this rendering, Lucifer is translated as "morning star." However, numerous traditional and standard translations, including the King James Version, the New King James Version, the Geneva Bible, the Living Bible, the Modern English Version, the Wycliffe Bible, specifically translate this as "Lucifer," and this, in fact, has been the traditional translation of Isaiah 14:12.

The name Lucifer means "light-bearer," and in Christian tradition, and throughout church history, Lucifer is the heavenly being who incited and then led the angelic rebellion against God (Isa 14:12, Rev 12:3–4). This angelic rebellion is the same event described in Revelation 12:7–8, whose conclusion shows Michael and his angels defeating the angelic rebellion, with the rebel angels being cast out of heaven and thrown down to the earth. Upon being cast out of heaven, Lucifer's name is changed to "Satan," which means "the Accuser." His name is changed to Satan not only because he is the accuser of man (Rev 12:10), but even more so because he accuses God of faithlessness and injustice. The name Satan appears often throughout the Bible, and he is described as the leader of the fallen angels and of the powers of darkness (Eph 2:2), and he is also called the devil (Rev 12:9), the serpent, and the dragon (Rev 20:2). Among the nine ranks of angels, among the entire created heavenly host, the Bible also makes clear Lucifer was God's greatest created heavenly being.

4

Description of Lucifer/Satan

IN A NUMBER OF passages, we are given information about Satan's character and position, but most of that information is describing him after his fall. In only two passages does the Bible talk about Lucifer *before* his fall: Isaiah 14:12–15 and Ezekiel 28:11–19.

The passage in Isaiah 14 describes what went on in Lucifer's heart as he was choosing to rebel against God, so even though it is describing Lucifer before his fall, it is in fact a description of his heart at the moment of his fall, describing for us the moment he chose, in his heart, to rebel against God.

The passage in Ezekiel 28, however, gives us some clear and detailed information about Lucifer before his fall, information about his original nature and character, describing him from the moment he was created and going on to describe his sin and his ultimate end, yet to come.

Ezekiel 28

Ezekiel 28 is divided into two clear sections. Ezekiel 28:1–10 is a prophecy against the *prince* of Tyre. Tyre was a great capital of the ancient world, and this prince of Tyre is its human ruler. This passage clearly tells us the prince of Tyre is a man, for we are told:

> And you say, 'I am a god,
> I sit in the seat of gods,
> In the midst of the seas,'
> Yet you are a man, and not a god. (Ezek 28:1–2 NKJV)

The passage continues to prophesy his destruction. The second section is Ezekiel 28:11–19, and it is here we find the description of Lucifer before his fall.

A Lamentation

Unlike the opening section of Ezekiel 28, which is clearly a prophecy, this second section is something different, for here God instructs Ezekiel as follows:

> The word of the Lord came to me: "Son of man, take up a *lament* concerning the king of Tyre and say to him: 'This is what the Sovereign Lord says.'" (Ezek 28:11 NIV)

God instructs Ezekiel to take up a lament concerning the king of Tyre. This is not a prophecy *per se*, but rather, at its heart, it is a lamentation of God over the king of Tyre. A lament is a song of weeping, a song of sorrow, so when God instructs Ezekiel to take up this lament over the king of Tyre, it is in fact God weeping over the king of Tyre.

The King of Tyre

Who is the king of Tyre? In the first section of Ezekiel 28, the prophecy is about a man, and that man is called the prince of Tyre. However, even though in the prophecy he is described as the prince of Tyre, that man was the earthly, or human, ruler of Tyre—in the eyes of the world, that man was the king of Tyre. So why then, in the second section of Ezekiel 28, does God take up a lament over the *king* of Tyre? If the earthly, or human, ruler of Tyre is called the prince of Tyre, then who is this king of Tyre?

As Ezekiel 28:11–19 continues, we see very clearly this king of Tyre is not a human being; rather, this king of Tyre is the real power behind the human ruler of Tyre. In fact, we are clearly told this king of Tyre is an angelic being who had set his power base over the city of Tyre. As the real power behind the earthly ruler of Tyre, this angelic being is called the king of Tyre. This king of Tyre is Satan.

Satan's Throne

The Bible tells us Satan sets up his throne at various places around the earth, moving it to various cities around the world. As a creature of time and space, Satan, just like you and I, can only be in one place at one time. He is not everywhere, for he is not God—he is a created creature. We are told the following in Revelation 2: "I know where you live—*where Satan has his throne*. Yet you remain true to my name. You did not renounce your faith in me, not even in the days of Antipas, my faithful witness, who was put to death in your city—where Satan lives" (Rev 2:13 NIV).

In this passage in Revelation 2, the apostle John is told to send a letter to the church in Pergamum, a city of the ancient world, being instructed by Jesus on what to write to the church in Pergamum. One of the things Jesus tells John to write is that they live in the city where Satan has his throne. This is the same situation as the one described in Ezekiel 28:11. Although by the time of Revelation 2:13, Satan had moved his throne to Pergamum, in the time of Ezekiel 28, Satan had his throne in Tyre, and so in Ezekiel 28 he is described as the king of Tyre, the real power behind the human ruler of Tyre. As a result, when God tells Ezekiel to take up a lament over the king of Tyre, he is instructing him to take up a song of weeping, a song of sorrow, over Satan.

Here is the passage from Ezekiel 28:11–19 in its entirety, giving us a very clear and detailed description of Lucifer before his fall:

> Moreover the word of the Lord came to me, saying, "Son of man, take up a lamentation for the king of Tyre, and say to him, 'Thus says the Lord God:
>
> "You *were* the seal of perfection,
> Full of wisdom and perfect in beauty.
> You were in Eden, the garden of God;
> Every precious stone was your covering:
> The sardius, topaz, and diamond,
> Beryl, onyx, and jasper,
> Sapphire, turquoise, and emerald with gold.
> The workmanship of your timbrels and pipes
> Was prepared for you on the day you were created.
> You were the anointed cherub who covers;
> I established you;
> You were on the holy mountain of God;
> You walked back and forth in the midst of fiery stones.
> You were perfect in your ways from the day you were created,

Till iniquity was found in you.
By the abundance of your trading
You became filled with violence within,
And you sinned;
Therefore I cast you as a profane thing
Out of the mountain of God;
And I destroyed you, O covering cherub,
From the midst of the fiery stones.
Your heart was lifted up because of your beauty;
You corrupted your wisdom for the sake of your splendor;
I cast you to the ground,
I laid you before kings,
That they might gaze at you.
You defiled your sanctuaries
By the multitude of your iniquities,
By the iniquity of your trading;
Therefore I brought fire from your midst;
It devoured you,
And I turned you to ashes upon the earth
In the sight of all who saw you.
All who knew you among the peoples are astonished at you;
You have become a horror,
And shall be no more forever.'" (NKJV)

The King of Tyre is an Angelic Being

As the passage begins, God describes the being he is lamenting, telling us in verse 13 that this being was *created*: "prepared for you on the day *you were created*" (Ezek 28:13).

Apart from Adam and Eve, human beings are not created, they are born, yet this being is described as being created. As a result, we know the being God is addressing here is not a human being; rather, this is an angelic being, for Psalm 148, when talking about the angels, tells us: "Praise him, all his angels . . . for he commanded and *they were created.*" (Ps 148:2, 5 NKJV) The king of Tyre is both a created and an angelic being.

The Anointed Cherub

As the passage continues, the rank and position of this angelic being is clearly described: "You were the *anointed cherub* who covers" (Ezek

28:14). Here we are told this angelic being, the king of Tyre, is a Cherub. The Cherubim (*cherubim* is the plural of cherub) are the greatest and most powerful angelic rank, with the closest association to God and to his throne. As a Cherub, this king of Tyre was an angelic being of the highest rank.

However, we are told not only was this king of Tyre a Cherub, but also he was the *anointed* cherub. This tells us not only was the king of Tyre of the highest and most powerful angelic rank, but even among the highest and most powerful angelic rank he was *anointed* above all of them, which means he was both set apart from them and was exalted above all the other cherubim. Since the Cherubim are the greatest and highest angelic rank, and since this king of Tyre was the *anointed* cherub, we know without a doubt this being was the greatest of the Cherubim, and therefore the greatest of God's created angels, the greatest of the created heavenly beings. This is Lucifer, later called Satan. As the passage continues, we learn about Lucifer's nature, his position, his role before God, and also, to some extent, what happened in the course of his rebellion.

Lucifer's Perfection

Ezekiel 28:2 tells us Lucifer was the "seal of perfection," that he was "full of wisdom and perfect in beauty." Lucifer was created absolutely perfect, utterly holy, magnificent. The term "seal of perfection" implies God created Lucifer as the very pinnacle of the entire angelic host, that he was God's greatest heavenly creature. When Lucifer is described as "full of wisdom," this tells us he, more than any other angelic being, would have known and understood God's goodness, his holiness, his love. When he is described as "perfect in beauty" this means not only was he the greatest and most powerful of the angelic beings by rank and position, but even physically he was breathtaking to behold. Furthermore, we are told: "You were perfect in your ways from the day you were created" (Ezek 28:15).

Not only was Lucifer perfect in beauty and full of wisdom, but, from the day that he was created, he was also perfect in all his *ways*. This means Lucifer, from the day he was created, was utterly and completely holy, good, and righteous, completely without sin—he was perfect in his nature.

From these verses we see God created Lucifer as his greatest angelic being, making him the greatest in rank and position above the entire angelic host. Lucifer was also filled with a deep wisdom, which allowed him to know and understand God better than any other angelic being, and he was made so physically beautiful he could only be described as the pinnacle of perfection. He was God's special, exalted, heavenly prince, his greatest heavenly creation, completely and perfectly holy, righteous, and good.

Representative of All Angels

One other very important thing we learn from this passage about Lucifer is that not only was Lucifer God's greatest heavenly creature, but he was also the *representative* of the entire angelic host before God, and he was also God's representative to the entire angelic host—he would speak to God on behalf of the entire angelic host, and he would speak to the entire angelic host on behalf of God. This is an exceedingly exalted position. How can we know this from the passage in Ezekiel 28? We can understand it from the following verse:

> Every precious stone was your covering:
> The sardius, topaz, and diamond,
> Beryl, onyx, and jasper,
> Sapphire, turquoise, and emerald with gold. (Ezek 28:13)

How, from this verse, can we conclude Lucifer was the representative of the entire angelic host before God, and also God's representative to the entire angelic host? This is an important truth to understand, and we can understand it as follows.

In Israel, the role of the high priest was to represent all twelve tribes of Israel before God, and, by extension, to represent God to all of Israel. The high priest, as well as all of the priesthood of Israel, came from the tribe of Levi, the tribe of Moses and Aaron, with Aaron, Moses' brother, being the first high priest. The Bible gives us many specific details on what was involved in the original institution of the high priest, including a detailed description of how the robes of the high priest were to be made. These were the robes the high priest would wear when he would go into the presence of God to represent all the people of Israel, and offer sacrifice for the sins of the people. This is described in Exodus 28:15–21:

> You shall make the breastplate of judgment. Artistically woven according to the workmanship of the ephod you shall make it: of gold, blue, purple, and scarlet thread, and fine woven linen, you shall make it. It shall be doubled into a square: a span shall

be its length, and a span shall be its width. And you shall put settings of stones in it, four rows of stones: The first row shall be a *sardius,* a *topaz,* and an *emerald*; this shall be the first row; the second row shall be a *turquoise,* a *sapphire,* and a *diamond*; the third row, a jacinth, an agate, and an amethyst; and the fourth row, a *beryl,* an *onyx,* and a *jasper.* They shall be set in gold settings. And the stones shall have the names of the sons of Israel, twelve according to their names, like the engravings of a signet, each one with its own name; they shall be according to the twelve tribes." (NKJV)

We are told in this passage that the high priest was to wear a breastplate as part of his priestly garment, and we are given the exact measurements of the breastplate that is to be made for the high priest. We are also told that, upon the breastplate the high priest was to wear when he entered into the presence of God, it was to contain settings of twelve precious stones, four rows of three stones. The precious stones are listed as *sardius, topaz, emerald; turquoise, sapphire, diamond; jacinth, agate, amethyst; beryl, onyx* and *jasper.* We are also told these twelve stones represented the twelve tribes of Israel.

This very clearly tells us the reason the high priest was to wear those twelve stones upon himself as he entered into the presence of God was to signify that he, as high priest, was representing all Israel—all twelve tribes—before God. This is exactly parallel to the description of Lucifer in Ezekiel 28. Further, in Ezekiel 28:13, we are told:

> Every precious stone was your covering:
> The sardius, topaz, and diamond,
> Beryl, onyx, and jasper,
> Sapphire, turquoise, and emerald with gold.

Where Aaron's high priest breastplate was adorned with twelve stones, we see that this "anointed Cherub's" covering was set with nine stones, all of which were also in gold settings, as were the stones on Aaron's breastplate. This means Lucifer, the anointed cherub, wore these nine precious stones upon himself, for they were his covering, which further denotes he was wearing the stones as part of some sort of covering garment.

What is the significance of the nine stones upon Lucifer's covering? We know the twelve stones on Aaron's breastplate represented the twelve tribes of Israel, one stone for each tribe. Why are there only nine stones on this anointed Cherub's covering? It is because, just as the twelve stones upon Aaron's robe represented the twelve tribes of Israel, so the nine stones upon Lucifer's covering represented the nine ranks of angels.

Also, we see that nine of the twelve stones on Aaron's breastplate are the same stones as the nine stones on the anointed Cherub's covering—sardius, topaz, diamond, beryl, onyx, jasper, sapphire, turquoise, and emerald. This is because the nine stones of the anointed Cherub's covering serve the same purpose as the twelve stones on the high priest's breastplate—just as the twelve stones being worn by the high priest upon his robe signify he is representing all twelve tribes of Israel before God, likewise the nine stones on the anointed Cherub's covering signify this anointed Cherub is representing all of the nine angelic ranks before God. This anointed Cherub is the representative of all the angelic ranks before God. Likewise, just as the high priest of Israel also represented God to the twelve tribes of Israel, so did the anointed cherub, Lucifer, represent God to all the angelic ranks.

As a result, we know from Ezekiel 28:13 that before his fall, this anointed Cherub, Lucifer, was not only God's greatest created heavenly being, but he was also in the position of representing all of the angels before God and representing God to all of the angels. Not only was that a position of highest exaltation, but it was also a position of highest creaturely authority and of the utmost trust. All of the other angelic beings would look to Lucifer, who was God's representative to them, to speak God's truth and God's will to them—they trusted him.

Everything about Lucifer's rank, power, position, wisdom and beauty was given to him by his creator, by God, and God specifically affirms this when he tells us the following: "I established you" (Ezek 28:14). Lucifer was established by God.

The Holy Mountain of God

As part of his exalted heavenly position, Lucifer is also described as follows:

> You were on the holy mountain of God;
> You walked back and forth in the midst of fiery stones." (Ezek 28:14)

The phrase "holy mountain of God" refers to the same mount as described in Isaiah 14:13:

> I will sit enthroned on the mount of assembly. (Isa 14:13 NIV)

This verse, Isaiah 14:13, is from the same Isaiah 14:12–15 passage which is a description of what was going on in Lucifer's heart as he was determining to rebel against God. In Isaiah 14:13, one of the things Lucifer desires is to sit enthroned on the "mount of assembly." This Mount of Assembly is the same "holy mountain of God" referred to in Ezekiel 28:14. The Mount of Assembly is in heaven, and it is the physical place in heaven upon which God had set his throne—God sits enthroned on the Mount of Assembly. The Mount of Assembly also seems to be the same place described in Job: "Now there was a day when the sons of God came to present themselves before the Lord, and Satan also came among them." (Job 1:6; also Job 2:1 NKJV)

The sons of God are described as coming to "present themselves *before* the LORD." This "presenting" or assembling themselves before the LORD, before his throne, is almost certainly the same Mount of *Assembly* referred to in Isaiah 14:13, which would also be the same as the "holy mountain of God" referred to in Ezekiel 28:14. It seems the reason this holy mountain of God, upon which God sits enthroned, is called the Mount of Assembly is because it was there, before God's throne upon the holy mountain, that the entire angelic host would come to present themselves, or to assemble, before God.

When Ezekiel 28:14 describes the anointed Cherub, Lucifer, as being on the holy mountain of God, this means he was positioned by the very throne of God, upon the top of God's holy mountain, upon the Mount of Assembly, before which the entire angelic host would gather and assemble. Again, this speaks to the exaltingly high position which Lucifer held in heaven.

The Fiery Stones

In Ezekiel, there is also a reference to the "fiery stones":

> You walked back and forth in the midst of fiery stones. (Ezek 28:14)

These fiery stones described here are described in the context of the anointed Cherub being on the holy mountain of God. This strongly suggests these fiery stones were also on the holy mountain of God, very likely right before God's throne. The Bible does not tell us the nature of these fiery stones, but they seem to be connected with the very presence of God and his throne. The passage in Exodus 24:10 may have a similar meaning:

> And saw the God of Israel. Under his feet was something like a pavement made of lapis lazuli, as bright blue as the sky. (NIV)

In the Exodus 24:10 passage, the seventy elders of Israel went up and they saw God, and when they saw him, they saw a pavement before him made of the precious stone lapis lazuli. This connects walking upon a precious stone pathway with the very presence of God.

When we are told Lucifer was on the holy mountain of God and walked among the stones of fire, it suggests these stones of fire could be similar to the lapis lazuli pavement the elders of Israel saw when they saw God—a pavement of precious stone before God's very presence. This suggests the stones of fire, in whose midst Lucifer walked upon in God's holy mountain, were likewise set before God's very presence. As a result, this is another description of the exceedingly exalted position of the anointed Cherub, Lucifer.

Why a Lament?

It is important to remember this entire passage of Ezekiel 28:11–19 is specifically called a "lament" (Ezek 28:12), a song of weeping, a song of God's sorrow over this anointed Cherub. Why does God weep over the anointed Cherub? The reason for this weeping starts to unfold in Ezekiel 28:15, "You were perfect in your ways from the day you were created, till iniquity was found in you."

This greatest and highest of God's creatures, his special "heavenly prince," his most beautiful and wisest creation, his seal of perfection, the one who was perfect in holiness and godliness, who was the representative of all the angels before God, sinned. Further, in that sin, he incited, and then led, a rebellion against God, which led to the fall of the angels. This was the origin of sin in the universe. God weeps over the fall of his highest creature.

5

The Angelic Rebellion

AFTER GOD'S CREATION OF time, space, and heaven, God created the angels, creating them in his own image (Ps 148:1–5), creating them in all their vast ranks and numbers. Among them was Lucifer, the greatest of all the created heavenly beings, the anointed Cherub, created holy, perfect, and good. All the sons of God watched God as he created the earth, and they all rejoiced and sang together as they witnessed that creation (Job 38:4–7), and Lucifer rejoiced and sang with them.

Heaven was a perfect world, as was the entire creation perfect. The entire universe was a place of light, beauty, and color, there was no darkness anywhere, and not even the concept of pain existed. Each and every one of God's angels was doing exactly what each was created to do, having perfect joy and fulfillment in the task. Each and every angel, across all ranks, knew only the love, goodness, peace, and joy of God, knowing total and complete fulfillment, living in perfect fellowship and harmony with God himself and with each other. Everywhere was only love and joy, and everything and everyone was only good and perfect.

Yet we are told there was rebellion in heaven. How and why would any angel rebel against God when all they knew was total love, peace, joy, goodness, and complete personal fulfillment? The Bible tell us the rebellion was instigated by one angelic being—Lucifer.

Lucifer Rejoices as God Creates

We know from Ezekiel 28 that Lucifer was created perfect in wisdom and beauty, that he was the greatest of God's angelic host, the seal of perfection. He was holy and righteous, and he was the representative of all the angelic host to God and God's representative to the entire angelic host. He was without sin, perfect in all of his ways. We also know from Job 38:4–7 that, during the original creation of the heavens and the earth (Gen 1:1), Lucifer had not yet rebelled, not even in his heart:

> Where were you *when I laid the earth's foundation?*
> Tell me, if you understand.
> Who marked off its dimensions? Surely you know!
> Who stretched a measuring line across it?
> On what were its footings set,
> or who laid its cornerstone—
> *while the morning stars sang together*
> *and all the angels shouted for joy?* (Job 38:4–7 NIV)

We are told in this passage that when God laid the earth's foundation (i.e., when he created Planet Earth) in Genesis 1:1, *all* the angels *shouted for joy*. When it says "all the angels" this includes Lucifer, and this does not mean *all except one* of the angels shouted for joy, or one angel shouted with deception or with the appearance of joy while actual rebellion was in his heart. Rather, it means exactly what it says, that all of the angels, including Lucifer, shouted with true, actual joy, as they watched God create the earth in Genesis 1:1. As a result of Job 38:4–7, we know with certainty that Lucifer's rebellion happened *after* Genesis 1:1.

Lucifer Sins

Yet, even though Lucifer rejoiced with God and with the entire angelic host as he watched God create the earth, we are told in Ezekiel 28:

> You were blameless in your ways
> from the day you were created
> *till wickedness was found in you.* (Ezek 28:15 NIV)

Although Lucifer was created perfect and blameless, somewhere along the way, Lucifer sinned. How was that possible? How could a holy, utterly sinless being, sin? How did Lucifer start to think in terms of rebellion? What was he rebelling against? What was he wanting to achieve? What was his goal? The Bible tells us:

> ... not a novice, lest being *puffed up with pride* he fall into the *same* condemnation as the *devil*. (1 Tim 3:6 NKJV)

> How you are fallen from heaven,
> O Lucifer, son of the morning!
> How you are cut down to the ground,
> You who weakened the nations!
> *For you have said in your heart*
> *'I will ascend into heaven,*
> *I will exalt my throne above the stars of God;*
> *I will also sit on the mount of the congregation*
> *On the farthest sides of the north;*
> *I will ascend above the heights of the clouds,*
> *I will be like the Most High.'* (Isa 14:12–14 NKJV)

> Your heart became proud
> on account of your beauty,
> and you corrupted your wisdom
> because of your splendor.
> So I threw you to the earth. (Ezek 28:17 NIV)

The Bible tells us Lucifer's heart became proud on account of his own greatness and beauty (Ezek 28:17). As a result, Lucifer wanted to exalt himself above the other angels and have their worship. Pride is exalting oneself over others, and so Lucifer began to think in terms of self-exaltation.

Isaiah 14:12–14 describes for us what was going on in Lucifer's heart as he chose this self-exaltation. We are told he wanted to exalt himself above all other angels ("the stars of God") and sit on his own throne; he wanted to sit on the seat of the mount, upon the Mount of Assembly, upon the holy mountain of God, the very same mount where God sat enthroned and before which all the angels would gather regularly before God (Job 1:6). The climax of Lucifer's desire was he wanted to *be like* God.

Lucifer's Pride

Lucifer's rebellion was not based on *hating* God; rather, Lucifer *envied* God—he wanted to be *like* God. This was the heart of his desire. In fact, since this is the heart of Lucifer's desire, he also believes it is the heart of everyone else's desire. This is why, in the garden of Eden, when he plans to tempt Adam by way of Eve, the serpent says to Eve:

> For God knows that in the day you eat of it your eyes will be opened, and you will *be like God*, knowing good and evil. (Gen 3:5 NKJV)

He tempts people with the very thing he himself desires. Lucifer believes everyone else desires what he desires—to be like God—and so he makes his temptations based on that appeal.

Here is what we can know: Lucifer was created perfect, holy, wise, good, and beautiful. He was God's greatest created being. He was God's representative to the entire angelic host, as he was their representative and spokesperson to God. He sincerely and righteously sang for joy with all the rest of the angelic host as he watched God create the earth in Genesis 1:1. He also knew and understood he was God's greatest creature—greatest both in beauty and wisdom. Ezekiel 28:17 makes it very clear it was on account of his *beauty* that he became proud.

How long did Lucifer linger over himself, over his beauty, before thoughts of self-exaltation started to swirl in his heart? Certainly it was a long time, perhaps many thousands of years—it did not happen overnight, but rather it happened step by step, little by little, and with every step along the way Lucifer knew clearly the choices he was making, also knowing the ramifications of those choices.

As God's wisest, most beautiful creature, Lucifer, above all others, knew and understood best of all God's perfect love, goodness, wisdom, and holiness. And yet, even with this understanding, he began to linger over himself, to linger over his own beauty and wisdom, coming to the point where he started to think "Look at how beautiful, wise, and great I am—I am greater than all the rest of God's creatures," and he would look at God and say "Look at how great you are! Magnificent! Beautiful! Worshiped by all," and then in the next step say, "I also deserve such worship and praise!" This progression did not happen in a moment; it took time, and Lucifer made a clear choice along every step of the way, ultimately resulting in a choice to try to exalt himself above all other creatures and to try to be like God. The defining moment of that choice being made is outlined in Isaiah 14:12–14:

> How you are fallen from heaven,
> O Lucifer, son of the morning!
> How you are cut down to the ground,

You who weakened the nations!
For you have said in your heart:
'I will ascend into heaven,
I will exalt my throne above the stars of God;
I will also sit on the mount of the congregation
On the farthest sides of the north;
I will ascend above the heights of the clouds,
I will be like the Most High.' (NKJV)

Lucifer's Rebellion

Lucifer, God's greatest angelic creation, the wisest, most beautiful, most exalted of the entire angelic host, was the author of rebellion. How could this be, since he was created holy, righteous, and good, and was perfect in all of his ways from the day he was created (Ezek 28:15)? And yet we are told in that same verse:

You *were* perfect in your ways from the day you were created,
Till iniquity was found in you. (NKJV)

How was it possible for sin to arise where there was no sin? Not only was there no sin within Lucifer or within any of the angelic host, but there was no sin or evil at all, anywhere, in the entire creation, and yet Lucifer sinned. This can only be understood by understanding that we all have been given free will.

The Choice of Free Will

Sin is the result of a choice a person makes. In its essence, sin is the choice to exalt oneself above others, to put oneself first, even above God. God did not create sin, but God did give free will. *All* of us—human and angel—have free will, this is the inviolate gift of God's making. No one can force us to choose anything—we can be tortured, manipulated, or deceived, we can even, under those circumstances, pay lip service to what a tormentor may want to hear, but ultimately, even in the midst of those things, within one's own heart, our choice always remains completely our own. This is what defines free will—it is our God-given ability to choose what we want to do and what we believe.

Why did God give free will? The answer is simple—without free will, there is no love. God loves us, and he wants us to love him. If we had no free will, then we could never love God. God gave free will to everyone whom he created in his image—this includes angels and man. The reason God gave free will is because God is love, and just as God loves us, he also wants us to love him. True love cannot be forced, predestined, or predetermined, it only exists when freely given by one person to another, given by their own free-will choice. Without free will, love from creature to creator cannot exist, so God gave us all an inviolate free will whereby we can choose to love him.

Imagine you really loved someone and wanted that person to love you back, and you tied that person up, held a gun to their head, and said "Say you love me or I will shoot," and they say "I love you." Is that love? Would there be any meaning to that? No, it would be meaningless since true love cannot be forced—true love is something that is given freely, as a matter of one's own choice, from one's own heart. The only way real love can exist, the only way love matters, is when the person you love looks back at you and, on their own, from their own free heart, says "I love you." That is love.

That is also what God wants—our true love. If God created a race of robot-humans, who were predetermined to do what he had ordained in advance, then any so-called love or faith is nothing of the kind—it is an illusion, a fiction, no different than holding a gun to someone's head and demanding they declare their love for you. There is no love in that situation. For this reason, God gave us free will—he did not give us the illusion of free will, or the deceiving impression we have free will when actually we do not (as some teach is the case, in which case God would be a deceiver). Rather God gave us real, true, actual free will, whereby we, on our own, can freely choose to love him. Everyone made in God's image, both man and angel, has free will.

However, by giving us free will, there is also a risk, and it is a risk God was willing to take. The risk is a creature may choose, of their own free will, to not love God, or that a creature will choose something else over God—a creature can choose to reject or hate God, rebel against him, or exalt himself above both God and others. This is the heart of sin—exalting oneself above others, an expression of complete selfishness. Sin is a possible outcome of having free will.

Sin's Nature and Origin

What exactly *is* sin? *How* can free will allow for it, and what is death? Why do sin and death go hand in hand? God's creation was perfect and flawless, it was only good and holy, completely without corruption or evil or stain. How then could sin or evil come into existence within a creation that was only perfect and good?

Since it is the nature of free will to allow for a choice, then just as we can choose to freely love God, we can also freely choose to not love him, and to reject him. We can choose to exalt ourselves above God and all others—an exaltation which is false, for we are not above God; no creature can ever be greater than its creator. This in fact was the sin of Lucifer. Lucifer, like us, had his God-given free will, whereby he could choose to love God or not. He lingered long over his own created beauty, his great wisdom, and his own perfection, all as created by God, and as he lingered upon himself, over time, he was presented with a choice—either love God, who himself is the source and creator of all that was good in Lucifer, or choose to try to exalt himself, the creature, over his creator. Lucifer chose self-exaltation. It was in choosing self-exaltation that sin was born in Lucifer—so we are specifically told in Ezekiel 28:15:

> You were perfect in your ways from the day you were created, till *iniquity was found in you*. (NKJV)

The Bible is very specific as to how it words this: it does not say "you sinned." Rather, it says "till iniquity *was found* in you." When Lucifer made his choice of self-exaltation, sin *came into existence* within him—it did not exist anywhere in creation until he made that choice. Once that choice was made, a choice born of his *selfish desire* to exalt himself over God, sin became present, or was found, within Lucifer, and it existed *only* within him, existing nowhere else in all creation. This is what is described in James 1:15:

> Then, *after desire has conceived*, it gives *birth to sin*; and sin, when it is full-grown, gives birth to death. (NIV)

Lucifer *desired* to be like God, and that desire led to a choice—a choice of either remaining loving and faithful to God, or choosing to reject God and exalt himself. Lucifer chose to reject God and exalt himself. Once that choice was made, sin existed in Lucifer, it was *born* of his desire, born of his choice. Lucifer's choice of self-exaltation resulted in the existence of sin.

What then is sin? Ultimately, sin is the *separation of oneself from God*, by an act of free will, and sin, in its very nature, results in *death*. But how can a *choice* of self-exaltation result in sin and in death? We can understand this by looking at Jesus' own words.

The Way, the Truth, the Life

Jesus tells us the following:

> Jesus said to him, "*I am the way, the truth, and the life.*" (John 14:6 NKJV)

We are also told the following:

> He is before all things, and in him all things *hold together*. (Col 1:17 NKJV)

Jesus specifically describes himself, and his own divine nature, as being "the life." He does not say he is merely "alive," but rather he is actually life itself. He himself, God Almighty, is the *source* of all life—*apart from him*, there is *no life*. This is further affirmed in Colossians 1:17, where Jesus is described as *holding all things together*—he *sustains* all things, he *makes them alive*. God and God alone is life, and life exists *only* in him and from him—apart from God, there is no life. To be apart from God, to be separated from him, is therefore to be separated from life, and to be separated from life is the definition of death. True death is to be separated, or cut off, from God, separated from the life that he *is*.

When Lucifer made the free-will choice of self-exaltation, choosing himself over God, in that moment there was an immediate, real, and practical consequence of that choice—with that free-will choice, he immediately *physically divorced himself* from God, he *separated* himself from God. With that separation from God, he simultaneously divorced and separated himself completely from *life*. The moment Lucifer chose self-exaltation, divorcing himself from God, he was no longer one with God, and was therefore no longer one with life. As a result, he no longer had life within him. His free-will choice of rejecting God broke his bond with God, broke his union with God, who is the source of life. As a result, Lucifer became immediately dead, for apart from God there is no life. Lucifer physically continued to exist, but only as something devoid of life.

All of this was the consequence of Lucifer's free-will choice—Lucifer's free-will choice of separating himself from God, separating himself from life, *actually* resulted in his separation from God, which then resulted in his separation from life, which then resulted in his immediate death.

By choosing self over God, one divorces oneself from God and thereby divorces oneself from life. By divorcing oneself from the source of life itself, one becomes dead. Sin is the choice to separate oneself from God, thereby separating oneself from the source of life. With that separation from life, sin always and only results in death.

It is exactly as when you clip a flower from a flower bush: the flower bush gives life to the flowers that grow from the bush, but once you clip one flower off of the flower bush, there is no longer any way for the flower to be sustained, and the flower dies, for it is removed from its source of life. This is the exact same scenario of choosing self over God. By choosing self over God, we cut ourselves off from the source of life, and, by becoming cut off from the source of life, cut off from God, we become separated from life, and so are dead.

When Lucifer chose self over God, chosen of his own free will, he sinned, and with that sin came death, for with his choice of self over God he immediately cut himself off from the source of life. His nature then became immediately corrupted, cut off from all that is good and holy, cut off from life, imbued *only* with complete selfishness, with nothing of love, life, or goodness existing at all within him.

Lucifer's Physical Being

As a created being, Lucifer is a physical being—a different kind of physical than flesh and bone, but physical nonetheless, being subject fully to time and space. As a physical being, Lucifer's very nature is a *physical* nature, and so the corruption of his nature by sin was itself a *physical corruption*. Lucifer's physical nature was created as perfect, holy, and good, completely one with God, and filled with the life that is God. By cutting himself off from God by choosing self over God, his physical nature was now no longer one with God, and so his created physical nature became *physically corrupt* and devoid of life. Just as God's entire creation is a *physical* creation, so also is there a *physicality* to sin. As a result, sin *always* has *physical consequences*. The selfishness and lifelessness that took up residence within Lucifer upon his choice of self over God was the innate result of sin, the result of separating himself from God. Being fully separated from God, that sin and selfishness then devoured him, for sin and selfishness now became his nature, with nothing of love, goodness, or holiness remaining. Sin and selfishness would devour him utterly until there was nothing left but the insatiable, unquenchable desire of self, impossible to satisfy. That is the nature of sin, and it is the full consequence of separating oneself from life.

Why Didn't Lucifer Physically Die?

The separation from God that results from sin, from choosing self over God, from divorcing oneself from God, is the definition of death, for it is a full divorcing of oneself from the Source of Life. If that is so, then why does Lucifer continue to exist? Why did he not decay and physically die, as humans do?

One very real possibility is Lucifer and all the other angels had eaten from the tree of life and therefore are incapable of physically dying. The Bible tells us the heavenly angels *do* eat: "Human beings *ate the bread of angels*; he sent them all the food they could eat" (Ps 78:25 NIV). Since Psalm 78:25 specifically tells us the heavenly angels do in fact eat, it is a very real possibility that the angels, all of them, before any fall or rebellion occurred, did eat of the tree of life and so are immortal. As a result, when Lucifer did sin, and cut himself off from God, from the Source of Life, he immediately died in his person, in his spirit, but he physically continues to live forever because he had eaten from the tree of life, and so he cannot physically die. The same would be true of the other fallen angels. This means that, upon sinning, Lucifer and all of the rebellious angels would forever be in a state of eternal sin (it is for this reason God drove man out of Eden after Adam ate of the forbidden fruit—Genesis 3:22—so that man would not live forever in his sin).

God is Truth

In addition to being "the life," God himself is also "the truth," so to divorce oneself from God means one will then also be divorced, or cut off, from truth. To be divorced from truth means one's nature will be a nature of only lies and deception. When Lucifer sinned by choosing self over God, he separated himself not only from life but also from truth, so that there was now nothing of truth remaining within him. As a result, with his separation from truth, his entire nature became a nature of only lies. This is why Lucifer is called the father of lies:

> When he lies, he speaks his native language, for he is a liar and the father of lies. (John 8:44 NIV)

Lucifer is described as the father of lies, with lies being his native language. This is *not* because he was created that way—he was not, he was created perfect and holy (Ezek 28:12, 15)—but he *became* a creature of lies as the direct result of sin. When Lucifer chose self-exaltation, not only did he divorce himself completely from the Source of Life, but he also divorced himself completely from truth. By separating himself from truth, truth no longer remained within him in any way whatsoever; rather, only lies took up residence within him and came to define his nature.

Sin is Completed in Death

Sin is choosing self over God. With that choice, one cuts oneself off from God, who is the Source of Life. By being cut off from the Source of Life, one no longer has any union with life, and so the result of sin is always and only death. Death goes hand in hand with sin—it is the immediate and natural result of sin, of being cut off from God, the Source of Life. We are told:

> For the wages of sin is death. (Rom 6:23 NASB)

> Then, when desire has conceived, it gives birth to sin; and sin, when it is full-grown, brings forth death. (Jas 1:15 NKJV)

Death is the only possible outcome of sin. Not only does death result from sin, but sin, once conceived, is actually *seeking* its fulfillment in death, sin is completed in death, death is the *final conclusion* of sin. The essence of sin is selfishness, for sin breeds an unquenchable *desire* for self. This is affirmed in the following Scriptures:

> But if you do not do what is right, sin is crouching at your door; *it desires to have you*, but you must rule over it. (Gen 4:7 NIV)

> Therefore do not let sin reign in your mortal body so that you obey *its evil desires*. (Rom 6:12 NIV)

> Abstain from *sinful desires*, which wage war against your soul.
> (1 Pet 2:11 NIV)

Sin itself, born of the free-will choice of self over God, has *desires*, and its *desire* is to continue to breed complete selfishness. These sinful desires of self are impossible to satisfy, and so sin keeps on consuming until there is nothing left to consume. As a result, sin leads to the full *consumption* of its host—for a physical, flesh-and-bone human being who has not eaten from the tree of life, that means we physically age, decay, and die, for the sin within us eats us alive. Our *physical death* is *sin achieving fulfillment*. Sin is *completed* in death, it has its full conclusion in death. Sin is relentless until it reaches death. Once sin results in death, that sin is then satisfied, is made complete, fulfilled, brought to conclusion.

Lucifer's Choice—A Choice Of Death and Lies

With his choice of self over God, sin was found in Lucifer, born in him, and he immediately became separated from God, separated from the Source of Life and from truth. As a result, he became entirely dead, filled only with lies. His physical nature changed as a result, being changed from holy, beautiful, and good, to dead, wretched, and corrupt entirely. Upon making his choice, and until he later began to spread rebellion, Lucifer was the only dead creature in all of God's creation, the only one filled with lies and the only one separated from truth. Consumed by lies, selfishness, corruption, and deception, Lucifer's sole plan was to pursue his own self-exaltation, for with the birth of sin within his nature, he was now consumed with complete and insatiable selfishness, and deceived by complete, devouring deception.

It is one thing to make the free-will choice to rebel and sin, and keep that within one's own heart, but another thing to try to accomplish the goal that is born out of that choice. Upon making his choice to exalt himself over God, to become a creature who himself would be worshiped, Lucifer now had to devise a plan by which he could accomplish his goal of self-exaltation.

Lucifer Spreads Rebellion

Lucifer had chosen in his heart to try and make himself like God, to receive the worship of angels. That choice remained private, known only to

God and no one else. But how was he to accomplish his goal? If he wanted to succeed, he had to devise a plan and a strategy to make it happen. What would be his strategy? What possible plan could Lucifer make that would incite God's angelic host, who knew only perfect love, peace, goodness, and happiness, as well as complete personal fulfillment, to rebel against God and worship Lucifer? What would be his angle? It was a question to which he applied the fullness of his God-given wisdom and intelligence.

Lucifer's Gamble

Before Lucifer could start to strategize a way to accomplish his goal, he first had to decide if he thought he could get away with it. Do you believe you personally could wage a war against God and win? Do you believe you could defy God and beat him? No one, not even the biggest fool, would seriously believe such a thing. If you and I, as imperfect as we are, can know enough to understand that a plan to fight God is complete folly, not even qualifying as futile, do you think God's greatest creature would be so stupid as to believe he could wage a war against God and win? It is impossible that Lucifer was so stupid—in fact, we are told in Ezekiel 28:12 that he was "full of wisdom." Lucifer, above all creatures, knew it would be impossible to wage a war against God and win.

That being the case, what possible strategy could Lucifer devise to succeed in his rebellious goals? Keep in mind the entire rebellion began, and happened, first and foremost, in Lucifer's heart (Isa 14:13) and it *stayed there* until he could figure out a way to accomplish it. God knew Lucifer's heart, and there is no question that at every step along the way of Lucifer choosing to sin, God was speaking love and wisdom to Lucifer's heart, so that every step of the way Lucifer had a clear choice, a clear understanding, of what he was doing, and was very clear about what choices he was making. When Lucifer, in his own heart, crossed the line from temptation to action, God knew it, though none of the rest of heaven did.

If Lucifer's rebellion could not be a rebellion of going to war against God, of trying to overpower God, trying to beat him in a fight, then what kind of rebellion could it be? Lucifer wanted to exalt himself above all other angels and receive their worship. How could he do this and get away with it? There is good biblical reason to believe Lucifer's strategy was to try and *outwit* God, that his rebellion consisted of trying to apply God's own character against God himself.

Lucifer's Rebellion and Strategy

Does God do anything without reason? No—everything God does he does with purpose and plan. This includes all the details of his creation, including the total number of angels he would create. The Bible tells us the very numbers of created things, the very numbers involved in his creation, are by God's design and plan:

> I do not want you to be ignorant of this mystery, brothers and sisters, so that you may not be conceited: Israel has experienced a hardening in part until the full *number* of the Gentiles has come in . . . (Rom 11:25 NIV).

> And even the very hairs of your head are all *numbered*. (Matt 10:30 NIV).

The Bible also tells us there is a "full number" of people that will come to believe. There is a *number* that is to be fulfilled. We are told even the hairs of our heads are numbered. Even such a small and seemingly insignificant detail as the number of hairs on our head matters to God and is part of his design. For some reason, there seems to be a perfect number for every aspect of God's creation.

Likewise, if even the number of hairs on our head have been predetermined by God, then the total number of human beings who will be given the gift of life has also been predetermined by God. This also means the total number of angels to be created had been predetermined by God—there was a *specific number* of *angels* God had determined to create, a number which was the *perfect number* for his creation.

God did not create an infinite number of angels, but a finite and specific number. Why did God create that specific number of angels? It seems the specific number of angels God created was the perfect number of angels for his plan and design of creation, just as there is a perfect number of people who will be born into existence and given the gift of life.

It seems this truth—God having a perfect number of created angels for his creation—was the truth upon which Lucifer gambled when he decided to rebel against God. He would reason as follows: if the specific number of angels created was the perfect number of angels for God's creation, then if he, Lucifer, rebelled against God, and tried to get other angels to rebel with him, what are the chances God would destroy him or the other angels, wiping them out of existence, since, if God did destroy him or any of the other angels, then God would no longer have that perfect number of angels?

As a result, based on the reasoning of there being a perfect number of angels for God's creation, Lucifer's gamble was that if he rebelled against God, God would *not* destroy him, because doing so would ruin God's perfect number of created angels.

Based on the biblical truth that God has specific numbers in mind for his creation, and based on the fact that Lucifer had to have thought about how he could get away with a rebellion against God, a rebellion that was not a rebellion of force, but a rebellion of wit, it is reasonable and in line with biblical truth to conclude this was Lucifer's thinking as he began to plan how to accomplish his goal. In fact, we know from both history and the rest of the Bible that Lucifer's reasoning was correct—Lucifer *did* rebel against God and God did *not* destroy him, nor did he destroy any of the rebel angels, for they rebelled and yet they remain alive, and so, even after the angelic rebellion, God's perfect angelic number remained.

Lucifer's Temptation to the Other Angels

For Lucifer to have an effective rebellion, it had to involve the other angels, since there were no other creatures from whom he could receive worship, and we know from Isaiah 14:12–14 that his goal was to raise himself above the "stars of God" (angels) and to be "like God" to them. For his rebellion to succeed, it would require that other angels rebel with him. We know from Revelation 12:9 and 12:3–4 that one-third of the angelic host *did* rebel with Lucifer:

> The *great dragon* was hurled down—that ancient serpent called the devil, or Satan, who leads the whole world astray. He was *hurled to the earth*, and *his angels with him*. (Rev 12:9 NIV)

> Then another sign appeared in heaven: an enormous red *dragon* with seven heads and ten horns and seven crowns on its heads. *Its tail swept a third of the stars out of the sky and flung them to the earth.* (Rev 12:3–4 NIV)

Revelation 12:3–4 tells us one-third of the angelic host rebelled with Lucifer. How did Lucifer incite rebellion among the other angels? What possible angle did Lucifer find that could tempt any angel to rebel against a life filled only with love, peace, happiness, joy, goodness, and complete personal fulfillment? We know from Genesis 3:5 that Lucifer believes the thing he desires is also what others will desire. He wanted to "be like God," and so he deceived Eve with that same desire. This was a desire that appealed to his pride and self-exaltation. As a result, this gives us a clue as to how Lucifer tempted the angels to rebel.

Pride Goes before the Fall

In God's plan of creation, man is second only to God in the entire created hierarchy. God's angels are, ultimately, beneath us:

> Are not all angels ministering spirits sent to *serve* those who will *inherit salvation*? (Heb 1:14 NIV)

> Do you not know that we will *judge angels*? How much more the things of this life! (1 Cor 6:3 NIV)

For the time being, fallen man is seemingly lower than angels, but that is only temporary. Our eternal place is ultimately above all angelic ranks and above all created things, for we, humanity, are to be God's special companion, his bride, and we will rule over angels.

The heart of Lucifer's own rebellion was pride, the desire to exalt himself over other creatures. We also know he applies that same strategy, the appeal to pride, when tempting human beings (Gen 3:5; also Matt 4:8–9). As a result, it is reasonable to conclude that Lucifer also applied that same strategy of temptation to the other angels—he wanted to instill in the angels an angelic pride and then appeal to that pride so as to incite discontent and, ultimately, rebellion. We know from Ezekiel 28:15–16 that Lucifer, in heaven, sowed the seeds of rebellion on a wide scale:

> You were blameless in your ways
> from the day you were created
> till wickedness was found in you.
> Through your *widespread trade*
> you were filled with violence, and you sinned. (NIV)

The term "widespread trade" carries with it the meaning that Lucifer was actively and calculatingly trying to spread his rebellion among the other angels in a planned and methodical way. This means he had devised a plan of how to spread rebellion, and it seems the way by which he planned to do that was by means of instilling, and then appealing to, angelic pride. This would somehow involve a strategy of deceiving the angels into thinking God was not being fair with them. In so doing, Lucifer would have a way of sowing discontent even where there was only love, peace, joy, and fulfillment.

What possible angle could Lucifer find to instill a sense of injustice among the angels, a sense that, somehow, God was not being fair to them? It seems the angle by which Lucifer would instill angelic pride was with the angle of man.

The Angle of Man

Somewhere along the way, either as God's own special confidant, or as his representative to the entire angelic host, Lucifer came into the knowledge that God was planning to create a new, second creature: man. Most likely, God himself announced this plan to the entire angelic host as they would gather before him at the Mount of Assembly (Job 1:6). God would have told of his plan to create a new creature who would be his companion, his bride (Rev 21:19; Eph 5:25–32), and who would be exalted to sit at his right hand (Eph 2:6). This creature man was to be made in both the image *and* the likeness of God (Gen 1:26), and would *rule* the creation with God (Gen 1:28). In this position, man would be exalted above all angels, and the entire angelic host would be subservient to man (Heb 1:14; 1 Cor 6:3). This was God's plan for creation and the angels would have rejoiced.

While this was yet a plan but not yet actually undertaken, it seems this was the angle Lucifer latched onto to sow discontent and rebellion among the angels. We know Lucifer approaches temptation by sowing seeds of doubt by asking questions:

> Now the serpent was more cunning than any beast of the field which the Lord God had made. And he said to the woman, "Has God indeed said, 'You shall not eat of every tree of the garden?'" (Gen 3:1 NKJV)

Lucifer sows seeds of doubt by asking subtle questions that carry within them seeds of destruction. This is not a thoughtless exercise, nor an unplanned undertaking, but a very clearly thought out and calculated strategy. Likewise, we could expect Lucifer's temptation of the other angels, using the angle of man, to go something like this: "Is it right that man should be above us? Aren't we the first of God's creation? Is that fair of God?" Since this was an appeal to pride, which was the very heart of

Lucifer's own rebellion, there is good reason to think this appeal to pride was the angle Lucifer decided to use to incite discontent, and then rebellion, among the angels.

We already know from Job 38:4–7 that all the angelic host knew of Earth, and there is no question they knew the earth was destined to be the uniquely special center of God's creation, which is why they shouted for joy upon its creation. In the revelation by God that he would be making man, it would also be revealed to the entire angelic host that the earth would be given to man to rule, to be his home, and this would only play into Lucifer's strategy of using man and his upcoming preeminence as his angle of angelic temptation. All of this is in keeping with Lucifer's clear strategy, as outlined in the Bible, of appealing to pride to foster a fall. By using the angle of man and his planned preeminence above angels as his strategy of temptation, we can understand how that basis could then be used to widen into rebellion against God, along the following line of questions Lucifer could pose to the angelic host:

> "Shouldn't we, as God's first creation, be preeminent over man? Is it fair that we, who were created first, should be subservient to this second creature? Why should the earth be given to man? We watched its creation—do we not have a prior right to it? How is this loving of God? He favors an uncreated second creature over you—is this just of him? Is this loving of him? Does he truly love you?"

This scenario represents a clear and biblical strategy of sowing discontent in a universe where only love, peace, happiness, joy, and fulfillment exist. Of course, the entire temptation, the entire strategy, is a complete lie—but the questions, once asked, sow the seeds of doubt.

It is also important to remember the one who is asking these questions, the one who is sowing these seeds of doubt, is the greatest angelic being among them all, one who is in fact their representative to God, and God's representative to them. As a result, there is an authority that goes with that position and standing. It is also almost certain Lucifer did not stand on a mountaintop in heaven and broadcast these questions en masse to the entire angelic host; rather, as is implied by the term "widespread trade" (Ezek 28:16, 18), he methodically, selectively, one by one, angel by angel, sowed the seeds of discontent over time, most probably over a very long period of time. His approach would have been subtle, careful and calculated. It is also important to understand that, during this entire time of subtle, long-lasting, calculated temptation of the other angels, God would have been aware of it, known of it, even though it was being done in secret by Lucifer. It is without a doubt that, as each angel was being tempted by Lucifer, God would have also been speaking truth to the heart of that angel so each angel was absolutely clear that what they were hearing from Lucifer were lies, and that they had the very clear choice of remaining in God's love. As is the case with us, God did not abandon his angels to deception, for he loved them.

After whatever length of time it took for such angelic discontent to become widespread, and certainly throughout that whole time of temptation, Lucifer was presenting himself as the answer and the alternative to God. He would lead the angels to their proper place of eminence, the position that they deserved as God's first created creatures. He was, after all, their representative. In all of this Lucifer gambled on the fact that God would not destroy them—neither destroy him nor any angels who would rebel with him, and so he calculated that he would get away with his rebellion.

The question then arises: If he could get angels to rebel with him, to choose to abandon God and to follow and worship him instead, where would they go? Would they remain in heaven, or would they leave heaven and go somewhere else instead? What alternative was there to their home, heaven? It seems if there was an alternative place to go to after their rebellion, the only alternative was Earth—and in fact, this seems likely based on subsequent events. It seems it was Lucifer's strategy that, upon succeeding in inciting rebellion against God, he and the other rebel angels would leave heaven and set up a domain on Earth, the very same home that was created for man.

As a result, we can summarize Lucifer's strategy as follows: use the angle of man's upcoming creation and his position of being God's companion and bride, and of his upcoming lordship of Earth and preeminence over angels, as the means by which to sow angelic discontent with God and thereby instill a sense among the angels that God was not being fair to them, and that they, the angelic host, deserved preeminence over man. From there, Lucifer would promise he would lead the angels to such a place of angelic preeminence, where they would fulfill their purpose as God's first and foremost creation, and that Earth would be the place where that could be fulfilled. In all of this, Lucifer was gambling that God would not destroy his angels and ruin the perfect angelic number of his making. The Bible tells us Lucifer succeeded in inciting rebellion against God. However, ultimately, it did not go as Lucifer had planned.

Which Angels Rebelled?

We know from Revelation 12:9 and 12:3–4 that one-third of God's angels rebelled, doing so with the full understanding of what they were doing. They chose to rebel against God, to dismiss his plan of man, choosing to exalt themselves, and to follow Lucifer. But did this rebellion occur among all nine ranks of angels, or was it more prevalent among certain ranks than it was among others? The Bible seems to say the rebellion happened among the lower six ranks of angels, and not among the highest three, as is indicated by the Bible's listing of ranks of fallen angels:

- *principalities* (Eph 6:12; Rom 8:38; Col 2:15 (KJV));
- *powers* (Col 1:16; 2:15; Eph 6:2, 12; Rom 8:38);
- *dominions* (Eph 1:21);
- *rulers* (Eph 1:21; 3:10; 6:2, 12; Col 1:16);
- *authorities* (Eph 1:21; 3:10; 6:2; Col 1:16; 1 Pet 3:22);
- *angels* (Matt 25:41)

Principalities, powers, dominions, rulers, authorities, and angels are the lower six ranks of the angelic hierarchy and are all listed in the various verses that list the ranks of fallen angels. With the exception of the Cherub Lucifer, who led the angelic rebellion, nowhere does the Bible ever include Cherubim, Seraphim, or thrones in any listing of fallen angels. As a result, we can conclude the angelic rebellion took place among the lower six ranks of the angelic hierarchy.

War in Heaven

Lucifer's rebellion was not a rebellion of force, for it is impossible he could have thought he could fight God by force, beat him, and take his kingdom. Rather, his rebellion was one of wit, strategy, and calculation, of trying to use God's own character, his own plan, against him. Lucifer had been sowing and fomenting the seeds of rebellion throughout the angelic ranks in secret (though not secret to God) over an extended period of time. In order

The Angelic Rebellion

to accomplish the plan of rebellion, sooner or later the time would come when the rebellion would have to be declared, and that time did come. The Bible does not tell us how the rebellion was declared, but it would have to have been declared before God himself and before the rest of the entire angelic host. It is reasonable to believe the rebellion was declared at one of the regular gatherings at the Mount of Assembly, when all the sons of God would gather before God (Job 1:6; 2:1).

What did Lucifer expect would happen when such a declaration was made? He was gambling that neither he nor the rebel angels would be destroyed, but rather, by avoiding destruction, they would live and continue upon their chosen path. If that would be the case and they were not destroyed, then it seems the only conclusion would be that the rebellion would succeed, and Lucifer and the rebel angels would leave heaven for Earth, and Lucifer would have the worship he wanted. But it did not go as planned. It is true that neither Lucifer nor the rebel angels were destroyed, so in that respect, Lucifer calculated correctly; but there was a whole world of consequences of which Lucifer was not aware and which he did not consider. Revelation 12 tells us:

> And war broke out in heaven: Michael and his angels fought with the dragon; and the dragon and his angels fought, but they did not prevail, nor was a place found for them in heaven any longer. So the great dragon was cast out, that serpent of old, called the Devil and Satan, who deceives the whole world; he was cast to the earth, and his angels were cast out with him. (Rev 12:7-9 NKJV)

When the rebellion was declared, it resulted in war in heaven. It is important to understand this war in heaven was *not* Lucifer's rebellion; that is to say, Lucifer did not rebel against God by force. Rather, the war in heaven was God's *response* to the declaration of the rebellion.

It is true that neither Lucifer nor the rebel angels would be destroyed or obliterated as a result of the rebellion, but there were other options Lucifer did not foresee. Rather than being destroyed out of existence upon declaring their rebellion, Lucifer and all the rebel angels were forcibly cast out of heaven. But to where were they cast? Revelation 12:9 tells us clearly the place to which Lucifer and the rebel angels were cast when they were thrown out of heaven—they were cast to Earth.

When Did the Angelic Rebellion Happen?

We know from Job 38:4–7 that the angelic rebellion happened *after* Genesis 1:1. We also know from other verses that the angelic rebellion happened *before* Genesis 1:2, and we know this as biblically true by looking at the state of Earth in Genesis 1:2 and comparing that to many other verses in the Bible that speak to the condition of darkness and a global flood.

We're told in Genesis 1:2 (NIV): "Now the earth was [or *became*] formless and empty, darkness was over the surface of the deep, and the Spirit of God was hovering over the waters." The earth in Genesis 1:2 was formless, empty, flooded with a global ocean, covered in complete darkness, and had the Holy Spirit hovering over it. The earth in Genesis 1:2 was uninhabitable—a ruined wasteland. Yet, the Bible is very clear—God did *not* create the earth as an uninhabitable, ruined wasteland—it was created in Genesis 1:1 to be *inhabited*, which also means it was created to be *habitable* for man, it was created perfect. Yet, in Genesis 1:2, the earth was completely *uninhabitable*—man could not live upon a global ocean. In addition to being covered by a global ocean, the earth was also covered in complete darkness. As discussed in the chapter on darkness, the presence of this darkness shows clearly that the earth in Genesis 1:2 was cursed.

Why was the earth cursed? It was cursed because of the rebel angels being cast out of heaven and thrown down upon the earth. The earth became the place upon which all the evil of the universe was thrown. As a result, God cursed the earth, cursing it as a place of uninhabitable desolation, covered by the curse of the global ocean, surrounded by the curse of darkness, and with the Holy Spirit himself being present to restrain the great evil that had been cast down (2 Thess 2:6–7 NKJV). As a result, we can know the angelic rebellion happened *after* Genesis 1:1 but *before* Genesis 1:2.

The Pit and the Abyss

When people talk about the fall of the angels, one very common and completely unbiblical understanding of this event is Lucifer and the rebel angels were cast out of heaven and were thrown into hell. This is completely false—neither Lucifer nor any of the rebel angels were cast into hell. Hell certainly exists, as Jesus himself tells us in Matthew 25:41 (NIV):

> Then he will say to those on his left, 'Depart from me, you who are cursed, into the eternal fire prepared for the devil and his angels.'

Hell is further described as a lake of fire:

> Then death and Hades were thrown into the lake of fire. The lake of fire is the second death. (Rev 20:14 NIV)

> Anyone whose name was not found written in the book of life was thrown into the lake of fire. (Rev 20:15 NIV)

However, no one—not devil, angel, or human—is currently in hell, nor has ever been in hell. Hell is empty, and it has always been empty. The Bible clearly tells us the first beings that will be thrown into hell, into the lake of fire, will be the beast (commonly known as the antichrist) and his false prophet:

> Then I saw the beast and the kings of the earth and their armies gathered together to wage war against the rider on the horse and his army. But the beast was captured, and with it the false prophet who had performed the signs on its behalf. With these signs, he deluded those who had received the mark of the beast and worshiped its image. The two of them were thrown alive into the fiery lake of burning sulfur. (Rev 19:19–20 NIV).

We are also told the devil, Satan, will not be thrown into the lake of fire until over 1,000 years *after* the beast and the false prophet are cast into the lake of fire:

> When the thousand years are over, Satan will be released from his prison and will go out to deceive the nations in the four corners of the earth—Gog and Magog—and to gather them for battle. In number, they are like the sand on the seashore. They marched across the breadth of the earth and surrounded the camp of God's people, the city he loves. But fire came down from heaven and devoured them. And the devil, who deceived them, was thrown into the lake of burning sulfur, where the beast and the false prophet had been thrown. They will be tormented day and night forever and ever. (Rev 20:7–10 NIV)

Revelation 20:11–15 continues to tell us that only *after* Satan is thrown into the lake of fire will there be the final judgment upon nonbelievers, who will only *then* also be cast into the lake of fire. (It is important to understand it is *not* God's will for *any* human being to be cast into hell—as we are very clearly told in 2 Peter 3:9 [NIV]—"The Lord is not slow in keeping his promise, as some understand slowness. Instead, he is patient with you, *not wanting anyone to perish*, but *everyone to come to repentance.*")

All of these events are yet to happen—no one is currently in hell, nor has anyone ever been in hell. Hell, the lake of fire, is empty. It is false to say Satan and the rebel angels were cast out of heaven into hell—they were not. When Lucifer and the rebel angels were cast out of heaven, they were *not* cast down to hell, rather, they were cast down to *Earth*:

> And war broke out in heaven: Michael and his angels fought with the dragon; and the dragon and his angels fought, but they did not prevail, nor was a place found for them in heaven any longer. So the great dragon was cast out, that serpent of old, called the Devil and Satan, who deceives the whole world; he was *cast to the earth*, and his angels were cast out with him. (Rev 12:7–9 NKJV).

Jesus himself also tells us: "I saw Satan fall like lightning from heaven [i.e., from the earthly sky]" (Luke 10:18 NKJV). Jesus spoke these words as he walked upon this earth. When he says "heaven" in this passage he is referring to the earthly sky. As a result, we can understand Jesus is saying he saw Satan fall from the earthly sky to the earth, in exactly the same way as a lightning strike falls from the sky down to the earth. This is a further affirmation that Satan was cast out of heaven and was thrown down upon the earth. Lucifer and the rebel angels, though, were not cast down *onto* the earth; rather, they were cast to a place *inside* the earth, a place which the Bible calls the pit, or in some translations the abyss.

The pit, or abyss, is inside the earth and is a place of imprisonment for the fallen angels, a place of chains and darkness (Isa 14:15, Jude 6, Rev 9:1, 2, 11; 11:7; 17:8, 20:1, 3). This is the same pit, or abyss, of Luke 8, to which the demons who possessed the man begged Jesus not to send them: "And they *begged Jesus repeatedly* not to order them to go into the *abyss*" (Luke 8:31 NIV). The pit is the place to where Lucifer and the rebel angels were cast—they were cast out of heaven and down into the pit, or the abyss, which is inside this Earth, a place of darkness and imprisonment. It was as a result of the rebel angels being cast down into the earth that the earth became cursed with a global ocean, by a covering of darkness, and with the Holy Spirit himself present to restrain the great evil that had been cast down.

Lucifer's Name Change

It is also upon that fall of the angels, upon the rebel angels being cast out of heaven and cast down to the pit inside the earth, that Lucifer's name was changed from Lucifer, which means "light-bearer," to Satan, which means "the accuser."

Unforeseen Consequences

Lucifer calculated and gambled that neither he nor the rebel angels would be destroyed if they rebelled, and as a result he expected to succeed in his rebellion and achieve his goal—to be worshiped by the other angels as a god. Although he was correct in calculating that neither he nor the rebel angels would be destroyed, he did not foresee, nor even remotely comprehend, other potential consequences of his actions.

First and foremost, he did not calculate that he and the rebel angels would be forcibly cast out of heaven—yes, cast to the earth, which would have been their goal, but they were thrown deep *inside* the earth to the pit, a place of darkness and chains. It is important to remember that neither Lucifer nor any angel had ever experienced such a thing as darkness. God's entire creation was full of light, for God himself is light: "God is light, and in him there is no darkness at all" (1 John 1:5 NASB). The entire angelic host were creatures of light, and even Lucifer's own name meant "light-bearer." All of God's creation was only good, wonderful, beautiful, perfect, and holy, and there was not even a dot of darkness upon the creation. Imagine then what it was like for these creatures of light to be cast into a prison of complete and utter darkness, cast into the pit—it would certainly have been a horror, an unimaginable experience, their first-ever experience of darkness. Until they were cast out of heaven and into the pit, they would not have known that such a thing as darkness could even exist—darkness was not a part of Lucifer's calculations.

But there was also a second thing that, like darkness, was totally and completely absent from their entire experience of life, completely absent from their experience of God and his creation, and that was the experience of *pain*. God's perfect creation was filled only with goodness, love, peace, fulfillment, and joy, there was not even a shred, not even an inkling, of pain within the creation, nor upon any angel in their experience of life. But upon being cast out of heaven, not only did the rebel angels experience darkness, but they also experienced, for the first time, pain.

Imagine what that was like—Lucifer had led the rebel angels to believe he was leading them to a liberation, to a place of exaltation, but instead they were thrown down to unimaginable darkness and experienced unimaginable pain. None of this was part of Lucifer's calculations. Although he may have been correct to gamble that neither he nor the rebel angels would be destroyed by God as a result of their rebellion, he was utterly wrong about everything else.

As a result of the angelic rebellion, the result of the rebel angels being cast out of heaven down into the earth, the earth became a cursed place, an uninhabitable place of darkness, a place utterly unfit for man—it became the earth as described in Genesis 1:2. But God's plan would not be abandoned, and he would not abandon the earth, neither would he abandon his plan for the creation of man. In time, God would begin a restoration of the cursed Earth.

6

The Restoration

WE ARE TOLD IN Isaiah 45:18 that God created the earth as a habitable place, a perfect place, a place to be inhabited by man. But in Genesis 1:2, the earth is uninhabitable, flooded with the global ocean, covered in thick darkness, and with the Holy Spirit himself present there—the earth in Genesis 1:2 is cursed. The reason the earth was cursed is because Satan and the rebel angels were cast down into the earth, into the pit. As a result of this angelic rebellion and casting down into the earth, both the earth and the universe were cursed. Upon the earth there are two elements of the curse—darkness and a global ocean. Upon the universe there is one great element of the curse: darkness.

As we have seen in chapter 2, darkness is always and only associated with either the curse or wrath of God—God is light, in him there is no darkness (1 John 1:5). God created the entire universe as a place of light—there was no darkness in existence anywhere in God's original creation, and yet as a result of the angelic rebellion, the entire universe is now under the curse of darkness, as was also the earth in Genesis 1:2.

What was the darkness? The darkness was the result of God withdrawing the light of *his presence* from his own creation. God himself is light, and by removing the light of his presence from the creation, as his judgment upon the rebel angels and upon the creation for the angelic rebellion, the creation was cursed with the resulting darkness.

In addition to the curse of darkness upon the entire universe (with the exception of the physical heaven, the seat of God's throne, which remained as the only place of light within the universe), the earth was further cursed with the global ocean, a global flood, making it entirely uninhabitable for humanity. We know that both the global ocean and the darkness surrounding the earth are elements of God's curse because both of these elements will finally be removed when God fully redeems Earth and his creation. We are told in Revelation 21:1 that when God redeems Earth there will, finally, no longer be any seas or oceans. We are also told in Revelation 22:25 that, upon God's redemption of the earth, there will no longer be any night. The curse of the oceans, and the curse of darkness, both present in Genesis 1:2, will finally be fully gone. Also, with the fact that there will be no more night, this means all the darkness throughout the entire universe will finally be gone—there will finally be no darkness anywhere, for God will fully lift the curse of darkness from the entire creation. However, as of Genesis 1:2, the curse of darkness was upon both the universe and the earth.

There is also a third element in Genesis 1:2 that is tied to the curse upon the earth, and that is the special presence of the Holy Spirit. Why is the Holy Spirit specifically mentioned here as being present over the earth? At least one main reason is because of the great evil that has been cast into the earth, down into the pit. The Holy Spirit was restraining that evil. This is to be understood in the same way we understand 2 Thessalonians 2:7 (NIV), which is talking about the power of lawlessness: "For the secret power of lawlessness is already at work; but the one who now holds it back will continue to do so till he is taken out of the way." No one knows how much time elapsed between Genesis 1:1 and 1:2, but it was very likely a long span of time, since the amount of time it would take Lucifer to foment rebellion would have been a slow, methodical process. Likewise, no one knows how much time elapsed between Genesis 1:2 and Genesis 1:3, for at Genesis 1:3, God begins to restore some of the cursed creation.

Let There Be Light

In Genesis 1:3, as the first act of restoration, God says "Let there be light." We know the sun, moon, and stars were created on the fourth day, so what was the light? It was, in fact, the light of God's *presence*—it was the light that was removed, or withdrawn, as a curse upon the creation, in response to the angelic rebellion, whose removal resulted in universal darkness. God, in Genesis 1:3, is letting the light of his presence begin to shine back upon his creation—not fully though, for the universe is still full of darkness end to end, but, within that, there is some light throughout, and that light is the hope of the final removal of all darkness, which will occur by Revelation 22:5. "Let there be light" is an act of restoration upon the creation.

God Creates the Sky

God then continues to specifically restore the earth itself, to make it habitable again for man, as it was upon its original creation in Genesis 1:1. His first act of earthly restoration, after he begins to let the light of his presence shine back upon the creation, is to make the "vault between the waters." It is not clear how "between the waters" is to be understood, but it is clear the vault described here is the earthly sky, with waters both above and below the sky.

The Waters above the Sky

It is easy to understand the waters below the sky—that would be the global ocean still upon the earth—but there are different ideas as to what the waters *above* the sky might be. Some have suggested it was a water or vapor canopy over the earth, but that is unlikely for the following reasons.

If it is true the waters *above* the sky were some sort of vapor canopy surrounding the earth, then the water canopy would be *above* the sky, which means that it would be outside of Earth's atmosphere, which means it would be in space. Water, or water vapor, could not exist outside of Earth's atmosphere—if water was outside and above Earth's atmosphere, in space, the liquid would become a gigantic globule, or ice, and if in a vapor form, it would dissipate since it is outside the atmosphere.

But the main reason the waters above the sky were not some sort of water/vapor canopy is the water/vapor canopy would have the effect of keeping the earth under *perpetual cloud*. This would then mean that neither the stars nor the moon would be visible from Earth, which then defeats the entire purpose of the creation of the moon and stars on the fourth day. The purpose of the creation of the moon and the stars on the fourth day is described as being to mark days, seasons, and years, which can only happen if the moon and the stars are visible from Earth. If there was a vapor canopy of cloud surrounding the earth, then neither the moon nor the stars would be visible, and therefore they could not fulfill their purpose of marking days, seasons, and years.

Also, the idea of a water vapor canopy above the sky is sometimes invoked as a way of explaining the source of the floodwaters of Genesis 7. However, we are clearly told in Genesis 7:11 that the primary source of the waters of the great flood of Noah's day was *not* from the sky, but rather, was from *beneath* the ground, from inside the earth:

> In the six hundredth year of Noah's life, in the second month, on the seventeenth day of the month, on the same day all *the fountains of the great deep burst open*, and the floodgates of the sky were opened. The rain fell upon the earth for forty days and forty nights. (Gen 7:11–12 NASB)

The primary, or *initial*, source of the water of the great flood of Noah's day was from the "fountains of the great deep," which "burst" open, and which was *followed* by the floodgates of the sky being opened—the fountains of the great deep bursting forth happened first. In fact, it has been put forth that the floodgates of the heavens being opened was the *result* of the explosion of the fountains of the great deep, which is to say that as the earth split open as a result of the exploding waters coming forth from within the earth, that same water, under enormous pressure, spewed very high into the sky and carried with it the sediment of the earth. Once at a high enough altitude, this sediment, together with the exploding water, then caused a reaction in the sky, a reaction of condensation, which then saw that same water fall back to Earth as rain.

Either way, the primary or initial source of the waters of the flood was from inside the earth, from the fountains of the great deep, and not from the sky. Therefore it is unnecessary to invoke a "water vapor canopy" above the sky as a way to explain the waters of the flood, for Genesis 7:11–12 already explains it for us—the waters for the flood came from the same place to which they receded to after the flood, which was inside the earth.

As a result, and especially due to the fact that such a water vapor canopy would cover the earth in a perpetual cloud, thereby obscuring the moon and the stars, we can conclude the waters "above" the sky are not some sort of water vapor canopy, but instead are something else.

God Brings Forth the Land

After God creates the sky, he then brings forth the land. About the third day, Genesis 1:9 tells us: "And God said, 'Let the water under the sky be gathered to one place, and let dry ground appear.' And it was so. God called the dry ground 'land,' and the gathered waters he called 'seas.' And God saw that it was good." In saying that the water under the sky was gathered to *one* place, this implies the land was also gathered to *another* one place, that is, that all the land itself was gathered to *one* place, raised together as one, great continent. If this is so, then why do we have the seven continents we have today? If God initially brought forth the land as one great continent, where did the current seven continents come from?

The continents we see today are the result of the flood of Genesis 7. At the time of the flood, the one continent was split by the enormous force of the water exploding out from beneath the earth (Gen 7:11), the result of the fountains of the great deep "bursting" forth. The waters of the flood exploded forth onto the earth up *through* the land, *through* the one continent. The result of this water exploding up through the land of the one continent was a crack in the earth, a crack upon the land, a crack upon the one continent. In fact, it is in this context we can understand Isaiah 24:20:

> The earth reels to and fro like a drunkard
> And it totters like a shack,
> For its transgression is heavy upon it,
> And it will fall, never to rise again. (NASB)

The earth is described here as "reeling" like a drunkard, while other translations use the word "staggers" (ESV). We are told the earth "totters like a shack." This is, in fact, describing the earth as it feels the enormous force of the water exploding forth from inside the earth, through the one continent, the result of the fountains of the great deep bursting forth to bring the great flood. The force of those fountains bursting forth was so great it literally rocked the earth to its foundations, causing the earth to stagger, to "reel" like a drunkard, to sway like a shack in the wind. As a result of those fountains bursting from within the earth, bursting through the land, the force of that event split the one continent, causing the divide that created the continents we see today. The mid-Atlantic Ridge, part of the longest mountain chain on Earth, all of which lies beneath the oceans, is the result of that "crack in the world" through which the floodwaters came.

The flood created that initial crack in Earth's one continent, and ultimately that crack caused the continents to *eventually* separate and form the continents we see today—and this ultimate separation is described in Genesis 10:25: "To Eber were born two sons: the name of one was Peleg, for in his days the earth was divided; and his brother's name was Joktan" (NKJV).

This description in Genesis 10:25 about the earth being divided in the days of Peleg is a reference to the ultimate splitting or breaking apart of the continents, which was initially begun with the flood, by way of the crack in the world resulting from the fountains of the great deep bursting forth.

All that to say that when God brought up the land and caused it to appear in Genesis 1:7, the land appeared as one great continent, all gathered in one place, just as were the waters gathered to another place. With the bringing forth of the land, the earth was once again being made habitable for man. The curse of the oceans still remained, as in fact it still remains today, with approximately 70 percent of the earth still flooded by the ocean waters, but the appearance of the land in Genesis 1:7 is God beginning to reverse the curse upon the earth, which will be fully reversed and redeemed in Revelation 21:1, "Now I saw a new heaven and a new earth, for the first heaven and the first earth had passed away. Also there was no more sea" (NKJV).

God Creates Vegetation

Also on the third day, God created the vegetation of the earth:

> Then God said, 'Let the earth bring forth grass, the herb that yields seed, and the fruit tree that yields fruit according to its kind, whose seed is in itself, on the earth'; and it was so. And the earth brought forth grass, the herb that yields seed according to its kind, and the tree that yields fruit, whose seed is in itself according to its kind. And God saw that it was good. So the evening and the morning were the third day. (Gen 1:11–13 NKJV)

God is now making the earth both habitable for man as well as making it able to sustain life. However, we are told the following in Genesis 2:5–6, which describes the events of the sixth day, the "day" of the creation of man:

> Now no shrub had yet appeared on the earth and no plant had yet sprung up, for the Lord God had not sent rain on the earth and

there was no one to work the ground, but streams came up from the earth and watered the whole surface of the ground. (NIV)

We are told in Genesis 1:11–12, on the *third* day, that God commanded that the land produce vegetation. How is it possible then that on the *sixth* day, as described in Genesis 2:5–6, we are told no shrub and no plant had yet appeared on the earth—is this not a contradiction? In fact, it is not a contradiction, as each of these passages are describing two different things. First, the vegetation created in Genesis 1:11–12 is a very specific kind of vegetation—it is specifically described as "grass, the herb [plants] that *yields seed*, and the *fruit tree that yields fruit* according to its kind, whose seed is in itself." Genesis 2:5–6, on the other hand, specifically describes a different kind of vegetation, described as "no *shrub* had yet appeared on the earth and no *plant* had yet sprung up."

The vegetation of Genesis 1:11–12 is specifically described as being seed-bearing plants and trees that produce seed-bearing fruit, whereas Genesis 2:5–6 specifically describes "shrubs" and "[non-seed-bearing] plants." Shrubs would be various bushes, while the non-seed-bearing plants would be things such as wheat, rye, other plants of the *field* (plants requiring cultivation, that is, a person to work the ground). In Genesis 1:11–12, God created, or *called forth*, seed-bearing plants and fruit-bearing trees (which also is exactly the food that God gave to Adam to eat in Genesis 1:29). As a result, there is no contradiction between Genesis 1:11–12 and Genesis 2:5–6 for the two passages are complementary, describing different things, and yet together they give us the big picture and the details as to the order in which the vegetation appeared. But if the plants and herbs of the field as described in Genesis 2:5–6 had not yet sprung up, does that mean God *created them* later on, creating them on the sixth day rather than on the third day?

Again, no, for the wording of Genesis 2:5–6 describes those plants and herbs of the field as not yet having *sprung* up, and gives the reason as being because it had not yet rained upon the earth. The phrase *sprung* up means the *seeds* and *germ* of the various plants and herbs of the field were *already there* on the sixth day, created by God, most likely also on the third day, but their seed and germ were *dormant* in the ground, awaiting the rain that had not yet come. Upon the coming of the rain, that seed would then spring up.

God Creates the Sun, Moon, Stars, Sea Creatures, and Birds

God continues to make the sun, moon, and stars on the fourth day, and on the fifth day he creates all the sea creatures and birds, in all their multitudes, and he blesses them, commanding them to be fruitful and multiply.

God Creates Land Animals

On the sixth day, God creates all the land animals—all of them, including all insects—in all of their kinds, or, as we might say today, in all of their species.

Restoration and Creation of Life

The account of Genesis 1, from verses 3 onward, is therefore not so much an account of the initial creation, for the initial creation took place in its entirety in Genesis 1:1; rather, it is an account of God restoring, to a degree, the cursed Earth so as to make it habitable again for man, as it was originally upon its creation (Isa 45:18). From there onward, it is also an account of God's creation of life upon the restored Earth.

Through all of this restoration of the earth, Satan and the fallen angels remained imprisoned within the pit, inside the earth, kept in chains and darkness. But God had now restored the earth, making it habitable again for man. Then, also on the sixth day, God created man.

7

The Creation of Man

THE PINNACLE OF GOD'S restoration of the earth, and the ensuing creation of life upon it, was the creation of man, described as occurring on the sixth day:

> Then God said, 'Let us make mankind in our image, in our likeness, so that they may rule over the fish in the sea and the birds in the sky, over the livestock and all the wild animals, and over all the creatures that move along the ground.' So God created mankind in his own image, in the image of God he created them; male and female he created them. (Gen 1:26–27 NIV)

The account in Genesis 1:26–27 is the general overview of God's creation of man, whereas Genesis 2 gives us a much more detailed account of this same event:

> This is the history of the heavens and the earth when they were created, in the day that the Lord God made the earth and the heavens, before any plant of the field was in the earth and before any herb of the field had grown. For the Lord God had not caused it to rain on the earth, and there was no man to till the ground; but a mist went up from the earth and watered the whole face of the ground.
> And the Lord God formed man of the dust of the ground, and breathed into his nostrils the breath of life; and man became a living being.
> The Lord God planted a garden eastward in Eden, and there he put the man whom he had formed. And out of the ground the Lord God made every tree grow that is pleasant to the sight

and good for food. The tree of life was also in the midst of the garden, and the tree of the knowledge of good and evil.

Now a river went out of Eden to water the garden, and from there it parted and became four riverheads. The name of the first is Pishon; it is the one which skirts the whole land of Havilah, where there is gold. And the gold of that land is good. Bdellium and the onyx stone are there. The name of the second river is Gihon; it is the one which goes around the whole land of Cush. The name of the third river is Hiddekel; it is the one which goes toward the east of Assyria. The fourth river is the Euphrates.

Then the Lord God took the man and put him in the garden of Eden to tend and keep it. And the Lord God commanded the man, saying, 'Of every tree of the garden you may freely eat; but of the tree of the knowledge of good and evil you shall not eat, for in the day that you eat of it you shall surely die.'

And the Lord God said, 'It is not good that man should be alone; I will make him a helper comparable to him.' Out of the ground the Lord God formed every beast of the field and every bird of the air, and brought them to Adam to see what he would call them. And whatever Adam called each living creature, that was its name. So Adam gave names to all cattle, to the birds of the air, and to every beast of the field. But for Adam there was not found a helper comparable to him.

And the Lord God caused a deep sleep to fall on Adam, and he slept; and he took one of his ribs, and closed up the flesh in its place. Then the rib which the Lord God had taken from man he made into a woman, and he brought her to the man.

And Adam said:
'This is now bone of my bones
And flesh of my flesh;
She shall be called Woman,
Because she was taken out of man.'
Therefore a man shall leave his father and mother and be joined to his wife, and they shall become one flesh. And they were both naked, the man and his wife, and were not ashamed."
(Gen 2:4–25 NKJV)

We are told God formed the body of the man from the dust of the earth, and that he then breathed into the man's nostrils the breath of life, and that man became a living being. We are also told in Genesis 1:26 that man was created in both the image *and* likeness of God. The Hebrew word for man is "adam," and so the name of the first man is called Adam.

The Image and Likeness of God

What does it mean to be created in the image and likeness of God? To be created in the image of God means that, like God, man, Adam, is a living, sentient, moral being—he has will, intelligence, emotions, personality, and a moral character that knows how to distinguish and choose between right and wrong.

To be made in the likeness of God means we *physically look* like him. We are told in Romans 8:3 that Jesus was sent in the *likeness* of sinful flesh: "Sending his own Son in the *likeness of* sinful flesh and as an offering for sin, he condemned sin in the flesh" (NASB). Jesus was not sent in the *image* of sinful flesh, rather, he was sent in the *likeness* of sinful flesh. To be sent in the "likeness" of sinful flesh means Jesus physically *looked* exactly like us, looked exactly as any sinful human would look. As a result, the term "in the likeness of" means to physically look like something. But isn't God spirit, and not a physical being? If so, then how can we physically look like him?

Jesus—The Agent of Creation

It's important to understand that Jesus Christ, God the Son, was the Agent of creation. The Trinity is one—Father, Son, and Holy Spirit—three distinct persons who together are the one God. Throughout the Bible, each of the three persons of the Trinity take on different roles, and the Bible clearly tells us Jesus, God the Son, was the one who executed the creation:

> Through him *all things were made*; without him nothing was *made* that has been *made*. (John 1:3 NIV)

> For *in him all things were created*: things in heaven and on earth, visible and invisible, whether thrones or powers or rulers or authorities; *all things have been created through him* and for him. (Col 1:16 NIV)

> But in these last days he has spoken to us by his Son, whom he appointed heir of all things, and *through whom also he made the universe*. (Heb 1:2 NIV)

Although the Trinity is one, Jesus, God the Son, was the Person of the Trinity who executed the creation, the one through whom all the universe was created. He is also called the Word of God (John 1), and it is no coincidence that in Genesis 1 God *speaks* the restoration and creation into being, that is, it is the *word* of God, the *speaking* of God, that restores and creates. Likewise, it is the Word of God, Jesus Christ, God the Son, who speaks in Genesis 1:26 when he says "Let us make man in our image."

The Divine Form

Based on this, and on the fact that to be made in the *likeness* of God means we physically *look* like him, we can conclude that Jesus, God the Son, had some sort of original divine form, the form in whose *likeness* humanity was created. This original form would have been his innate and divine form prior to the creation of the universe and prior to his incarnation, with that divine form being part of the essence of his uncreated and eternal nature. It was not a form of flesh or bone, but rather, was his innate *uncreated* divine form, yet it was a form which would have had the *appearance* of a physical form, but which was absolutely not physical in the sense that it was an uncreated form and was in no way subject to time and space.

This original divine form of God the Son is referenced repeatedly throughout the Bible. We regularly read about the hand of the Lord (Exod 6:1; 7:5; and many others), the face of the Lord (Exod 33:11; Deut 5:4; Ps 4:6; and many others), the arm of the Lord (Exod 6:6; and others), the eyes of the Lord (Gen 6:8; 33:8, Deut 11:12; Ps 33:18; 34:18; and others), and the back of the Lord (Exod 33:23). Some try and make these to be only poetic expressions, but they are not—they are in fact factual descriptions, as the Bible clearly describes God's hand, arm, eyes, face, and back in a literal way. What is important to remember is these are all descriptions of God the Son, the Agent of creation, the one in whose likeness man was made—we *physically look* like him.

Adam Created from the Dust of the Earth

We often seem to take it for granted, but there is a profound truth in the fact that Adam was created from the dust of the earth. Adam was not made from the dust of heaven, nor from the ground of heaven; rather, he was made from the dust of Earth. As a result, it is important to understand that man, humanity, has a permanent tie to this Earth, we are made for Earth, and Earth has always been destined to be our eternal home, just as it is destined to be the eternal home of God himself (Rev 21:3), to be the place of God's eternal kingdom, the seat of his throne and of his New Jerusalem. Adam was made from the dust of Earth for a reason.

Another important point to remember, and one which is often overlooked, is that Adam was not created in the garden of Eden. The Bible very clearly tells us man was created from the dust of the earth, and then, *after* man was created, God "planted" a garden in the East, in Eden, and put the man into the garden (Gen 2:7–8). Eden was especially made as the place in which God was to put Adam, being "planted" by God himself, and only *after* man was made. Man, Adam, was *not* made in Eden.

Adam was Made Alone

If I were to choose the single most profound verse in the entire Bible, it would be this: "It is not good for the man to be alone" (Gen 2:18 NASB) How many times have we read this verse, passed it right by as just a detail in a narrative, without deeply considering it?

Consider this: at the conclusion of the first day in Genesis, God looked at what he had done and saw it was good. Likewise, at the conclusion of the third, fourth, and fifth days. In each and every case God saw his restoration and creation was good. On the sixth day, God saw his entire creation—man included—was very good. God only does what is good, he cannot do what is wrong, and neither does God make mistakes.

How then can God say "It is *not good* for the man to be alone?" How can God do something that is "not good?" What happened? Did God make a mistake? Did God screw up? Or, was this *intentional*?

We know God does *not* make mistakes, he *always* knows what he's doing and he *never* screws up. So then, when God made Adam alone, even though it was "not good," it must have been intentional, by design. Why?

Think of the utter uniqueness of the situation. God himself is a Trinity—Father, Son, and Holy Spirit. The great, vast, numberless multitude of the angelic host were all created en masse, all created at one time, in their entirety, not one by one, and never alone. All the animals upon the earth were created at the very least in pairs of male and female, and in Genesis 1:20 we are told God made the waters *teem* with life, with the remainder of the verse implying it was the same for the birds of the air. Not one creature in God's entire creation, and not even God himself, the Trinity, was alone. Only Adam was alone. Adam was the *only* creature in the entire universe that had no other companion creature like himself—he was absolutely unique in all the creation, the only one who was *alone*. And God said it was "not good."

In fact, God seems to emphasize just how alone is Adam. When we are told it was not good for Adam to be alone, it also implies strongly that Adam was feeling sad and depressed that there was no one like him. Even though he was a perfect man and had a perfect fellowship with God, he was still the only one of his kind. So what did God do? He brought before Adam *all* the wild animals and *all* the birds of the air, to see if a companion would be found that would be suitable for Adam (Gen 2:19–20). God of course knew that no suitable companion for Adam would be found among the animals or the birds, but he wanted *Adam* to know that, and to experience that as well. Adam, during that same time God brought all the wild animals and birds before him, also *named* all the wild animals and birds—all of them, not some of them, and not just whatever few happened to be in his vicinity—but *all* the wild animals and birds created by God, who made a point of bringing them all to Adam.

Of course, no suitable helper was found for Adam. So why did God do this? Why did he make Adam alone, even though it was not good for Adam to be alone, and why did he then drive the point home of just how alone and unique Adam was by bringing before him all the wild animals and birds, emphasizing how none of them was a suitable helper for Adam? The answer is in Ephesians 5:31–32 (NIV): "For this reason a man will leave his father and mother and be united to his wife, and the two will become one flesh. This is a profound mystery—but *I am talking about Christ and the church*." God wanted Adam to know what it felt like to desire a companion that was like himself, because he wanted Adam to know how God felt. Just as Adam wanted a companion, a companion that was like himself, a companion with which to share himself, so God also wanted a companion with which to share himself, a companion that was like him, made by him and for him.

God Wants a Companion

It is often said "God does need anything." There is nothing in the Bible that specifically says, or even talks about, what God does or does not need. We are told there is nothing we can give to God that isn't already his (Ps 50:9–12), which is to say we cannot make something to give to God that he does not already have, but the Bible never talks to us about what God may or may not need. In fact, the concept that God does not *need* anything is not biblical: rather, it is born of Greek philosophy, particularly Plato, whose description of "perfection" is that perfection is self-sufficient and needs nothing.

It may very well be that God does not *need* anything, or does not *need* a companion, but, one thing is certain and inarguable: whether or not God *needs* a companion, God *wants* a companion, whether he needs one or not, he *wants* one, and this is why there is a creation, and why God created man.

This is also the reason why God initially created Adam alone—so Adam would know what it felt like to desire a companion like himself, so he would understand how God also wants a companion like himself, and in fact, man—Adam—is that companion for God. God wanted Adam to know how he felt.

But God didn't leave Adam alone. After making Adam alone, God fulfilled Adam's desire for companionship. The real pinnacle of creation was not just the creation of Adam, it was the creation of Eve, the woman.

The Uniqueness of Eve

Eve was the final thing God created—she was the pinnacle of his creation. Unlike Adam, she *was* made in the garden of Eden. Unlike Adam, and unlike all the other creatures on Earth, she alone was *not* made *directly* from the dust of the earth, from the ground, rather, she was made *from Adam*, from his side, from his own flesh. This creation of Eve took place after God had put Adam into a deep sleep. When Adam awoke, he beheld Eve, he drank her in, and he named her, just as he also had named all the birds and wild animals, naming her "woman." In seeing Eve, Adam's heart was satisfied, for in her he finally had his companion—bone of his bones, and flesh of his flesh—a companion that was just like him, and this was the institution of marriage.

This is what God wanted Adam to experience—the desire of wanting a companion that was like himself, a companion with whom to share himself, and then to experience the joy, love, and satisfaction in seeing that desire fulfilled. Additionally, this is also why human marriage is sacred and holy, because it is a picture of what God is doing in the universe, of what God is doing for himself—he is making his own singular companion, his own bride.

There is also a beautiful poetry in God's creation of Eve, for just as Eve was made from Adam, with the woman coming from the man, now, and ever since, every man comes from the woman, comes from inside her, given birth by his mother.

Adam before Eve

After God created Adam, making him alone, we are told God then planted a garden in the East, in Eden, and that he placed the man in the garden to look after it, care for it, and tend it (Gen 2:15). We are told after God planted a garden in Eden, he then made grow out of the ground, in Eden, every tree that is pleasant to the sight and good for food (Gen 2:9). We are then told, as a separate point, in the middle of the garden there were *also* two other trees—the tree of life and the tree of the knowledge of good and evil.

The Bible is very specific in how it words the growth of the trees in Eden, and then also how it talks about those two special trees—the tree of life and the tree of the knowledge of good and evil. The Bible tells us in Genesis 2:9, "And out of the ground the Lord God made every tree grow that is pleasant to the sight and good for food" (NKJV). It then tells us, as a separate and distinct point: "The tree of life was also in the midst of the garden, and the tree of the knowledge of good and evil" (NKJV).

These other two, special trees are *not* described as *growing* in the garden, or as being "made to grow" in Eden, or as "coming up from the ground" in Eden. Rather, after being told how God made every tree that was "pleasant to the sight" and "good for food" grow in Eden, we are then told those other two special trees were "also" there. The entire wording and structure of that account strongly conveys the tree of life and the tree of the knowledge of good and evil did *not* grow in Eden but rather they were *placed* in Eden after the garden was planted.

After God had put Adam into the garden of Eden, and *before Eve was even created*, God gave Adam a command: "And the Lord God commanded the man, saying, "Of every tree of the garden you may freely eat; but of the tree of the knowledge of good and evil you shall not eat, for in the day that you eat of it you shall surely die" (Gen 2:16–17 NKJV). It is very important to recognize this command was never given by God to

Eve; rather, it was given *only* to Adam, and given to him *before* Eve was even created.

Adam's Perfection

In the 1830s, a new idea, a new teaching, was invented, called "dispensations." The teaching of dispensations is a view which states that throughout all history, God engages with humanity in successively changing ways, ways that are, in essence, a continual testing of humanity, with humanity always failing each test.

There is nothing wrong with coming up with and discussing ideas about God and how he is working in the world and with man, but the teaching of dispensations has in some circles transformed from an idea of discussion into a doctrine. We will hear teachers, pastors, and others refer to dispensations as if they were some sort of truth, as if they are fact. However, the teaching of dispensations is a new idea—not even 200 years old—whereas the church is almost 2,000 years old. For almost all of the church's existence, the notion of dispensations did not exist. In fact, the teaching of dispensations is not an idea supported by the Bible. The Bible never talks about God changing his plan or his approach to humanity—God is not a meandering schizophrenic—rather, the entire Bible, from Genesis to Revelation, is always and only about the expression and unfolding of God's one plan, which ultimately is the creation of his companion and his one plan of salvation.

The reason it's important to have some familiarity with the invented concept of dispensations is, in its scheme of anywhere from three to eight dispensations (depending on who you are talking with, though most people talk in terms of seven dispensations), the first dispensation is called the dispensation of innocence, and it is a reference to Adam. Of course, as is the case with most such arbitrary invented ideas, neither the concept of innocence, nor the word as a description of man or God's plan, exists in the Bible (and neither do the words or concepts of any of the other two to seven dispensations—dispensationalism is a man-made notion that, ultimately, is contradictory to the Bible's clear unfolding of God's one and only plan). But by use of the word "innocence," as in the "dispensation of innocence" as a reference to Adam, it carries within itself many implications about the nature of Adam, implications which lead to false and wrong understandings. In the dispensation of innocence, Adam and Eve are described as "innocent" (even though, again, the Bible never uses any such word or description of Adam), and the very word "innocence" leads to a seriously flawed understanding of Adam.

The major and erroneous implication conveyed by the word "innocence" is its implication that Adam was like some sort of child, someone who had no experience, someone who had a limited maturity. In this description, Adam is something less than us, and in fact this is exactly how in many cases the concept of innocence has been applied to Adam. And yet we are told, "Honor your father and your mother, as the Lord your God has commanded you, so that you may live long and that it may go well with you in the land the Lord your God is giving you" (Deut 5:16 NIV). When we speak of Adam as if he was in some way less than we are, when we consider him as less wise or less capable than us, or as being in any way ignorant or childlike, we are in fact dishonoring our first father. The fact remains Adam was absolute perfection—he was emotionally perfect, intellectually perfect, spiritually perfect, and physically perfect. Furthermore, Adam was the son of God (Luke 3:38), and he was fully indwelt by the Holy Spirit, exactly the same as was Jesus Christ, and more so than is any Christian currently.

Adam is clearly described as being "the Son of God" (Luke 3:38). God was Adam's Father. Adam was the *created* son of God, whereas Jesus was the *begotten* Son of God, but *both* Adam and Jesus were sons of God, and *both* were fully indwelt by the Holy Spirit, whereas we Christians currently only have a *deposit* of the Holy Spirit as a guarantee of our salvation (2 Cor 5:5), with his full indwelling yet to come, which will happen upon our resurrection.

As a result, Adam's relationship with God, his Father, was vastly closer and more intimate than what any Christian currently has. In fact, Adam's relationship with God, his Father, was just as close, just as intimate, and just as perfect as was Jesus' relationship with his Father.

Adam was no naïve child, he was the greatest man who has ever lived. If we took the greatest thinkers, artists, athletes, poets, statesmen, and leaders that have ever existed, and combined them all into one man, Adam was greater than all of that. He was total and absolute perfection, just as was Jesus, except in Adam's case he was also physical perfection, whereas the Bible tells us Jesus, physically, looked like an ordinary man (Isa 53:2). If we were to see Jesus, he would physically look like any other man, whereas if we were to see Adam, we would swear we were looking physically at a god.

So when the word "innocence" is used in reference to Adam, it carries with it some very unbiblical connotations that can lead us away from the truth of who Adam was and from the truth of his nature, his perfection, and his capacity in wisdom and understanding.

One way in which Adam's great capacity and astounding intellect are demonstrated is in the fact he named all things. It is important to realize in this act of naming all the animals and birds, Adam was in fact *participating* with God in the act of creation. It's just as when a mother bakes a cake and the little girl ices the cake—God created all things, and Adam's act of naming the animals is man putting the icing on God's creation.

The fact Adam named all the animals shows us two things. First, even at the outset it is man's role to be a companion with God, to share with him in the lordship of creation. Second, it shows man shares God's creative nature, all of which further testifies to man being made in the image of God.

The Naming of Animals

The Bible clearly tells us Adam named *all* the wild animals and birds of the air. There are some who disregard this, because it doesn't fit into their preconceptions about Genesis. As a result, they say Adam rather named only *some* of the animals, only the relatively few who happened to be near him or close to him in Eden. But that is not what the Bible says—the Bible tells us in Genesis 2:19 that God formed out of the ground *all* the animals of the earth and birds of the air, and that he brought *all* of them before Adam so Adam would name them.

How many animals did Adam name? In today's science, it is stated that there are about 6.5 million *land* animal species, including birds. However, the definition of species was greatly changed in the early twentieth century for the sole reason of trying to make it look like the philosophy of evolution was true. Some people just *wanted* the philosophy of evolution to be true, regardless of the fact of there being no evidence to support the evolution philosophy. So they changed the definition of species, vastly expanded it so any differences between animals came to signify a new species. Not long afterward, this led to the invention of a new propagandist term—*microevolution*. The fact remains there is a very clear way to define a species, or a *kind*, and that is the definition first created by Carl Linnaeus (1707–1778), the father of modern taxonomy, which is the ordering and classification of species.

Linnaeus had a very clear and true definition of what constitutes a species. If two creatures can mate, and produce *viable* offspring, then those two creatures are the same species. For example, a dog and a wolf can mate, and they can have viable offspring (*viable* means their offspring can also mate and have offspring), therefore a wolf and a dog are the same species. On the other hand, a horse can mate with a donkey, and they will have an offspring, a mule, but that mule is sterile and cannot reproduce, and the mule is therefore *not* a *viable* offspring, and therefore a horse and a donkey are not the same species, but are two different species, or, to use the Bible's words, are two different *kinds*.

When we take into account that the true definition of a species is if the two creatures can mate and produce viable offspring, then the real number of actual different species or kinds of land animal and birds is vastly less than the 6.5 million that is enumerated today. If we were to be enormously conservative, we can say maybe there is no more than 50,000 actual different kinds or species of land animals and birds. We can even be ridiculously conservative, just to be on the safe side, and say maybe it's not more than 30,000. All that to say that Adam would have named *all* of these created land animals and birds, creating their names from nothing *and* giving them names that were thoughtful, informed, and perfect for each creature, with each name defining the essence and nature of each creature, just as the name "woman" defined the nature and essence of Eve.

In naming Eve, Adam first named her woman (Gen 2:23) and then later he named her Eve (Gen 3:20), and the Bible gives us a detailed description of *how* Adam went about naming her woman. First he looked upon her, considered her, drank her in. Next he spoke aloud the name he was giving her, and then he spoke aloud the *reason* why he was naming her so. This is an example of how Adam would have named all the land animals and birds—all the 30,000-plus animals God would have brought to him. It takes a vast and powerful intellect to accomplish the naming of all the land animals and birds, and to do so in a meaningful, thoughtful, and definitive way, and it is an intellect Adam possessed in full.

Did Adam Understand Right from Wrong?

Just as some people seem to think of Adam as a sort of naïve child, in the same vein they often consider Adam as lacking any real capacity to distinguish good from evil. This idea is then further embellished by appealing to the fact Adam ate from the tree of the knowledge of good and evil, suggesting that until Adam ate from the tree of the knowledge of good and evil, he didn't really comprehend evil.

This, of course, is not true since if Adam did not have the real capacity to distinguish good from evil, then neither would he have been capable, nor guilty, of sin. In fact, Adam would have known absolutely how to distinguish between good and evil, just as did the sinless angels before him, and just as did the sinless Jesus Christ.

The angels as created by God were created in his image, which is why in the Old Testament they are called the "sons of God" (Job 1:6; 2:1; 38:7). All of the angels were created perfect, holy, and sinless, yet they all had the capacity to distinguish between good and evil and to make an informed choice between good and evil. The angelic rebellion was born out of angels making such a choice, and, in their choice of choosing evil, they were guilty of sin. They were guilty of sin because they could distinguish and choose between good and evil—they were moral creatures.

In Revelation 19:10, the apostle John, during the course of receiving the revelation, was in awe before the great things being revealed to him, and he was accompanied by an angel during the course of the revelation. In his awe, John fell face-down to worship the angel and the angel instantly told him, "*See that you do* not *do that!* I am your fellow servant, and of your brethren who have the testimony of Jesus. Worship God" (NKJV).

This clearly shows that God's unfallen, holy angels can very clearly distinguish between good and evil, even though, like the unfallen Adam, they have no sin or any experience of sin in their own being. But having no sin or any experience of sin within their own being has no bearing on being able to distinguish between or choose right from wrong.

Likewise, Adam, the son of God (Luke 3:38), being made in both God's image and in his likeness (Gen 1:26), had the complete and full capacity to know good from evil, know right from wrong, and recognize and distinguish between the two.

Also, Jesus Christ, the Second Man and Last Adam (1 Cor 15:45), was, just like the First Adam, the son of God (Luke 3:38). Like the First Adam, Jesus also had no sin. Jesus Christ was, like the First Adam, spiritually, intellectually, and emotionally perfect, fully indwelt by the Holy Spirit—and yet, though just like Adam Jesus had no sin, Jesus fully knew and understood good from evil, right from wrong.

We must also remember Jesus, by becoming human as incarnate God, had let go of his equality with the Father (Phil 2:5–8), which is to say that as the fully human, incarnate Son of God, Jesus was human in every way and lived as a human in every way, living by faith in the Father, and not living according to his divinity. Just as the perfect, sinless, and fully human Jesus knew how to distinguish between right and wrong, between good and evil, so did the perfect, sinless, and fully human Adam know fully how to distinguish between good and evil, between right and wrong. To say Adam did not know fully how to distinguish between good and evil is unbiblical and is nothing more than a position of contemporary arrogance, whereby we demean Adam, God's first and completely perfect man, our first father (Isa 43:27), making ourselves greater than him. But we are not greater than Adam, not in any way. Adam was neither naïve nor childlike, but was, just like Jesus Christ, intellectually, emotionally, and spiritually perfect, the created son of God, fully indwelt by the Holy Spirit, the greatest man to ever live. Adam absolutely and fully knew and understood right from wrong, good from evil. It is for this reason that, upon his creation, Adam was placed in Eden, the place of testing.

8

Eden and the Testing of Man

As a result of Lucifer's rebellion, one-third of the angels chose to rebel with him and were cast out of heaven and into the earth, into the pit (Rev 12:7–9). Yet, Satan, the serpent (Rev 20:2) is found roaming freely in the garden of Eden (Gen 3:1). How can this be? The pit is a prison, a place of chains and darkness (Jude 5–6, Rev 20:2–3) and no one can get out of the pit unless God has allowed them out (Rev 9:1–2; 20:3). This being the case, then it is without question that God allowed Satan out of the pit after he was cast out of heaven—but why, and when, was he allowed out? All of this is essential if we are to understand the events of the garden of Eden.

Satan Allowed Out of the Pit

The Bible does not give us a direct account of Satan being allowed out of the pit, nor of the ensuing conversation God would have had with Satan, but the Bible does give us other similar accounts of Satan before God and of God's conversations with him, and we can use those accounts to begin to understand what must surely have occurred prior to the creation of man, and the ensuing events in Eden. The key passage that can help our understanding of this is Job 1–2.

In Job 1, Satan comes before God, together with the other sons of God (in this case God's holy angels) to present themselves before God. The Bible tells us God's angels, the sons of God, would regularly assemble in heaven before God's throne, the purpose of which would seem to be to share with each other their discoveries of God's creation, fellowship with God, and to love him and each other. The Bible tells us this place in heaven is called the Mount of Assembly (Isa 14:13). In Job 1–2, and this is quite a while *after* the fall of man, Satan is also there, in heaven, standing before God, and God speaks to Satan, asking him to consider his servant Job. This incident in Job is a good illustration of what was involved in Satan being allowed out of the pit after his fall and after being cast out of heaven.

We know Satan and all the rebel angels were cast out of heaven down upon the earth, being cast into the pit (Rev 12:9). Since we know that no one can escape from the pit unless they have been allowed out by God, we can conclude with certainty that God had allowed Satan out of the pit after casting him out of heaven. This would have occurred sometime *before* the creation of man and the planting of Eden, since we know from Genesis 3:1–5 that Satan, in the body of the serpent, was present in Eden, deceiving and giving temptation.

Before the creation of man, before Eden was planted, we can conclude God allowed, or called forth, Satan from out of the pit to come stand before him in heaven, in a similar way as is described in Job 1–2. It is possible, at the very least, one reason for this was to have Satan give account and answer for his rebellion, and to do so at the Mount of Assembly before all of God's holy and unfallen angels. It seems reasonable that, during that exchange, Satan would have made defense of his actions, a devious and calculating defense. It is reasonable to expect at least some part of his calculating defense would almost certainly have been to declare he was only acting according to his nature, acting according to the nature God had made in him. This would be saying in effect that he, Satan, was not responsible for doing anything wrong but rather, if there was any fault, it was with God for making Satan the way he made him. This in fact is a common accusation across human history—"If God is so great, why then does he allow evil?," as if God were to blame for all the evil we do. This human accusation against God can be seen as being an echo of the initial accusation Satan would have leveled against God in defending his own rebellion.

Satan's Accusations against God

The name Satan means "the accuser," and not only does Satan accuse humanity constantly before God (Zech 3:1; Rev 12:10), but he also accuses

God to humanity and to the angels. In fact, it seems very likely the essence of his original rebellion was to accuse God of injustice, the injustice of making man, and of planning to make man to be greater than the angels. In saying the fault of any angelic rebellion ultimately lay with God, Satan would have accused God of being flawed and unjust.

During the course of this exchange in heaven, just as in the similar scenario described in Job, Satan would certainly have brought up the injustice of the making of man, since, as described, there is good reason to believe that was the angle Satan had used to incite the angelic rebellion against God. Satan would have accused God again of being unjust, of creating a second creature, man, who was destined to be greater than and superior to the entire angelic host (Heb 1:14; 1 Cor 6:3); he would have accused God of planning to make man to be his special companion, his own bride, while leaving his angelic host, his first creatures, to be subservient to man. In the course of this defense and accusation against God, Satan would again have defended his own actions as being no fault of his own, but rather, as having come from the nature in which God had made him, thereby declaring it God's fault for making Satan the way he did.

Further to that defense, and as a proof of it, Satan would argue *any* creature made in God's image, including man, would also *naturally* rebel against God. Once that accusation is made, then the scene becomes an exact parallel of Job 1–2, where Satan tells God that if God removed his favor from Job, Job would curse him to his face. God, as a result, allows Satan to tempt Job by bringing calamity upon him. This is an exact parallel to the events that would have transpired in heaven before the creation of man and the planting of Eden, with Satan called before God from out of the pit to account for his rebellion.

It is in the course of this conversation between God and Satan that the nature of man would have been questioned and, in so doing, the nature and justice of God as well. In fact, by making the accusation that *any* creature made by God would ultimately choose to *naturally* rebel against him (which would then be a justification of Satan's own rebellion), including man, who was to be made as God's own companion and bride, to be set above the entire angelic realm in position, authority and greatness, Satan is further accusing God of an even greater injustice. If man, like Satan, would choose to rebel against God, then God is mistaken to declare man is a greater being than the angels, and therefore God's very creation of man is an act not only of injustice, but also of error—God does not know what he is doing.

It is extremely important to remind ourselves that Satan's rebellion against God was not one of force, though it was concluded by force as is described in Revelation 12:7-9. Rather, it was a rebellion of calculation and an attempt to try to outwit God, using God's own character against him. We are told very clearly in 2 Corinthians 2:11 that to "outwit" is at the heart of how Satan operates: "In order that Satan might not outwit us. For we are not unaware of his schemes" (NIV).

As a result, the nature of man then becomes the very testing ground of God's own character and justice, just as it was on a much smaller scale in Job 1-2. Satan would have accused God of injustice and wrong judgment, of being flawed, and he would have done so at the Mount of Assembly before the entire host of God's holy and unfallen angels. God's holy and unfallen angels, though, would certainly have known enough to recognize Satan's lie, since they had already made the clear and permanent choice of remaining faithful to God at the time Satan was instigating the rebellion. However, Satan's accusation was against both God and man, and it is possible Satan would have challenged God to prove his justice and wisdom by showing that man was deserving to be his companion and bride, was deserving to be greater and above the entire angelic host.

The Bible does not give an account of that specific exchange between God and Satan, but based on Job 1-2, based on the various verses about the pit as a prison, the Bible's clear teaching that Satan's own fall was due to his pride and selfishness—the same pride he appeals to in his temptation of man (Gen 3:4-5)—and occasions when Satan even requests of God to be allowed to target specific people for temptation (Luke 22:31), we can piece together that the above scenario is at least a general outline of what must have happened, for we know Satan was cast out of heaven into the pit, that the pit is an inescapable prison, and yet Satan is present in Eden to tempt man. This can only have occurred if God allowed Satan out of the pit, called him forth, and agreed to a scenario in which Satan would be allowed to tempt man. Ultimately, we have very clear reason to conclude such a scenario did occur in heaven between God and Satan before the creation of man and the planting of Eden.

We know for certainty that however the details of the conversation would have transpired, God ultimately agreed to allow Satan to tempt man (since, if that was not the case, then there would never have been any temptation of man in Eden).

The Test

We know from the Bible how man was to be tested—man would be given just one command to obey, and Satan would be allowed, just once, to tempt man to disobey. If man resisted Satan and did not disobey, then the test would be over and Satan would be defeated. If however man did disobey, then the authority man would have received of lordship over the earth (Gen 1:26) would be transferred to Satan, and then all of the fallen angels, who had been cast into the pit with Satan and who were still imprisoned therein, would also be allowed out of the pit to freely inhabit the earth, where Satan would then claim a right to rule. We must remember it was always the goal of Satan's rebellion to be like God, to be worshiped.

What we see then, in this test situation, is that, from Satan's perspective, not only would this be a test of man that is meant to be a justification of Satan's own rebellion, not only would it be a test that is designed to show God as unjust, and designed to break or bring down the very concept of man as God's companion or bride, it would also be a test designed to allow Satan and all the fallen angels to be released out of the prison of the pit, and to give Satan a claim of lordship over the earth. This would ultimately allow him to try and garner worship from God's created creatures, whether from the fallen angels or from the race of man. In every way, such a test targets virtually every goal of Satan's rebellion against God. This testing would take place in Eden.

Implementation of the Test

It is after the parameters of the test were established that the test was implemented, and the Bible gives us some very clear details on the many aspects of this implementation, each of which further affirms the scenario of Eden being made specifically as a testing ground for man.

The Bible tells us God created man from the dust of the earth (Gen 2:7). It is also very important to realize that man, Adam, was *not* created in Eden—Adam was created *outside* of Eden, before Eden was even planted, for we are told in Genesis 2:8 that after God had created Adam, *then* he planted a garden in Eden, and put the man into the garden. Adam was created *outside* of Eden and then *placed* in the garden.

Also, unlike the language used in Genesis 1 to describe God's restoration of the cursed Earth and his creation of both plant and animal life, as well as the creation of man, the language that refers to Eden's existence is unique. We are not told God *created* Eden or spoke it into being and *brought it forth*, which is the language used for his various acts throughout Genesis 1; rather, we are told, "The Lord God *planted* a garden toward the east, in Eden; and there he *placed* the man whom he had formed" (Gen 2:8 NASB). In this instance, and in this instance alone in the entire Genesis account, we are told Eden was *planted* by God, rather than "called forth."

We are told in Genesis 2:9 that *after* God planted the garden, God caused trees to grow in Eden: "Out of the ground the Lord God caused to grow every tree that is pleasing to the sight and good for food" (NASB). This is distinct from *planting* the garden in the first place, and to say that God causing the trees to come forth and the act of planting the garden are in fact just two ways of describing the same thing is not accurate. In the Genesis account there is a clear distinction between the planting of the garden and God subsequently causing the trees to grow within it.

Also, the fact Adam was made *outside* of Eden, and then the fact Eden was *planted* by God after Adam's creation, and *then* the man was *placed* in the garden, strongly conveys the idea that there is a special reason for the existence of Eden. In fact, as we shall see, Eden is planted specifically as a place of testing, and this is further affirmed by the remainder of Genesis 2:9. After God created Adam, the perfect man, and after he planted Eden, and after he put Adam in the garden and called forth the trees which were pleasing to the eye and good for food, we are then told the following, as a *separate* detail of the account: "The tree of life was also in the midst of the garden, and the tree of the knowledge of good and evil" (Gen 2:9 NASB).

The way this is worded strongly suggests the tree of life and the tree of the knowledge of good and evil did *not* grow in Eden, were *not* brought forth out of the ground in Eden, since these two trees are mentioned *separately* from the description of God bringing forth the trees of Eden that were pleasing to the sight and good for food. Rather, the wording suggests these two trees were *placed* in Eden after the fact, for we are told the two trees were just "there," described as "also" there, separate from the point of God bringing forth the other trees of Eden that were pleasing to the sight and good for food.

The "also there" strongly suggests those two trees were not part of the group of trees created or brought forth by God in Eden. Some have said the statement of the two trees being "also" in Eden is just an expansion of the previous verse describing God's bringing forth of the other trees of Eden; however, the wording of the text strongly suggests otherwise.

The phrase "good for food" specifically *proves* the tree of the knowledge of good and evil was certainly *not* created in Eden, nor was it among the trees God "called forth" or "caused to grow" in Eden. We are told in Genesis 2:9, "Out of the ground the Lord God caused to grow every tree that is pleasing to the sight and good for food; the tree of life also in the midst of the garden, and the tree of the knowledge of good and evil" (NASB). The trees God made in Eden, or "called forth," or "caused to grow" in Eden, are specifically described as being "good for food." We know the tree of the knowledge of good and evil was certainly *not* good for food: "But of the tree of the knowledge of good and evil you shall not eat, for in the day that you eat of it you shall surely die" (Gen 2:17 NKJV).

Since the trees God made to grow in Eden are all described as being "good for food," and since the tree of the knowledge of good and evil is *not* good for food, this affirms the tree of the knowledge of good and evil is *not* among the trees God made grow in Eden. Rather, as Genesis 2:9 tells us, both the tree of the knowledge of good and evil, as well as the tree of life, were just "there"—that is, they were *placed* in Eden *after* Eden was planted, placed there *after* the trees that were good for food were made to grow.

Also, not only were the two "special" trees "also" in Eden, they were in fact placed in the *middle*, or center (midst), of Eden. Not only were they in the midst of Eden, they were also, generally, *side by side*. Their being side by side does not necessarily mean they were inches from one another, but rather they were together, in the midst of Eden, in the close vicinity of each other.

Consider then the scene: Adam is created *outside* of Eden; Eden is then *planted* by God; Adam is then *placed* in Eden; in the *middle* of Eden were *placed* the tree of life and the tree of the knowledge of good and evil, and the two trees are generally *side by side*. Every aspect of this scenario strongly conveys Eden as a place specifically *designed* to be a place of testing for man.

Nature of the Test

The nature of the test was simple: "And the Lord God commanded the man, saying, "Of every tree of the garden you may freely eat; but of the tree of the knowledge of good and evil you shall not eat, for in the day that you eat of it you shall surely die" (Gen 2:16–17 NKJV). It is extremely important to recognize that this command was given by God *only* to Adam—it was *not* given to Adam *and* Eve, but to Adam *alone*. In fact, this command was given to Adam *before* Eve was even created. The sole responsibility to obey the command was *only* Adam's, *not* Adam and Eve's, but Adam's alone.

Yet, when Eve encounters the serpent, she repeats to the serpent that same command that God gave to Adam. How are we to understand this, if the commandment was given only to Adam before Eve was created? The Bible affirms Eve did not get the commandment from God but rather, she got it from Adam, for when the serpent begins to deceive her, Eve answers:

> And the woman said to the serpent, 'we may eat the fruit of the trees of the garden; but of the fruit of the tree which is in the midst of the garden, God has said, 'You shall not eat it, nor shall you touch it, lest you die.' (Gen 3:2–3 NKJV)

Eve's reply to the serpent is not quite the same as the commandment that God gave to Adam. God did *not* say to Adam "nor shall you touch it"—he just said do not eat of it. So where did the "nor shall you touch it" come from?

It came from Adam—Adam conveyed God's command to Eve after Eve was created. When Adam conveyed to Eve the commandment that God had given *him,* Adam *added* the "you shall not touch it" to protect his wife from the danger of the tree. This further supports the fact that not only did Adam fully understand and recognize the distinction between right and wrong, between good and evil, but that he also had the wisdom and foresight to understand how to try to help and protect Eve as well.

The commandment from God about not eating from the tree of the knowledge of good and evil was given only to Adam, and Adam *alone* was responsible to keep the commandment. We see from the rest of the entirety of the Bible that this is in fact exactly the case—it is Adam alone who is responsible to keep the commandment, and it is Adam alone who must disobey for there to be any fall of man.

The Two Trees

The two special trees that were placed in the middle of the garden of Eden, together in its midst, were the tree of life and the tree of the knowledge of good and evil. What was the nature of these two trees? Some have said these two trees were just regular, nothing-special trees, that they were just symbolic and representative of obedience or disobedience. However, that is an impossible argument, for it contradicts the very clear words and actions of God, especially in regards to the tree of life. In Genesis 3:22–23, we are told:

> Then the Lord God said, "Behold, the man has become like one of Us, to know good and evil. And now, lest he put out his hand and take also of the tree of life, and eat, and live forever"—therefore the Lord God sent him out of the garden of Eden to till the ground from which he was taken. (NKJV)

God specifically says if Adam, after his fall, was to take the fruit of the tree of life and eat it, he would live forever. God clearly tells us that to eat of the fruit of the tree of life would result in living forever—the fruit of the tree of life would give physical immortality. It is for *that* reason that God drives Adam out of the garden of Eden, so Adam would *not* eat from the tree of life.

Some have said God drove Adam from the garden because he was angry with Adam, but that is absolutely false. Rather, God drove Adam from the garden because God was *merciful* and *loving*. Once Adam ate from the tree of the knowledge of good and evil, he was in sin, and if he *then* also ate from the tree of life, then that would mean that Adam, and all humanity to follow, would never die and, as a result, would *forever* be in a state of eternal sin. God driving Adam out of the garden of Eden ensures man will *not* remain in a state of eternal sin, it is God making possible the salvation and redemption of man, and this is the love and mercy of God.

Also, the tree of life appears again, in Revelation, after this eternal Earth (Mic 6:2; Ps 104:5) is redeemed, after Jesus sets up his eternal kingdom upon Earth upon his second coming after the New Jerusalem comes down to Earth from heaven (Rev 21:2), after God the Father moves his throne from heaven to Earth, to dwell here with us on Earth in the New Jerusalem forever (Rev 21:3; 22:3). The same tree of life that is in Genesis 2 is also in Revelation 2:7, 22:2, 22:14, and 22:19. In Revelation 22:1–2, we are told:

> Then the angel showed me the river of the water of life, as clear as crystal, flowing from the throne of God and of the Lamb down the middle of the great street of the city. On each side of the river stood the *tree of life*, bearing twelve crops of fruit, yielding its fruit every month. And the leaves of the tree are *for the healing of the nations*. (NIV)

Once again, we are told the tree of life is described as having special properties, in this case we are told its leaves are for the "healing of the nations." God himself in Genesis 3 tells us eating of the tree of life will impart immortality to the eater, and in Revelation 22 we are told the leaves of this same tree of life will heal the nations. As a result, it is inarguable the tree of life is an actual special tree, one that it is not merely symbolic nor a metaphor, but rather it is a tree that does in fact have special properties of immortality and healing.

Likewise, if the tree of life is an actual special tree that is neither symbolic nor a metaphor, but is rather a tree that does in fact have special properties, then the same must be true of the tree of the knowledge of good and evil. In the case of the tree of the knowledge of good and evil, the special property is to impart an *actual* knowledge of good and evil.

The Tree of the Knowledge of Good and Evil

Why is this tree called the tree of the *knowledge* of good *and* evil? Why isn't it called the tree of the knowledge of evil? Or the tree of evil? Or the tree of death? This tree has a very specific name, and to understand that name is key to understanding both the test of Eden and the fall of man.

Knowledge

In the Bible, to have *knowledge* of a thing is to have an intimacy of the thing, a special experiential understanding of the thing. For example, in Genesis 4:1, we are told, "Now Adam knew Eve his wife, and she conceived and bore Cain" (NKJV). The term "knew his wife" is the literal and deepest translation of the phrase, and both the KJV and NKJV keep that translation. Other translations use phrases such as "made love to" (NIV) or "had relations with," (NASB) but the actual, literal, and deepest translation is the phrase "*knew* Eve his wife."

For Adam to *know* his wife is for Adam to have the deepest, most intimate experience of his wife, and that is what the word, and concept of, knowledge means in the Bible—to know something intimately and by experience. It isn't just to recognize a thing, or to discern it, or to intellectually respond to it; rather, it is to know it at its heart, to have the taste of it, the experience of it in its essence.

Imagine you met a man who had never in his life tasted an orange, and you wanted to describe to him the taste of an orange. You can give him all kinds of examples, all kinds of metaphors, show him all kinds of pictures, and the man can recognize an orange when he sees one, but until he actually *tastes* the orange, he will never truly *know* what the orange tastes like—to have a true knowledge of a thing is to *experience* the thing.

God, of course, already truly *knows* all things—he himself has absolutely no evil or darkness within him, nothing bad (1 John 1:5), he is totally, completely, and absolutely all goodness and all love (1 John 4:8). Yet by virtue of being God he has a complete understanding and knowledge of evil and the nature of evil, not because he is evil or has any evil in him, but because he is the Almighty, All-knowing God, who himself *defines* goodness and love. There is *nothing* he does not know or understand, including the *nature* of evil, for it is he himself who defines all that is good:

> No one is holy like the Lord,
> For there is none besides You,
> Nor is there any rock like our God.
> 'Talk no more so very proudly;
> Let no arrogance come from your mouth,
> For *the Lord is the God of knowledge*;
> And by him actions are weighed.'
> (1 Sam 2:2–3 NKJV)

So, in one real sense, the tree of the knowledge of good and evil can be called the tree of the *experience* of good and evil, for the *knowledge* that eating from the tree imparts is the intimate knowledge gained from experience.

The Knowledge of Good *and* Evil

But why is it called the tree of the knowledge of *good* and evil? Does eating from the tree somehow make one also understand goodness? Doesn't Adam already *know* goodness, since he himself is completely without sin and since he is the son of God (Luke 3:38), fully indwelt by the Holy Spirit, and with his entire experience being only of God's goodness and love?

This is one of the unique characteristics of this tree, and of eating from it. It is not just the knowledge of good *or* evil, or the knowledge of evil, but the knowledge of both good *and* evil. What does that mean?

Who in all of creation knows both good *and* evil? God of course knows the nature of everything, since he is the Almighty, All-loving, All-knowing Creator, and he himself defines all that is goodness and love. He also fully understands the nature of what it is to rebel against that goodness and love, so God, certainly, fully knows and understands *both* good and evil. But how about the angels? Do the angels have a *knowledge* of *both* good *and* evil?

All of the angels, like unfallen Adam, would have recognized and discerned good and evil. But one-third of those angels rebelled (Rev 12:4), while two-thirds remained faithful to God, holy and unfallen. Did those angels who remained faithful, holy, and unfallen, even though they were *witness* to evil, come to have any actual *innate knowledge* or *inner experience* of evil? That is, did they come to have a personal experience of the nature of evil within their own hearts?

The answer is no—the holy, unfallen angels certainly saw evil, they were witness to the birth of evil and its aftermath, they were faced with making a choice to either trust God or rebel against him, and they chose to trust and to love him, and so they remained holy and blameless. Yet the holy, unfallen angels, although they witnessed evil, and can discern its existence, have never had any innate personal experience of evil within themselves or within their own beings. They have only ever *known* only what is good, but they themselves have never *tasted* of evil.

The fallen, rebellious angels, on the other hand, were created holy and knew what it meant to be holy, but in their rebellion and sin their natures were permanently changed according to the choice each freely made. As a result of that choice—the choice of rebellion, sin, selfishness, pride, and hatred—every vestige of what used to be holy and good within them was gone, and they were left with *no* goodness within them anymore, they were left with *only* evil, so that if they were even to try and recall what holiness or goodness meant, they could not, for all their understanding was now corrupt and poisoned. The fallen angels now have *only* the experience of evil, and yet, with that, not even any true understanding of it, since their understanding is now fully corrupt, perverted and poisoned. The fallen angels can no longer recall what goodness or holiness meant since, as a result of their fall, all such knowledge had been completely corrupted, and they were left as only evil, yet having no understanding of that evil. So neither the holy, unfallen angels, nor the fallen rebellious angels, actually *know* both good *and* evil—the holy angels know *only* good, while the fallen angels know neither. So, only God himself *truly* knows *both* good *and* evil.

This is one of the unique defining characteristics of the tree of the knowledge of good and evil. That tree was placed in the garden, together with the tree of life, to be a test for man—not to be a test for angels nor for any other creature—*only* for man. Man was created in both the image and the likeness of God, and he was created supreme and perfect in every way. Being created in God's image, man was created having God's nature—full of his goodness, love, and wisdom, created as holy and fully good. And here's the thing, if man was to eat from the tree of the knowledge of good and evil, then evil—or sin—would take up residence in man, and it would be there *together with* the goodness within man, which man had as a result of being created in God's image. Evil and sin would *coexist* with the goodness of God's image in man's nature. As a result, in eating of the tree of the knowledge of good and evil, man, and man alone among God's creatures, would come to have an *experiential* and *intimate* knowledge of *both* good *and* evil, with *both* good *and* evil coming to reside together within him, unlike any other creature in the universe. And so man alone would become like God, knowing *both* good and evil.

The Nature of the Tree of the Knowledge of Good and Evil

Both the tree of life and the tree of the knowledge of good and evil are without question real trees with special properties they impart to the eater—the tree of life imparts immortality, while the tree of the knowledge of good and evil imparts the residence of evil that would come to coexist with good within the eater. Both of these trees were *placed* in Eden, in the middle of the garden, side by side, to be a test. Being *placed* in Eden means the two trees were created outside of Eden. So, where were they created, if not in Eden and not on Earth?

It is easy to understand God being the creator of the tree of life, especially as that tree seems like an eternal tree, one which will have a permanent place in the coming New Jerusalem in God's kingdom to come upon this Earth (Rev 22:2). The strong implication of this is the tree of life, which imparts immortality and whose leaves heal nations, was a tree originally created in heaven, and then placed in Eden, and which now remains eternally here on Earth (it remains on Earth to this day, still guarded by the Cherubim with the flaming swords, who will stop guarding the tree of life and reveal it at the coming of the New Jerusalem).

If this is the case for the tree of life, then how do we understand the tree of the knowledge of good and evil? If, like the tree of life, it was placed in Eden and not created in Eden, then where was it created? And was it created having evil within it? The Bible does not give any details on the creation or origin of the tree of the knowledge of good and evil, but it does give us some details on the tree of life, as well as details on Satan and how he operates. The Bible also affirms to us that God is just, just to all, which would include him being just to Satan. Putting all of this together, we can arrive at some conclusions.

First, like the tree of life, the tree of the knowledge of good and evil was *placed* in Eden, not created there. This is the strong conclusion when looking at the various verses describing Eden, the two trees, and other verses describing the tree of life. If the tree of the knowledge of good and evil was placed in Eden, not created there, then where was tree of the knowledge of good and evil created? It seems reasonable to conclude this special tree, like the tree of life, was created originally in heaven. Does that mean God created something evil, that he created a tree that could impart evil? No, God never creates anything evil, God *only* creates what is holy and good. How then can we explain or understand a heavenly tree that imparts evil?

The key to understanding this is to remember that by the time the testing of man would have been agreed upon in heaven during Satan's audience with God, evil was already in the universe—the angelic rebellion had already happened, the rebel angels were already cast out of heaven into the pit, and war had already occurred in heaven (Rev 12:7–9).

During the audience Satan would have had with God in heaven when Satan, the instigator of the rebellion, was called forth to present himself in heaven before God, the parameters of man's test were decided, and the parameters of that test are exactly what is outlined in Genesis: a place of testing would be made on Earth—Eden—and in that place of testing two trees would be placed. Man would then be placed in Eden and only one command would be given to man, to not eat from one of the trees, and Satan would be allowed to tempt man to freely choose to rebel, just as he tempted the angels, so as to instigate rebellion. One of the trees would be the tree of life, but what would be the other tree? It was decided the other tree would be the tree of the knowledge of good and evil—a tree that, if eaten from, would impart, together with the knowledge of good and evil, death.

Where could such a tree be found? In light of the certainty that the two trees in Eden were neither symbolic nor a metaphor, it is reasonable to conclude God either allowed Satan to somehow infect a created, heavenly tree—one originally created as holy and good, but which was then allowed to be infected by Satan for the purpose of testing man—or that such an infected tree may have already existed as part of the aftermath of the angelic rebellion. In either case, such an infected tree would in fact be a tree we could consider poisoned, a tree that had, within its infected fruit, the very nature of sin. To physically eat from the tree of life would bring *physical* immortality. Likewise, to physically eat from the tree of the knowledge of good and evil would bring actual *physical* sin and death to the eater. The further result of that physical sin and death would be spiritual death, true death, which is separation from God.

The result of eating from such an infected tree would be that man would have, within himself and within his own nature and being, the simultaneous coexistence of both God's goodness (the result of being made in God's image and likeness) and also the actual physical presence of evil and sin, coexisting within man and at war with each other within his whole being, within his own flesh. This is exactly what we see as the result of Adam eating from that tree (Rom 7:5, 18, 25; 8:5; 13:14; Gal 2:20; 5:16–17, 24; Eph 2:15), and the whole history of humanity affirms the aftermath of it.

The scenario is this: God put Adam in a place of testing, in Eden, in whose midst were placed both the tree of life and the tree of the knowledge of God and evil, side by side, both real, actual trees with special properties—the tree of life with the property of giving physical immortality, and the tree of the knowledge of good and evil, an infected tree, with the property of imparting actual, physical sin and death. God gave to Adam—and only to Adam, before Eve was even created—one command: to not eat from the tree of the knowledge of good and evil. Satan was allowed to go into the garden to try and tempt Adam to freely choose to disobey God and break his command. The stage was set.

9

The Temptation and Fall of Man

MAN WAS MADE THE lord of the earth, given dominion over it and over all the living creatures upon it (Gen 1:26)—Adam, the son of God (Luke 3:38) was literally the king of the earth. Adam was put into the place of testing, Eden, in whose midst were the tree of life and the tree of the knowledge of good and evil. He was given only one command—to not eat of the tree of the knowledge of good and evil. After God had given Adam the one command, and after naming all the land animals and birds, Adam was put into a deep sleep, and then, there in Eden, from Adam's own flesh and bone, Eve was created. Adam named her woman, later naming her Eve.

The one commandment to not eat from the tree of the knowledge of good and evil was given by God only to Adam, before Eve was ever created. Adam later conveyed God's commandment to Eve, which is affirmed in Genesis 3 during Eve's conversation with the serpent. Since the commandment to not eat from the tree of the knowledge of good and evil was given only to Adam, it was Adam who was responsible to keep the commandment. It was Adam and Adam alone who had to choose whether or not to obey God's commandment. Adam and Adam alone was the target of Satan's strategy in Eden.

Upon the declaration of his rebellion in heaven, Satan was cast out of heaven and thrown down into the pit, a prison of chains and darkness within the earth. He was subsequently allowed out of the pit and brought before God in heaven to account for his rebellion. During that exchange between God and Satan in heaven, the testing of man would have been determined and its parameters set. Satan would be allowed into Eden to tempt man to disobey God, to sin against God, to rebel against him.

But this would not be an ongoing string of temptation; rather, as it was with the angels in heaven, once Adam would make his choice to obey or disobey, his choice would be permanent. The angels in heaven all had to eventually make a choice—rebel against God or remain faithful to him and to his love. Once an angel made that choice, that choice was permanent and absolute, for those angels who chose to remain faithful to God and to his love would never again be tempted to make that choice. Likewise, for the angels that chose to rebel against God and his love, who chose the lie of self-exaltation over the truth of love, once they would have made their choice it too was absolute and permanent—they would not have the chance to choose again.

The same was true of Adam. Satan only had one chance to try to incite Adam to sin—if Adam resisted the devil and said "no" to Satan's temptation, then the test was over, done and finished, and Adam's choice of obedience to God would be permanent and absolute, inviolate, never to be tested again. If Adam chose to sin and to rebel against God, then that choice would also be absolute and permanent in the sense that it could not be undone, and all the consequences from making the choice to rebel would ensue.

The potential fall of man was of enormous importance to Satan because in essence it was Satan's way of justifying his own rebellion to God, of ultimately blaming God for the angelic rebellion. If Adam were to sin, then Satan could argue the propensity to sin was in the created nature, and God was responsible for creating that nature, a nature whose natural propensity was to sin. As a result, Satan could then argue his rebellion, like Adam's, was only the result of him acting according to the nature with which he was created. Therefore, since it was God who created him and who created his nature, then he, Satan, did nothing wrong, and if there was anyone to blame for the rebellion, it was God. In Satan's reasoning, if Adam were to sin, then Satan would be justified and God would be at fault. Adam's potential fall was of enormous importance to Satan.

Also, a secondary result of the fall of man would be Adam relinquishing his dominion and lordship over the earth, relinquishing it to Satan. If Adam sinned, then, as a result of that sin, of that rebellion against God, Satan would have a legal claim to the lordship of the earth because, in sinning, by choosing sin over God, Adam would give the dominion of the earth over to Satan, the author of sin.

For Satan, the stakes of the potential fall of man were colossal, and trying to elicit Adam's sin was perhaps Satan's single most important undertaking. Adam had one choice to make, and Satan had one chance to evoke sin, and so Satan had to try and figure out how to tempt Adam to sin against God, to get Adam to eat from the tree of the knowledge of good and evil.

Satan's Strategy

Satan was the greatest of God's heavenly creatures, the anointed Cherub, representative of all the angelic ranks before God, their spokesman, and God's representative to them (Ezek 28:11–19). He was created full of wisdom and perfect in beauty. When he in his own heart decided he wanted to be like God (Isa 14:12–15), he sinned and died and became a creature of complete corruption and lies. He then began to plan and strategize how to actually try and realize his ambition to be like God and to be worshiped, applying his whole mind and intellect to achieving that goal. This resulted in a long and subtle plan, his "widespread trade" (Ezek 28:16) of sowing doubt in the minds of the other angelic sons of God so as to try and incite rebellion. Lucifer did nothing stupidly—even after his fall, he still retained his rank and intellect. In looking to incite the fall of man, the rebellion of Adam, this also would not be done stupidly, but rather would be the result of applying every aspect of his mind and intellect to creating a strategy to accomplish that end.

This is important to understand, for too often people seem to think of the events of Eden as just something that sort of happened one day as Satan was walking through the garden. But this is not so, for the events of Eden were the result of extreme and thorough calculation and strategizing on the part of Satan, and this strategizing happened over an extended period of time, being the result of much observation and thought.

Satan Sees Adam and Eve for the First Time

We read the events of Eden, in Genesis, as a familiar story, and as a result we take many things for granted and forget there is a whole deep background behind those events. For example, Genesis 3 just starts to talk outright of the serpent and Eve, but that conversation between the serpent and Eve was the result of a deep, calculated process. As part of that process, certain things took place which are not related in Genesis, but which certainly must have occurred. One of those events which certainly preceded any encounter of Satan with either Adam or Eve was the very first time Satan saw Adam and Eve. What was that like? What did Satan think when he saw them for the very first time? What was he expecting? What did he feel? He knew man was created to be God's bride and companion, but what exactly was man? He did not know anything about man until he saw man firsthand, and that would have happened for the first time in Eden.

After the parameters of the test in Eden were set, and after Eve was created in Eden, then was Satan allowed to go from the presence of God to Eden to tempt man (exactly as he was allowed to go to the desert to tempt Jesus, the Second Adam). As Satan was on his way to Eden to encounter man, what was he expecting to find? His entire experience of creation was as follows: God himself is a Trinity—Father, Son, and Holy Spirit—the eternal, uncreated God and Creator of all things, Almighty and All-knowing. All the angels—their entire vast number—were created en masse, they were not born. This was Satan's experience of God and of his creation—no one was created alone, and even God himself is a Trinity. So what did Satan think when he first entered Eden, when he was looking for man, and then found Adam—only *one* man? Was he expecting to find a great company of men, as numerous in number as were the angels? Most likely he was, since that was the entirety of his experience, and yet he found only *one* man: Adam.

What did he see in Adam? There is no question that, in seeing Adam, Satan would have instantly recognized the image of God, but he also would have recognized the *likeness* of God, which is probably something he did not expect since angels, though also made in the image of God, and hence called the sons of God, were not made in God's likeness. There is no question that, in seeing Adam, Satan would have seen and recognized the great glory of God. In fact, Satan, for the first time ever, would have seen and recognized a creature greater than himself, which almost certainly would have filled him with both an overwhelming envy and also an overwhelming hatred.

And then Satan would have seen something he could not ever have even remotely imagined—a *woman*. There is no question that in seeing Eve, Satan was astounded. There were no female angels; God himself is Father, Son, and Holy Spirit—Satan would have had no experience whatsoever with seeing a female "image and likeness" of God. There is also no question that in seeing Eve, Satan, for the first time ever, would have seen a creature even more beautiful than himself. It has been said that, as a result of encountering Eve's indescribable beauty, a beauty that exceeded Lucifer's own unfallen beauty, a particularly vicious hatred toward the woman was born in Satan's heart.

In all of this, Satan would have been overawed encountering man—Adam and Eve. It is almost certain he did not know what to make of them—both a man *and* a *woman*—and there were only the *two* of them, not a vast host of humanity. All of this was completely outside of Satan's entire experience. It is Satan's nature to first apply his mind and intellect to understanding a situation, and then to strategize and plan how to accomplish his goal. As a result, Satan would undertake to observe Adam and Eve, to study them, to understand them, and then strategize how to incite Adam to sin.

Satan's Observations

From the description the Bible gives us of ensuing events, we can come to some very clear and certain conclusions. First, we know Adam and Adam alone was the target of Satan's strategy, for only Adam was given the commandment to not eat from the tree of the knowledge of good and evil. Therefore the fall of man, the sin or rebellion of man, is dependent *only* on Adam eating from the tree. Satan had to strategize on how he could lure *Adam* into eating from the forbidden tree. Satan had only one chance to accomplish his goal.

One other thing is certain—during the course of his observation and study of Adam, Satan came to conclude if he were to tempt Adam *directly*, Adam would resist him and Satan would fail and be defeated. We know for a certainty this is true because of the ensuing events as recounted in Genesis 3. Satan saw that to try and tempt Adam directly would lead to failure.

So what was he to do? How could he accomplish his goal? What sort of calculated strategy could he devise that would somehow lead to Adam eating from the forbidden tree? There is no question that, during the course of his study and observation of Adam, and after realizing that to try and tempt Adam directly would lead to failure, Satan discovered an angle that would form the basis of his strategy, an angle that would be an *indirect* way of tempting Adam, an angle that had at least the chance of success. Satan discovered that at one time Adam had been *alone*, that he had been without Eve, and Satan discovered that Adam did not want to be alone again. That discovery would be the key to Satan's strategy of devising an indirect way to tempt Adam to eat of the forbidden tree.

The Angle of Eve

Eve was Adam's wife, his companion, his helper, made by God from him and for him, made from his own flesh and bone—she was his joy, his love, his happiness. In making Adam alone, God wanted Adam to know what it was like to desire a companion with whom to share oneself. In God's creation of Eve, Adam then had that desire fulfilled, a perfect picture of how God's desire for his own companion is fulfilled in man. Adam and Eve lived in perfect joy, harmony, and fulfillment, together with each other and with God—sinless people, perfect in every way, full of wisdom, power, and beauty, and fully indwelt by the Holy Spirit. They were in a patch of paradise called Eden, and they lacked nothing. God gave Adam one commandment, to not eat from the tree of the knowledge of good and evil. When Adam later relayed that commandment to Eve, he also *added* to that commandment for the sake of protecting his wife. God's commandment to Adam was:

> And the Lord God commanded the man, saying, "Of every tree of the garden you may freely eat; but of the tree of the knowledge of good and evil you shall not eat, for in the day that you eat of it you shall surely die." (Gen 2:16–17 NKJV)

This is the commandment as given by God. But when Adam relayed that commandment to Eve, it was as follows:

> The woman said to the serpent, "We may eat fruit from the trees in the garden, but God did say, 'You must not eat fruit from the tree that is in the middle of the garden, *and you must not touch it*, or you will die.'" (Gen 3:2–3 NIV)

God did *not* say to Adam that he must not *touch* the tree or its fruit, but when Adam relayed God's commandment to Eve, Adam added the "you must not touch it" as an added measure to protect Eve from the danger of the tree. Adam had perfect wisdom and perfect intellect, and perfect love for both God and Eve, and he understood the need for, and the importance of, obeying God and staying away from even the vicinity of the tree. In adding the "you must not touch it," Adam was being wise and protective of Eve.

Satan, in discovering that at one time Adam had been alone, now devised his strategy. He somehow had to set up a situation wherein Adam would believe he might lose Eve. Satan's strategy of trying to set up that situation would be to try to get *Eve* to eat from the tree. Satan knew Eve eating from the tree would mean nothing, for there would be no fall until Adam ate of the tree, so the angle of Eve was a calculated plan of an unfolding sequence of events that could indirectly lead to Adam eating from the tree. Satan thought this through deeply, he calculated exceedingly, for he would only have one attempt to try and engender the fall of Adam. With his strategy developed, being the result of deep, lengthy observation, immense thought, and great calculation, he set the plan in motion by targeting Eve.

Eve Must be Alone

The very heart of Satan's strategy was that somehow he must encounter Eve *alone*, without Adam being there, for the whole point of approaching Eve was to avoid tempting Adam directly, for any such direct attempt upon Adam would surely result in failure. Satan had to try to set up a sequence of events that would lead to an indirect temptation of Adam, and this would be impossible if Adam was present with Eve when he, Satan, would approach Eve.

Furthermore, we already know Adam was particularly vigilant about the forbidden tree, since he went out of his way to add the "you must not touch it" to God's original commandment, so as to protect Eve from any possible danger. With all of this taken together, it is without question Satan had to encounter Eve when she was *alone* near the tree, to encounter her when Adam was not close enough to be looking out for Eve—to do otherwise would go against the very heart of his strategy.

Adam and Eve were together in Eden, and there is no question Adam was at least in the general vicinity when Eve found herself close to the tree of the knowledge of good and evil. We know this because we are told in Genesis 3:6, "When the woman saw that the fruit of the tree was good for food and pleasing to the eye, and also desirable for gaining wisdom, she took some and ate it. She also gave some to her husband, *who was with her*, and he ate it" (NIV).

The Temptation and Fall of Man

The phrase "who was with her" does *not* mean Adam was there beside Eve throughout the whole time of Eve's temptation. Again, the whole point of Satan approaching Eve was so he would *not* approach Adam directly, for Adam would resist him and Satan would fail. Yes, Adam was "there with her," but this only means he was in the general area with her, for the alternative, that he was right there beside her, is impossible, for it would make Satan a fool—and Satan was not a fool. Adam being present with Eve would defeat the whole point of Satan's strategy of approaching *Eve*—Satan approached Eve as an indirect, calculated way of getting to Adam. Adam was *not* beside Eve through the time of her deception, but he *was* in the general area. Satan did not approach Eve stupidly or thoughtlessly, but with extreme calculation. Satan saw his opportunity, and Eve was alone by the tree when the serpent spoke to her.

Why was Eve Alone Near the Tree?

While Adam and Eve were in the same general area of Eden at the time of Eve's deception, Satan knew he somehow must encounter Eve while she was alone *by the tree*, with Adam out of earshot so he would not hear the conversation. Satan somehow would have to lure Eve away from Adam and toward the tree. The details of the luring are not outlined in Genesis, but again, in looking at the ensuing events, some conclusions can be drawn. The key to both the luring of Eve and the deception that followed is the serpent.

The serpent was created by God, like all the other animals of the earth. The serpent was *not* a snake—the serpent *became* a snake after it was cursed (Gen 3:14). The serpent, before it was cursed, had legs and, according to the Bible, was an exceptional creature, for we are told "now the serpent was more cunning than any beast of the field which the Lord God had made" (Gen 3:1 NKJV).

The serpent stood out from among God's other creatures—various translations describe the serpent as more cunning, or more crafty, or more subtle, or more shrewd that any of God's other creatures, affirming the serpent was an exceptional creature. It is also likely the serpent was physically more beautiful, or at least more striking to behold, than the other creatures. Satan would have discovered the serpent and its qualities during his time of studying and observing Adam, Eve, and Eden. All of this taken together shows the serpent would prove a powerful choice as a means of luring and then deceiving Eve.

The serpent in and of itself, as a creature of God's making, neither lured nor seduced Eve. Rather, Satan designated the serpent as the means by which *he*, Satan, would lure and then ply Eve with temptation. To do that, Satan strategized to possess the serpent. We know Satan possessed the serpent because the serpent spoke to Eve in a human language and had a reasoned conversation with her. Animals do not have human speech, nor can they engage in reasoned conversation, and so the "talking serpent" is witness to the fact Satan did possess the serpent, both working and speaking through it. Also, this is further affirmed in Revelation 12:9 where Satan is described as "that *serpent* of old, called the Devil and Satan, who deceives the whole world" (NKJV).

This description of Satan as "that serpent of old" is a reference to the garden of Eden and to his possession of the serpent. As a result of his long observation, deep thought, and intricate calculation, Satan devised a strategy to possess the serpent as the means by which to lure Eve to the tree and then to deceive her to eat from it.

So the scenario is as follows: Adam and Eve are together in Eden, with the tree of the knowledge of good and evil relatively near, but not so near that they are exposed to it. Satan possesses the serpent, perhaps the most exceptional creature in Eden, both in appearance and certainly in manner and substance. Satan has Eve in his sights, so he, in the body of the serpent, approaches Eve, who may very well have been close to Adam. The serpent approaches Eve, in every respect looking and acting as a regular creature of Eden. Eve notices the serpent, and whether it was through some sort of intriguing playfulness, or some engaging movement on the part of the serpent (though playfulness is most likely), the serpent attracts Eve's attention and Eve is engaged by the serpent's mood and movements. It is reasonable to conclude Eve would have engaged with the serpent as a response to its playfulness, engaging it with a joyfulness of heart. But the serpent's playfulness was only a ruse, for Satan was possessing the serpent, and Satan had his plan, and the serpent's playfulness was a lure. Once Eve was engaged, the serpent would have "playfully" led her in the direction of the tree of the knowledge of good and evil. And then, soon enough, both Eve and the serpent would have been by the tree, alone. It is at that point that the deception begins.

The Deception of Eve

When we look at the deception of Eve by the serpent, it can only be described as a masterpiece of temptation. Here is the account in Genesis 3:1–6:

> Now the serpent was more cunning than any beast of the field which the Lord God had made. And he said to the woman, 'Has God indeed said, "You shall not eat of every tree of the garden?"' And the woman said to the serpent, 'We may eat the fruit of the trees of the garden; but of the fruit of the tree which is in the midst of the garden, God has said, "You shall not eat it, nor shall you touch it, lest you die."' Then the serpent said to the woman, 'You will not surely die. For God knows that in the day you eat of it your eyes will be opened, and you will be like God, knowing good and evil.' So when the woman saw that the tree was good for food, that it was pleasant to the eyes, and a tree desirable to make one wise, she took of its fruit and ate. She also gave to her husband with her, and he ate. (NKJV)

There are many elements of the temptation outlined in this account. First, once the serpent "happens" to lead Eve to the tree, the serpent stops, turns, and *speaks* to Eve. What did Eve make of this? There is no question she would have been astounded—serpents and animals do not talk with human speech. To hear the serpent *speak* to her, in a reasoned way, would have been both shocking and incredible. Remember, Satan's goal was to have Adam eat of the tree, and so he calculated this whole scenario, beginning with Eve, many steps in advance. In Satan's masterful temptation, notice how the serpent is *not* the one who brings up the tree of the knowledge of good and evil, rather, he just asks the general question, "Has God indeed said, 'You shall not eat of every tree of the garden?'" Satan had designed his question so as to allow *Eve* to bring up the tree, which she does in her reply to the serpent. This results in making it seem like bringing up the tree of the knowledge of good and evil was *Eve's* idea. This is a masterfully subtle stroke. In her reply to the serpent, she includes God's commandment regarding that tree, also adding the extra proviso given to her by Adam that not only are they not to eat of the tree but they also must not *touch* it.

This was Satan's opportunity, for he responds, "You will not surely die. For God knows that in the day you eat of it your eyes will be opened, and you will be like God, knowing good and evil." Eve is now being told, by a talking serpent, she will *not* die if she eats of the tree. Rather, if she eats of that tree, she will have her eyes opened, which is to say she will become wise and in fact become like God, knowing both good and evil. Remember it was the essence of Lucifer's own fall, the very heart of his ambition, to make himself be like God (Isa 14:14). As a result, Satan believed everyone else also desired to be like God, and so he made that exact same temptation to Eve, that in eating of the forbidden tree she would become *like God*.

There is no question Eve would then have been confused. Adam had relayed to her God's commandment, and told her to stay away from the forbidden tree, telling her also to not even touch it. The serpent was telling her eating of the tree would make her wise. Consider the scenario—a *talking* serpent was telling Eve that eating of the fruit of the forbidden tree would make her wise. Think of the extreme cleverness of this strategy—neither serpents, nor any animal, can talk and have reasoned conversation, and yet here is a serpent *talking* with Eve, in human speech, conversing and reasoning with her. This was a powerful part of Satan's strategy in tempting Eve, for the implication is clear: How did the serpent acquire the power of speech and reason? Perhaps by eating of the forbidden tree? There is no question such a thought would have been in Eve's mind, and that was part of Satan's plan—that the speech of the serpent was witness to the power of the forbidden tree to give wisdom.

Eve was now in the midst of temptation, and we are told the following: "So when the woman saw that the tree was good for food, that it was pleasant to the eyes, and a tree desirable to make one wise, she took of its fruit and ate." How did Eve see the tree was desirable for making one wise? Almost certainly by the fact of encountering a *talking* serpent. Following the words of the serpent, Eve would have looked upon the tree, looked upon its fruit, lingered upon it, and wondered what was the truth. This is how Satan so often operates—by engendering and instilling doubt. As she looked upon the tree, she saw it was a beautiful-looking tree with beautiful-looking fruit. It was probably the very first time she ever actually, in any deep way, looked at that tree and its fruit, and she saw it looked good and beautiful. She also saw its fruit could also be eaten just like the fruit of any other tree. And then she considered the serpent's words—that the tree would make her like God, that the tree would make her wise. And then the moment of truth—she reached out and took the fruit, she *touched* the fruit. Adam's added proviso was they must *not touch* the fruit, but that was not part of the command God gave to Adam; it was

Adam's added warning so as to help protect Eve. But that added warning, given by Adam in wisdom and in love, was used by Satan as the means of strengthening the deception, for when Eve eventually reached out and *touched* the fruit, by taking it in her hand, *before* eating of it, she would have noticed something astounding—nothing happened. She touched the fruit, and nothing bad happened, she did not die. This would have emboldened her to believe the rest of the serpent's words and, by seeing that touching the fruit had no effect on anything, she then ate of the fruit. And she again noticed something even more astounding—upon eating the fruit of the forbidden tree, nothing happened. She did not die, there was no fall, she had no experience of sin (since the commandment was never given to her, it was given only to Adam). In fact, in eating of the fruit of the forbidden tree, in seeing it was beautiful and good for food, in touching it and eating of it and with nothing bad happening, it would have affirmed the serpent's words, and she would have thought the serpent was telling her the truth.

It is important to recognize every word the serpent spoke *to Eve* was, in fact, *true*. There was *no lie* in his word, at least not as it applied to Eve. It was *true* that eating of the tree would *not* lead to *Eve's* death. Satan knew this—he knew the power of sin was in the commandment (1 Cor 15:56) and since Eve was not given the commandment, the sin within the fruit of that tree would not be aroused and as such it would have no power upon her. But he was thinking far beyond Eve, for he was thinking ultimately of Adam. Yes, if Eve ate of the tree, nothing would happen and she would not die, but if *Adam* ate of the tree, then both Adam and Eve would die. Once again, Satan's strategy of temptation was calculated and exceedingly clever.

Upon eating of that fruit and seeing that nothing bad happened, but rather, seeing that the fruit tasted good, Eve went to Adam, who would have been in the general area with her but not close enough to hear or see her engagement with the serpent. She would have approached Adam, bringing him the fruit, and she would have told him she ate of the fruit, that nothing had happened, that it was good for food, that it would make them wise, and she would then offer him the fruit. Setting up that scene between Eve and Adam was the entire purpose of Satan's strategy of approaching Eve. Adam's temptation would be presented not by Satan, but by Eve.

Adam's Temptation

What did Adam think or feel when Eve came up to him, coming with the fruit, having eaten from it and giving it to him to eat of it as well? The Bible gives us an account of the general facts, without all the shades of detail, and so this whole scenario is presented in a few words, for we are told "she also gave to her husband with her, and he ate." The fact that this is related as an event that happened, as a factual presentation of the event, can lead one to think that Adam just thoughtlessly and immediately took the fruit and ate of it, but that is impossible, for many reasons.

1. Adam was a perfect man—perfect in wisdom, intelligence, emotion, physicality, and spirit, and he was fully indwelt by the Holy Spirit, as was Eve and as was Jesus Christ. Adam named all things, his mind was the most powerful human mind ever, and he was no fool.

2. Adam understood the danger of that tree, for it was he who added the proviso to Eve that not only should she not eat of the tree, but also that she should not even touch it—those were wise and loving words of warning for the woman he loved.

3. Satan had already seen that if he were to approach Adam directly with the temptation to eat of the tree, Adam would have resisted him, and Satan would have failed. We know this is true because of the events that ensued, as outlined in Genesis 3, made clear by the very fact that Satan approached Eve rather than Adam.

As a result, it is certain Adam would have understood completely what it would have meant to eat of the forbidden tree, and that it must not be done under any circumstance. He also would have understood that to eat of the tree would have been to break God's commandment. So when Eve walked up to Adam, with the partially eaten fruit in her hand and offered it to him to eat, it is an absolute certainty there was war in Adam's heart—and this is exactly the scenario Satan was hoping to set up.

On the one hand, God's commandment was clear—do not eat of the tree of the knowledge of good and evil, for to eat of that tree would be to die. Adam may not have known the fullness of what it would have meant to die, because there was no experience of death on Earth, but he certainly would have known to die would not have been good, and to die would mean loss.

On the other hand, Eve, his one and only human companion, made of his own flesh and bone, the fulfillment of his desire, *did* eat from the tree. What do you suppose Adam thought as he looked upon Eve with the partially eaten fruit in her hand? There is no question there was fear in his heart—fear of what would now happen to Eve, fear that Eve would die, fear that he would lose her and that he would, again, *be alone*—and this was the heart of Satan's strategy. Adam did not want to be alone again, so what would he do? Would he leave Eve to die, whatever the fullness of that would mean, though he would have understood enough to know that death would at least mean losing Eve and he would again be alone? Or would he rather choose to *share Eve's fate* with her, whatever that would be, and so not be alone again?

That was the temptation: Does Adam choose God, or does he choose Eve? Adam's choice was no fleeting, momentary thing—it was the result of a powerful war within his being, a great turmoil, the product of fear and confusion. Adam would have stood before Eve for at least some length of time as the war raged within him. But Adam recalled what it meant to be alone, and that it was not good, and Adam did not want to be alone again, to be without the companion who was the fulfillment of his desire. And so Adam made his choice, in the midst of the raging battle within his heart—he chose Eve over God, and so he took of the fruit and ate.

Adam could have trusted that God would somehow redeem Eve's actions, which he certainly would have, but Adam did not trust God in this, and so he chose to share Eve's fate, whatever it would be. When Adam ate of the fruit of that tree, sin entered into him, and man fell.

10

The Aftermath of the Fall

WHEN ADAM ATE OF the forbidden fruit, there were immediate and devastating consequences for humanity. It is essential to understand it was Adam and Adam alone who was responsible for the fall of man—it was not Adam and Eve, but only Adam, and this is key to understanding what happened on the cross.

Adam Alone Responsible for the Fall

The commandment to not eat of the fruit of the forbidden tree was given to Adam and only Adam, before Eve was ever created (Gen 2:16). The commandment was never given to Eve—Eve received the commandment from Adam, with his own "and don't touch it" proviso added, added so as to help protect Eve. At the very worst, Eve disobeyed her husband, whereas Adam sinned against God—Adam sinned, and as a result of Adam sinning, Eve became a sinner. God specifically and only lays the fault of the fall of man at Adam's feet:

> Your first father sinned. (Isa 43:27 NKJV)

> Therefore, just as *sin entered the world through one man*, and death through sin, and in this way death came to all people. (Rom 5:12 NIV)

> Nevertheless, death reigned from the time of Adam to the time of Moses, even over those who did not sin by *breaking a*

command, as did Adam, who is a pattern of the one to come. (Rom 5:14 NIV)

Romans 5:12 is very specific when it tells us sin entered the world through *one man*—it does not say "though one man and one woman," rather, only through one *man*—this is a clear affirmation sin entered the world *only* through *Adam*.

Likewise Romans 5:14 is very specific when it tells us breaking the commandment that caused sin was the fault of *Adam*—it does not say it was the fault of Adam *and Eve*—rather, it was the fault of *only* Adam.

Romans 5:17 also tells us the following: "For if, by the trespass of the *one man*, death reigned through that *one man*, how much more will those who receive God's abundant provision of grace and of the gift of righteousness reign in life through the *one man*, Jesus Christ!" Once again, we are told the sin of Eden was caused by one *man*, not by one man and one woman, but by one man *only*—Adam alone was responsible.

We are also told the following: "For as *in Adam* all die, so in Christ all will be made alive" (1 Cor 15:22 NIV). Here again, Adam alone is held responsible for the death of the world. There is no mention whatsoever of Eve, only of Adam as being responsible for the death that came to humanity. The Bible is very clear: Adam and Adam alone caused the fall—not Adam and Eve—Adam alone was responsible for breaking the commandment, for the commandment was never given by God to Eve, it was given only to Adam.

Eve Became a Sinner

However, we are also told the following: "And Adam was not the one deceived; it was the woman who was deceived and *became a sinner*" (1 Tim 2:14 NIV). We are told Eve was deceived, and that Eve *became a sinner*. If Eve was not given the commandment, and if Eve did not sin, then how could Eve have become a sinner?

This verse is in complete agreement with the fact that it was Adam alone who caused the fall of humanity. The very specific phrasing of this verse, when contrasted with the phrasing of Isaiah 43:27, affirms that upon eating of the fruit of the tree, Eve did not sin.

When the Bible describes Adam eating of the tree, it very clearly and specifically states "Your first father sinned" (Isa 43:27). We are also specifically told Adam *broke the commandment* (Rom 5:14). This is unequivocal. However, when describing Eve, it does *not* say Eve *sinned*, or that she *broke* the commandment; rather, we are told Eve was *deceived* and she *became* a sinner.

How are we to understand this? Why this very specific language? It is obvious how Eve was deceived—she was deceived in her encounter with the serpent. But what does it mean she *became* a sinner? It means Eve *became* a sinner only *after Adam ate of the fruit*, which is exactly what we see:

> She also gave some to her husband, who was with her, *and he ate it. Then* the eyes of *both of them* were opened, and they realized they were naked . . . (Gen 3:6–7 NIV)

It is only after *Adam* eats of the fruit Eve has *her* eyes *opened* and sees she is naked, and so it is only after Adam eats of the fruit Eve *becomes* a sinner. This contrasts with the Bible's description of when Adam eats of the fruit, for when Adam eats of the fruit, it does *not* say Adam *became* a sinner; rather, we are told specifically Adam *sinned* and he broke the commandment. When Adam ate of the fruit, Adam sinned, but when Eve ate of the fruit, she was deceived and then later *became* a sinner only after *Adam* ate.

Once again, this clearly affirms the fall of man was solely and exclusively Adam's responsibility. The consequences of Adam's sin were immediate and tragic, a devastation upon humanity. The main immediate consequence of Adam eating of the forbidden fruit was it brought sin and the sinful nature into Adam, and, through him, to all humanity.

The Physicality of the Sinful Nature

When Adam ate of the forbidden fruit, sin *physically* entered into Adam and took up residence in his body, in his flesh—we call this habitation of sin the "sinful nature." The term "sinful nature" describes the sin residing *physically* within us—it is the sin that came to *inhabit* Adam immediately upon his eating of the forbidden fruit. The Bible repeatedly affirms the physicality of the sinful nature within us, the sinful nature which we inherited from our first father, Adam, for the Bible repeatedly speaks of our sinful nature in physical terms. It is very important to understand the sinful nature is *not* a spiritual state, it is *not* a spiritual condition; rather, it is an actual, *physical thing* that took up *physical residence* within Adam, and, through Adam, was passed on to all of his descendants. All of this is the result of Adam eating the forbidden fruit, of Adam ingesting the habitation of sin within the fruit of the tree of the knowledge of good and evil, of ingesting the substance within it that was a substance of sin.

The Residence of the Sinful Nature

If the sinful nature is a physical thing and came to enter physically into Adam upon his eating of the forbidden fruit, then where did the sinful nature take up residence within Adam? The Bible affirms the sinful nature took up physical residence within Adam's *blood*.

Blood

Sin and blood are inextricably linked throughout the Bible, as the following verses affirm:

> For the wages of sin is death. (Rom 6:23 NASB)

> Splash some of the blood of the sin offering against the side of the altar; the rest of the blood must be drained out at the base of the altar. It is a sin offering. (Lev 5:9 NIV)

> This is my blood of the covenant, which is poured out for many for the forgiveness of sins. (Matt 26:28 NIV)

> In him we have redemption through his blood, the forgiveness of sins. (Eph 1:7 NIV)

Blood and sin, and especially the forgiveness of sin, are inextricably linked throughout the entire Bible. Why are blood and sin inextricably linked throughout the Bible? It is because the sinful nature that inhabits humanity resides physically in our blood.

Mortal Life is in the Blood

We are told a creature's life is in its blood:

> The life of every creature is its blood. (Lev 17:14 NIV)

> But be sure you do not eat the blood, because the blood is the life. (Deut 12:23 NIV)

This is very clear: the life of a creature, the life of every creature, is in its blood, and this includes the life of all humanity, of Adam's descendants—our life is in our blood. But what kind of life is in our blood? Is it eternal life, or is it *mortal* life? There are at least two things we can understand from Leviticus 17:14 and Deuteronomy 12:23. First, the thing that keeps our bodies physically alive is our blood, for if our bodies did not have blood, we would be dead. But there is also a second and more important truth to understand from these verses. The life that is in the blood is *not* eternal life; rather, it is *mortal* life, it is a life that has within it *mortality*. The blood does *not* give eternal life; rather, it gives only *mortal* life. This also means not only does the blood keep us physically alive, but it is also the mortality *within the blood* that *makes us mortal*, that makes us die—our *mortality* is in our blood. This truth is absolutely implicit in the understanding of each of these verses, and it is an important truth.

As a result, we can understand the following. Yes, it is the blood that gives us physical life, but it is also the blood that *makes* us *physically die.* It is the blood that makes us *mortal,* it is the *blood* that gives us *mortality*. How does the blood give us mortality? Because it is the blood that carries *within it* the *thing that makes us mortal.* What is the thing that makes us mortal? The thing that kills us, that brings us death, that makes us mortal, is *sin*, the sinful nature. Our *sinful nature* is what brings us death, it is the *sinful nature* that makes us *mortal.* Our physical death is solely and exclusively the result of sin:

> For the wages of sin is death. (Rom 6:23)

> Then, after desire has conceived, it gives birth to sin; and sin, when it is full-grown, gives birth to death. (Jas 1:15 NIV)

Since it is our sinful nature that brings us death and makes us mortal, and since it is the blood that carries within it our mortality, there is no question the sinful nature resides physically in our blood.

The Flesh

The fact that the sin within us is a physical thing, physically residing within our flesh, is constantly affirmed throughout the letters of the apostle Paul. The apostle Paul constantly equates sin, our sinful nature, with "the flesh." Here are just a few Scriptures where Paul equates sin with "the flesh":

For when we were in the realm of *the flesh*, the sinful passions aroused by the law were at work in us, so that we bore fruit for death (Rom 7:5 NIV)

The mind governed by *the flesh* is death, but the mind governed by the Spirit is life and peace. The mind governed by the flesh is hostile to God; it does not submit to God's law, nor can it do so. Those who are in the realm of the flesh cannot please God. (Rom 8:6–8 NIV)

For if you live according to *the flesh*, you will die; but if by the Spirit you put to death the misdeeds of the body, you will live. (Rom 8:13 NIV)

Rather, clothe yourselves with the Lord Jesus Christ, and do not think about how to gratify the desires of *the flesh*. (Rom 13:14 NIV)

Are you so foolish? After beginning by means of the Spirit, are you now trying to finish by means of *the flesh?* (Gal 3:3 NIV)

You, my brothers and sisters, were called to be free. But do not use your freedom to *indulge the flesh*; rather, serve one another humbly in love. (Gal 5:13 NIV)

So I say, walk by the Spirit, and you will not gratify the desires of *the flesh*. For *the flesh desires* what is contrary to the Spirit, and the Spirit what is contrary to the flesh. They are in conflict with each other, so that you are not to do whatever you want. But if you are led by the Spirit, you are not under the law. The acts of the flesh are obvious: sexual immorality, impurity and debauchery (Gal 5:16–19 NIV)

Those who belong to Christ Jesus have crucified *the flesh* with its passions and desires. (Gal 5:24 NIV)

Whoever sows to please their *flesh*, from *the flesh* will reap destruction; whoever sows to please the Spirit, from the Spirit will reap eternal life. (Gal 6:8 NIV)

All of us also lived among them at one time, gratifying the *cravings of our flesh* and following its desires and thoughts. Like the rest, we were by nature deserving of wrath. (Eph 2:3 NIV)

> In him you were also circumcised with a circumcision not performed by human hands. Your whole self ruled by *the flesh* was put off when you were circumcised by Christ. (Col 2:11 NIV)

> This is especially true of those who follow the corrupt desire of *the flesh* and despise authority. (2 Pet 2:10 NIV)

> For they mouth empty, boastful words and, by appealing to the lustful desires of *the flesh*, they entice people who are just escaping from those who live in error. (2 Pet 2:18 NIV)

The Bible constantly equates our sinfulness with our *flesh*. Our flesh is absolutely physical. Why does Paul constantly speak of the sinful nature as being "the flesh?" It is because the sinful nature is physically residing within our blood, and our blood imbues and inhabits every cell of our physical bodies, of our flesh. As a result, the term "the flesh" is synonymous with the sinful nature within our blood. To describe our sinful nature as being our flesh is to affirm our sinful nature is a physical thing residing physically within our flesh, specifically within our blood.

Subject to Death

Furthermore, Paul specifically equates our physical death with the fact our *bodies* are subject to death, all as a result of *the sin within us*, the sin *within our flesh*: "But if Christ is in you, then even though your *body* is *subject to death* because *of sin*, the Spirit gives life because of righteousness" (Rom 8:10 NIV). Why are our physical bodies subject to death? Because our sinful nature resides physically within our bodies, within our flesh, within our blood, and so we are told it is "because of sin" our *bodies* are subject to death. Why does sin make our bodies subject to death? It is because death is the only conclusion of sin—sin is seeking its fulfillment, its completion, in death. In fact, sin is relentless until it is fulfilled in death. By having sin physically residing within us, we are subject to the inescapable death that will result from that sin coming to completion. As a result, our physical death is our sin coming to completion. This is a profoundly important truth to understand as it speaks directly to what happened on the cross. Our bodies die, are subject to death, because of the sin within us—our physical death is the *result* of the physical sin within us.

Are Our Bodies Evil?

When Paul equates sin with flesh, does that mean our human bodies are evil? No; our bodies are holy, for we are made by God in both his image and likeness. Being made in God's image means we are like him in our nature, and being made in God's likeness means we physically look like him. Even though we are fallen, we retain both the image and likeness of God. As we are told in Genesis 9:6: "Whoever sheds human blood, by humans shall their blood be shed; for in the image of God has God made mankind" (NIV). Genesis 9:6 was spoken after the fall of man. Even after the fall of man, we all still retain God's image and likeness, which means our bodies remain holy unto God (which is why our bodies are resurrected, not reincarnated). To equate sin with "the flesh" is *not* to say our bodies are evil; rather, by equating sin with "the flesh," it is *affirming* there is *something within our flesh* that *should not be there*, namely, the sinful nature.

By equating sin with the flesh, it means our human bodies have, residing within them, the physical substance of sin, which now physically *coexists* with the goodness of the image of God we all retain, which we all have by virtue of being made in God's image and likeness. Our bodies are holy, which is why, even after the fall, God tells us murder is still wrong (Gen 9:6). However, ever since the fall, within our holy bodies there now also resides, physically within our blood, the sinful nature. Our blood imbues every part of our flesh, every cell of our bodies, and so, by physically residing in our blood, the sinful nature is literally inhabiting every cell of our flesh.

Paul and Peter constantly use the term "the flesh" in talking about our sinful nature, and the reason for that is because it is an exact and literal description of the situation—it is a constant reaffirmation the sinful nature is a physical thing that physically resides in our physical bodies, residing in our *flesh* by way of our *blood*. The sinful nature does *not* reside in our spirit, it does *not* reside in our soul, it does *not* reside in our minds, it is *not* a spiritual state; rather, it resides physically *only* in our *flesh,* in our physical *bodies*. This is why we *physically* decay and die, because we have sin *physically* residing within us, exactly as if it were a terminal disease. It is the sin that resides within our physical bodies that *kills* the body and, ultimately, brings physical death.

The Shedding of Blood and Forgiveness

It is because of the fact our sinful nature resides physically within our blood that throughout the Bible the shedding of *blood* is *always* connected to the *forgiveness* of sin:

> In fact, the law requires that nearly everything be cleansed with blood, and *without the shedding of blood there is no forgiveness.* (Heb 9:22 NIV)

> This is my *blood* of the covenant, which is *poured out* for many for the *forgiveness of sins.* (Matt 26:28 NIV)

> In him we have redemption through his *blood,* the *forgiveness of sins*, in accordance with the riches of God's grace. (Eph 1:7 NIV)

The shedding of blood is *required* for the forgiveness of sins. Why? Because our sinful nature resides within our blood. In one sense, by shedding one's blood, it is as if one is getting rid of, or shedding, the sinful nature (except in such a case such a shedding of blood also means death, which again shows death as the inevitable result of sin).

Holding the Power of Sin and Death

When Adam ate the fruit of the forbidden tree, it is at that exact moment that he ingested the *physical* sinful nature from the fruit of that tree. As outlined earlier, there is a very strong reason to conclude the tree of the knowledge of good and evil was, like the tree of life, a tree created in heaven and that was subsequently allowed to be poisoned, by Satan. As a result, the tree of the knowledge of good and evil carried within it an actual "sin" substance, brought to the tree by the devil. This is further affirmed in Hebrews 2:14: "Since the children have flesh and blood, he too shared in their humanity so that by his death he might break the *power of him who holds the power of death*—that is, the *devil*" (NIV).

We are told sin is the *power* of *death*, since death comes from sin (Rom 6:23). Hebrews 2:14 also specifically tells us it is Satan, the devil, who himself *holds* the *power* of *death*. Since sin is the power of death, and since Satan holds the power of death, Satan therefore must also have authority, or power, over sin.

Sin—and its ensuing death—were in the fruit of the tree of the knowledge of good and evil, not in a symbolic or metaphoric way, but in an actual, real, and physical way. Hebrews 2:14 specifically affirms it is Satan who holds the power of death. Since Satan holds the power over sin and death, and since sin and death were both within the fruit of the tree of the knowledge of good and evil, this then is a further affirmation it was Satan who was responsible for infecting the tree of the knowledge of good and evil with the power of sin and death. Sin and death were both *physically* present within the fruit of that tree.

When Adam ate the fruit of that tree, he physically *ingested* the sin and death within its fruit. Once Adam ate of that fruit, sin, together with its ensuing death, took up physical residence within him. It is no accident the physical presence of sin within Adam is the result of him physically eating, and ingesting, the fruit from the forbidden tree. Upon eating the fruit of that tree, the physicality of sin took up residence within Adam, within his flesh, within his blood.

Ingesting the Fruit of the Tree

The tree of the knowledge of good and evil was infected physically with a sinfulness that took up residence within it, a sinfulness that was present within its fruit, as though it were a poison, and so for Adam, it was not just the *choice* to eat of the fruit that caused the full aftermath of the fall, but rather the fact Adam *ingested* what was within that fruit, ingesting a physicality of sin, a physicality which came to take residence within him, within his flesh upon his eating of the fruit.

Sin and Death within the Fruit of the Tree

As we have seen, the tree of life was an actual tree, a tree having both the property to give eternal life to the eater and to heal the nations. Likewise, the tree of the knowledge of good and evil was also an actual tree, having the property to impart the knowledge, or *experience*, of *actual sin* and evil to the eater, thereby bringing the full consequences of that sin to the eater.

It seems certain the tree of the knowledge of good and evil was in fact an infected or poisoned tree, infected or poisoned with an actual sin substance or sin nature. It's not that the sin substance within the fruit of the tree was the *cause* of the sin and death within that tree; rather, that sin substance within the tree was the *result* of the tree being infected with sin and death by Satan, who himself held the power of sin and death (Heb

2:14). Originally, this tree was almost certainly a created heavenly tree, created holy and pure, as was all of God's creation, but it was infected by Satan either during his angelic rebellion, or subsequently so as to establish the conditions of the testing of man in Eden, as a result of Satan's heavenly dialogue with God in the wake of the angelic rebellion.

How are we to understand such an infection? It can be understood in the same way we can understand the existence of violence and death among animals and the existence of poisoned plants within nature.

The Infection of the Tree

God did not create death, yet there is violence and death in nature. If God did not create death, then how did death come to be in nature? In God's original creation of life upon Earth, animals did *not* kill or eat each other—*all* animals ate plants:

> And to all the beasts of the earth and all the birds in the sky and all the creatures that move along the ground—everything that has the breath of life in it—I give every green plant for food. (Gen 1:30 NIV)

Likewise, God did *not* create poisonous plants—*all* the plants he created were *good* and were good for food.

> Then God said, "I give you every seed-bearing plant on the face of the whole earth and every tree that has fruit with seed in it. They will be yours for food. And to all the beasts of the earth and all the birds in the sky and all the creatures that move along the ground—everything that has the breath of life in it—I give every green plant for food." (Gen 1:29-30 NIV)

And yet there are *many* plants of all kinds that are poisonous, and *many* animals that kill each other and eat each other for food. How did this happen, since God did *not* create it this way? It happened as follows.

God gave Adam dominion, or lordship, over the earth (Gen 1:28). When Adam sinned, *he gave the dominion and lordship of the earth to Satan*. This is why Satan tells Jesus all the kingdoms of the earth are his to do with as he wishes (Luke 4:6). The reason Satan had this authority, or lordship, is because Adam gave it to him.

As a result of Adam giving the lordship of the earth over to Satan, the plants and animals of the earth were now no longer subject to

Adam's dominion; rather, they now became subject to *Satan's* dominion. It was upon becoming subject to Satan's dominion—a dominion of sin and death—that animals began to kill and eat each other, and plants became infected with poison—poisonous plants are infected plants and are the result of Satan's dominion over the earth, a dominion given him by Adam. These very same plants were created by God as holy and good, but upon coming under Satan's dominion they became infected with death and became poisonous plants.

As a result, we can understand the infection of the tree of the knowledge of good and evil in exactly this same way. The tree of the knowledge of good and evil was a created, heavenly tree, created holy and good, but, in order to establish the testing in Eden, was put under, or brought under, Satan's authority, and made subject to his holding the power of sin and death. By coming under Satan's authority and by becoming subject to his power over sin and death, that tree then became an infected or poisoned tree—just as the perfect plants of God's earthly creation came to be poisoned plants upon becoming subject to Satan's dominion. In the case of the tree of the knowledge of good and evil, that infection was with a substance of sin. We may not fully understand the substance of sin, but it was, and is, certainly a physical thing, and there is no question the tree of the knowledge of good and evil had within its fruit a habitation of sin.

Eve Did Not Sin—The Power of Sin is the Law

If there was an actual physical habitation of sin within the fruit of that tree, then why was not Eve infected by that same sin which was physically inhabiting the fruit of the tree, when she ate of its fruit?

It is because Eve was never given the commandment to not eat from the fruit of the tree, for it was the *commandment itself* that *activated* the power of sin within the fruit of the tree. The Bible tells us: "The sting of death is sin, and the *power of sin is the law*" (1 Cor 15:56 NIV). Sin is the power of death, but *the law* is the power of sin. Sin gets its *power* from the commandment; the *commandment*, the very holiness of the commandment, causes sin to *react* against the commandment and to become *active* (Rom 3:20; 5:13). Even though sin might itself be present, if the commandment is not given, the sin is not *activated*, for it is the very holiness of the commandment that brings out, arouses, or *exposes*, sin. Since Eve was not given the commandment to not eat from the tree, then the sin that was present within the fruit of the tree when she ate of it was not aroused, it was not activated. As a result, the sin within the fruit of the tree would have no power over her. Only the *commandment* would cause sin to *activate*. So, when Eve eats of the fruit of the tree, nothing happens.

Adam however *was* given the commandment, which means the sin that was present within the fruit of the tree when *Adam* ate of it *was* aroused, was activated, by that commandment. As a result, when Adam eats of the same fruit of which Eve had already eaten, the power of sin within that fruit is aroused and present *for Adam*. When Eve eats of the fruit, nothing happens, because she was never given the commandment, and therefore sin was not aroused, was not activated, for her. But when Adam eats the fruit, the sin *is* aroused and activated for *him*, because the commandment *was* given to Adam. As a result, when Adam eats, Adam sins and they *both* fall.

Eve Under Adam's Authority, Made of His Flesh

When Adam ate of the forbidden tree, he ingested the sinful nature, and the sinful nature took up physical residence within Adam. Upon taking up residence within Adam, the sinful nature *simultaneously* took up residence within *Eve*. Eve was under Adam's authority, being made of his flesh and bone—when the sinful nature entered first into Adam, into his flesh, it also simultaneously entered into Eve, for her flesh was literally Adam's flesh. As a result, when Adam sinned by eating from the forbidden fruit, *both* Adam and Eve fell in that moment and sin entered into *both* of them.

Adam's Descendants

Eve did not experience any fall or sin until *Adam* ate of the forbidden fruit. It was only after Adam ate of the fruit that Eve fell, for she was made of Adam's flesh and bone, and so was under his authority in regards to Adam keeping, or not keeping, God's one commandment. When Adam ate of the fruit, when he sinned, when he broke God's one commandment, only then did Eve also fall, and only then did the sinful nature take up residence in Eve—Eve got her sinful nature from Adam.

Adam is the physical father of all human beings, we are all his physical descendants, having his physical blood flowing through our veins. As a result, we also, all humanity, have the sinful nature now residing within us, residing in our blood, for we, like Eve, are Adam's descendants. Where Eve was created from Adam, we are born of Adam, and so we are told:

> For since *death came through a man*, the resurrection of the dead comes also through a man. For as in Adam all die, so in Christ all will be made alive. (1 Cor 15:21–22 NIV)

> Therefore, just as *sin entered the world through one man*, and *death through sin*, and *in this way death came to all people* (Rom 5:12 NIV)

The Bible does not say death came into the world through one man and one woman; rather, it says death came into the world through one *man—Adam*.

The Bible does not say "as in Adam and Eve all die"; rather, it says "For as in *Adam* all die . . . ." Once again, the Bible is very clear it is *Adam* and Adam *alone*, the *man*, who is responsible for our sinful natures—we inherit our sinful natures from Adam, *not* from Eve.

The Sinful Nature Comes through Our Human Father

There is a very important and profound truth contained in these verses, which is as follows—we, humanity, do *not* inherit our sinful natures from our human *mothers*; rather, we inherit our sinful natures *only* from our human *fathers*.

Think of it in terms of genetics. All human beings, both male and female, have their father's blood within them. Each human father is, of course, male, and so each father's blood contains the Y chromosome that gives maleness to himself. All of the father's offspring, all of his children, including his daughters, have their father's blood flowing through their veins. Yet even though a father's blood is flowing within his daughter, his daughter did *not* get her father's Y chromosome passed on to her, even though that Y chromosome is in the father's blood. Even in genetics there is a selective transmission of nature.

Likewise, all women have the sinful nature within their blood. Yet even though all women have the sinful nature residing within their blood, the mother does *not* pass on that sinful nature to her offspring, just as the father does not pass on his Y chromosome to his daughters. Even though the mother has the sinful nature residing within her blood, she does not transmit that sinful nature to her children; it is only the father who passes on the sinful nature to the children. This is completely in accordance with 1 Corinthians 15:21–22—we do not inherit sin or death from Eve, our mother, but only from Adam, our father. This means we inherit our sinful natures *only* from our human *fathers,* not from our human *mothers.*

Sin and the Image of God

God created man in both his image and likeness (Gen 1:26). Did this change after Adam ate of the forbidden fruit? Is it possible man is now no longer made in God's image as a result of Adam's fall and as a result of the sin that now lives within each of us, in our blood? This is an important question since there are some who teach exactly that—that as a result of Adam's fall, man is now no longer made in God's image, that the sin that is now within us has obliterated God's image within us, and we are now totally depraved.

Such a teaching is a perversion. It is a completely false and unbiblical teaching, contradicting a host of Scripture. Even after he sinned, even after the fall, Adam, and all humanity, continue to bear God's image and continue to have *both* good *and evil* residing within us—the Bible makes this clear.

Jesus' own words address this subject: "If you, then, though you are evil, know how to give good gifts to your children, how much more will your Father in heaven give good gifts to those who ask him" (Matt 7:11)! In this verse, Jesus tells us that, though we are evil (that is, we are fallen and have the sinful nature within us), we still know not only *how* to do good but also *actually* can *do* good. According to Jesus' own words, fallen man retains the capacity to both *know* good and to *do* good.

We are also told in Genesis 9:6, "Whoever sheds human blood, by humans shall their blood be shed; for in the image of God has God made mankind." God made this statement thousands of years *after* the fall of man, and here God himself affirms that, even though man is fallen, he still retains the image of God despite his fallen, sinful state. As a result, it is inarguable that man in his fallen state has both good (God's image) and evil (the sinful nature) residing within him, coexisting.

Nakedness and Shame

The strongest affirmation of this truth, of the coexistence within humanity, within our flesh, of *both* the goodness of God's image together with the fallen sinful nature, is outlined in Genesis 3:6–10:

> When the woman saw that the fruit of the tree was good for food and pleasing to the eye, and also desirable for gaining wisdom, she took some and ate it. She also gave some to her husband, who was with her, and he ate it. Then the eyes of both of them were opened, and they realized they were naked; so they sewed fig leaves together and made coverings for themselves. Then the man and his wife heard the sound of the Lord God as he was walking in the garden in the cool of the day, and they hid from the Lord God among the trees of the garden. But the Lord God called to the man, 'Where are you?' He answered, 'I heard you in the garden, and I was afraid because I was naked; so I hid.' (NIV)

Immediately after Adam ate of the forbidden fruit, we are told *both* the eyes of Adam and Eve were opened and they *both* saw they were *naked*. Adam later says to God, upon hearing God walking in Eden, that he, Adam, was *afraid* because he was *naked*, and so he hid from God. What does it mean when we are told they both realized they were naked? And why was Adam scared by being naked before God? All of this is due to the physical presence of the sinful nature now residing within Adam's flesh.

When Adam ate of the forbidden fruit, the physical sinful nature entered into his body and took up physical residence within his blood, in his *flesh*. This is why we are told, upon eating of the forbidden fruit, *both* Adam and Eve saw, or became aware, they were *naked*, for now there was something wrong living within their flesh, residing within their physical bodies, and they became immediately *conscious* of it.

In fact, not only did they become *aware* of being naked, but they also immediately became *ashamed* of being naked, which is why they tried to cover up their nakedness by sewing together fig leaves. Then, when God was walking through Eden, Adam's shame, which was his consciousness of the sin now physically residing within him, turned into fear, and because of that fear, Adam went into hiding. Adam was ashamed of his nakedness before God, a shame which the fig leaves could not cover up, and he was now scared of God. All of that was the result of Adam eating the fruit of the forbidden tree, and of sin entering into his flesh, into his blood. What does this all mean? What does it tell us?

There are at least two things we learn from this. First, the fact that Adam and Eve became aware of being physically naked, becoming immediately ashamed of their physical nakedness, affirms the sinful nature took up residence within their physical flesh, all via Adam. Something bad was now residing within their flesh, and they were aware of it.

But *why* were they *ashamed*? If Adam, upon sinning, was now totally and completely corrupt, totally depraved, and no longer retained God's image and had nothing good whatsoever living within him, as some teach, then we would expect both Adam and Eve, upon Adam's fall, to exult in their sinfulness, in their nakedness, to have no shame in it, but rather indulge in it in every perverted, sinful, and evil way. But they did not—rather, they were *ashamed*.

The reason they were ashamed is because they retained the image of God, the moral conscience of good, and it was the living presence of that moral conscience of good they had by virtue of being made in God's image that caused them to be ashamed of the sin now living within them.

The fact Adam and Eve were ashamed of their nakedness is a clear affirmation that *both* good *and* evil were now living within them, coexisting in their humanity. God's goodness remained present within them by virtue of them being made in both the image *and* likeness of God. Evil was present in their blood by way of the physical sinful nature now residing within them as a result of Adam eating the fruit of the forbidden tree. So the fact Adam and Eve became aware of their nakedness, and then were *ashamed* of it, affirms the sinful nature was physically resident in their physical bodies *together with* being made in God's image and likeness—they now had *both* good *and* evil living *together within them*. Upon Adam eating of the fruit of the forbidden tree, man would now know *both* good and evil. This is an affirmation of God's own words: "And the Lord God said, 'The man has now become like one of us, knowing good and evil'" (Gen 3:22 NIV).

The Power of Sin—Death

What is the power of sin (1 Cor 15:56)? What *effect* did the sinful nature have on Adam upon entering into his body, into his blood? There are some very clear results of the immediate effects of sin upon Adam. We are told in the Bible:

> For the wages of sin is death . . . (Rom 6:23)

> So that as sin reigned in death, even so grace might reign through righteousness to eternal life through Jesus Christ our Lord. (Rom 5:21 NKJV)

Death is an immediate result of the sinful nature, and there are two kinds of death. The first kind of death is the slow, decaying physical death we all experience. Physical sin, living within us, residing in our blood, is like a disease, physically eating away at us, seeking its fulfillment and completion in death, destroying our bodies until our physical life is destroyed. This is why we all physically age, decay, and eventually die, because we have sin living within us—our decay, aging, and eventual death is sin devouring its host.

The second kind of death is one where our *relationship* with God is broken, where we become separated from God—it is the death of our spirit. This is our *spiritual* death, where we are cut off, divorced, from the Source of Life. This is in fact the *immediate* experience of Adam upon eating of the forbidden fruit. By eating of the forbidden fruit, Adam made a choice to sin. In making a choice to sin, Adam separated himself from God, for with his choice to sin he chose his own selfishness over God. With that free-will choice of self over God, Adam separated himself, divorced himself, from God. His free-will choice had an immediate practical consequence—in *choosing* self over God, in *choosing* to separate himself from God, Adam in fact literally *did* separate himself from God—his free-will choice was made real. By separating himself from God, Adam was separating himself from life, for God is life (John 14:6). As a result, with his choice of separation from God, of separation from life, immediate death resulted, for separation from God, from the Source of Life, is what defines death. Immediately upon eating of the forbidden fruit, Adam became dead in his spirit, for that death was the immediate manifestation of his choice to separate himself from God. This separation from God, death, was the result of sin. The power of sin is death.

The Power of Sin—Fear

Another immediate result of sin is fear. Sin, in breaking or killing our relationship with God, instills in us a *fear* of God. The reason for this is sin is an accursed thing, it is under God's judgment, since sin is evil and destructive. As a result, sin carries within it an *innate* fear of its own destruction. Sin *knows* it is under judgment. This means when sin takes up residence within us, it causes us to fear God, to fear his judgment, for sin causes us to know we are deserving of God's judgment and that God's judgment is right. This fear is seen immediately in Adam in his response to God walking in Eden:

> Then the man and his wife heard the sound of the Lord God as he was walking in the garden in the cool of the day, and they hid from the Lord God among the trees of the garden. (Gen 3:8)

After his fall, Adam's response upon hearing the approach of God was to run and hide from him. Adam was now *afraid* of God. This fear of God within Adam was new, and was the immediate result of the sin now residing within him. But haven't we been told we are to *fear* God?:

> The fear of the Lord is the beginning of knowledge, but fools despise wisdom and instruction. (Prov 1:7 NIV)

Isn't this a contradiction? No; for in this case what is translated as "fear of the LORD" in fact means to "stand in awe" of the LORD. So yes, we are to stand in awe of God, but when the power of sin is broken, we no longer *fear*, or are *scared*, of God, for, as we are told in 1 John 4:18, perfect love casts out fear. Fear was the result of sin. The power of sin is fear.

The Power of Sin—Deception

Walking hand in hand with sin's power of fear is its power of deception. Deception is tied in with fear, for sin deceives us into thinking of God as our condemning judge. In doing so, sin deceives us into thinking God is out to destroy us, rather than to love us. As a result, this power of deception blinds us to the knowledge of God's wonderful and infinite love for us, and to the knowledge of his forgiveness and salvation. The Bible clearly tells us sin is deceitful: "but exhort one another daily, while it is called 'Today,' lest any of you be hardened through the *deceitfulness of sin*" (Heb 3:13 NKJV). We are also told in Luke 1:77 ("To give his people the *knowledge of salvation* through the forgiveness of their sins" [NIV]), the *knowledge* of salvation comes as the *result* of the forgiveness of, or the *removal* or *breaking the power* of, sin. This affirms the deception of sin is what *blinds* us to the knowledge of God's love for us, to his forgiving nature, and to his desire to give us salvation. The power of sin is deception.

The Nature of Sin—Selfishness

Selfishness is the nature of sin. The opposite of love is not hate; rather, the opposite of love is selfishness. Love puts others first, whereas selfishness puts oneself first. Selfishness is the nature, the essence, of sin. It is the heart of the sinful nature. Sin, residing in our flesh, in our blood, is always trying to gratify itself, but that gratification is impossible because sin can never be satisfied—no matter how much it gets, it always wants more. Sin is insatiable, and this insatiable drive is also its own destruction. It is this insatiable drive to its own destruction that leads sin to result in death. It is also what drives us to destruction as we pursue the impossible sin-satisfaction. This insatiable desire, or lust, of sin is affirmed throughout Scripture:

> Therefore do not let *sin reign in your mortal body*, that you should *obey it in its lusts*. (Rom 6:12 NKJV)

> Dear friends, I urge you, as foreigners and exiles, to *abstain from sinful desires, which wage war against your soul*. (1 Pet 2:11 NIV)

> Rather, clothe yourselves with the Lord Jesus Christ, and do not think about how to gratify the *desires of the flesh*. (Rom 13:14 NIV)

> So I say, walk by the Spirit, and you will not gratify *the desires of the flesh*. (Gal 5:16 NIV)

In its complete and total selfish nature, sin is at war against anything that is born of love, born of God, born of his Holy Spirit, for love is the contradiction to sin. Sin and selfishness are the opposite of love.

The Power of Sin—The Law

Since sin and the sinful nature are *at war* against anything born of goodness or love, it is at war with everything holy. In fact, the very nature of holiness—its total goodness, its perfect love, its complete selflessness—will arouse sin, and the sinful nature, to react against that very holiness. This is why the Bible tells us the following:

> The sting of death is sin, and the *power of sin is the law*. (1 Cor 15:56 NIV)

> Therefore by the deeds of the law no flesh will be justified in his sight, for by *the law is the knowledge of sin.* (Rom 3:20 NKJV)
>
> For until the law sin was in the world, but *sin is not imputed when there is no law.* (Rom 5:13 NKJV)
>
> But sin, *taking opportunity by the commandment,* produced in me all manner of evil desire. For apart from the law sin was dead. (Rom 7:8 NKJV)
>
> For sin, taking occasion by the commandment, deceived me, and by it killed me. (Rom 7:11 NKJV)

God's very holiness, his goodness, his love, is the foundational nature of his law. As a result, when God gives his commandment, whose sole purpose is always to protect us from harm and encourage us in the freedom of goodness and of love, sin *reacts* against the commandment, reacting against the law of God, *reacting* against its *holiness,* thereby resulting in the law *exposing* sin. By exposing sin, the law fulfills its purpose toward us—it shows us, by its very holiness, we cannot fulfill the law, for the sinful nature residing within us makes that fulfillment impossible—just by encountering the law, the commandment, our sinful nature is aroused and exposed.

The entirety of this power of sin—the power of death, fear, deception, and its nature of selfishness—are manifest almost immediately in Adam upon his eating of the forbidden fruit, upon ingesting the sinful nature contained within it, which then immediately takes up residence in his flesh, in his blood.

The Devastation of the Fall

In the immediate aftermath of the fall, we are told of how Adam encountered God, and of how both he and Eve responded to God's questions:

> Then the man and his wife heard the sound of the Lord God as he was walking in the garden in the cool of the day, and they hid from the Lord God among the trees of the garden. But the Lord God called to the man, 'Where are you?' He answered, 'I heard you in the garden, and I was afraid because I was naked; so I hid.' And he said, 'Who told you that you were naked? Have you eaten from the tree that I commanded you not to eat from?'

The man said, 'The woman you put here with me—she gave me some fruit from the tree, and I ate it.' (Gen 3:8–12 NIV)

In this conversation between God and Adam we see the immediate and devastating effect of the fall. Consider the situation: the reason Adam ate of the fruit from the forbidden tree, the reason he sinned and rebelled against God, was because he did not want to lose Eve. He did not want to be alone again. Rather, he chose to share Eve's fate than to live without her—he chose Eve over God. And yet look at how Adam responds when God asks him, "Who told you that you were naked? Have you eaten from the tree that I commanded you not to eat from?" Adam replies "The woman you put here with me—she gave me some fruit from the tree, and I ate it." If I were to pick what I would consider the single most tragic verse in the entire Bible it would be Genesis 3:12, Adam's reply to God. It is no exaggeration to say every time I have heard this verse referenced in a sermon, it has been treated as a joke—the speaker says something like "Isn't it just like the man to blame the woman," and then he and the congregation laugh. But this is no joke; rather, this verse, more than any verse in the Bible, shows the immediate devastation of sin.

Adam chose Eve over God because he didn't want to lose her, choosing instead to share her fate, and yet, when God asks Adam, "Who told you that you were naked? Have you eaten from the tree that I commanded you not to eat from?," Adam, in his reply, is actually giving up Eve to destruction in order to save himself.

This is incomprehensibly tragic—to go from choosing Eve over God, choosing to sin and share her fate rather than be without her, and then to so quickly be willing to give up Eve to possible destruction in order to save himself, is a striking example of how quickly and how deeply sin had infected Adam. The essence of true love is to put the other person first, whereas the essence of all sin is to put oneself first. Here, in Adam's reply to God, we see Adam's complete selfishness, even to the point of being willing to potentially sacrifice the woman for whom he sinned rather than to face that potential himself. This is a powerful example of the immediate devastation of the sinful nature upon Adam.

Adam's Confession

However, in this same exchange with God, one other profound and powerful truth is seen, which once again affirms the coexistence of both good and evil within fallen man: "The man said, 'The woman you put here with me—she gave me some fruit from the tree, *and I ate it*'" (Gen 3:12). Not only do we see here the tragic and devastating impact of sin within Adam, but Adam here does something beautiful and great—he confesses. Not only was he quick and willing to offer up Eve to destruction to save himself, but he immediately confessed his sin to God—"and I ate it."

This is no small thing—Satan never confessed his sin before God; Satan continues to this day to blame God for his own evil, for Satan, in his fall, became totally depraved, becoming only evil, having no longer any remnant of goodness left within him.

Not so with man. Adam, as with all fallen humanity, now had *both* good and evil residing within him, coexisting. It is because of the goodness of God's image within him that Adam was ashamed of his nakedness, ashamed of the sin that became resident within his flesh, and it is because of the goodness of God's image within him Adam confessed his sin to God. Adam's confession was made with no prodding, but was made clearly, quickly, and on his own. I have no question when God heard Adam's confession, God's heart melted with deepest compassion in the fullness of his endless love.

We also see the same confession from Eve:

> Then the Lord God said to the woman, "What is this you have done?" The woman said, "The serpent deceived me, *and I ate.*" (Gen 3:13 NIV)

Eve, like Adam, confessed her sin to God. Both Adam and Eve confessed their sin to God immediately, while Satan has never done so. This is further witness to the fact that man now had both good and evil resident within himself, coexisting.

Immediate Death

In addition to the immediate presence of the sinful nature within Adam and Eve as a result of Adam eating from the fruit of the forbidden tree, there was also another immediate affect—the immediate spiritual death of man in relation to God.

Man was created perfect in every way, including spiritually. Adam was fully indwelt by the Holy Spirit, just as was Jesus Christ, for Adam, like Jesus, was the human "Son of God" (Luke 3:38). Adam was the *created* son of God, and Jesus was the *begotten* Son of God, but both were the son of God—God was the Father of Adam, as he is the Father of Jesus Christ. Just like Jesus, who was fully indwelt by the Holy Spirit, is the Son of God, so was Adam also fully indwelt by the Holy Spirit as God's created son. But, when Adam sinned, that spiritual oneness with God was severed, and in that moment Adam instantly died—he died to God in his spirit, for by his choice to sin he became separated from God, the Source of Life, which is the definition of death. Adam would also *eventually* physically die because of the sin which now took up residence in his body, within his flesh, but he *instantaneously* died spiritually—he immediately was no longer in communion with his Father, his Maker. When Adam sinned, the Holy Spirit no longer remained dwelling within him. This spiritual death, this separation from God, is what both Adam and Eve experienced immediately upon Adam eating the fruit of the forbidden tree.

The Lordship of the Earth

Adam was named lord of the earth, ruler of the planet, lord of all creatures on the face of the earth (Gen 1:26), and it was Adam's responsibility to implement that lordship. All the earth, and all of the living creatures upon the earth, were under Adam's lordship, under his dominion. But Adam sinned—he rebelled against God. When Adam did this, not only did the sinful nature take up physical residence within his body, not only did Adam instantly die a spiritual death before God, but Adam, in that moment, also gave the *legal* authority and dominion of the earth to Satan. This is why we read of Satan:

> Now is the time for judgment on this world; now the *prince of this world* will be driven out. (John 12:31 NIV)

> I will not say much more to you, for the *prince of this world* is coming. He has no hold over me. (John 14:30 NIV)

> Because *the prince of this world* now stands condemned. (John 16:11 NIV)

> We know that we are children of God, and that *the whole world is under the control of the evil one*. (1 John 5:19 NIV)

Satan, the devil, is called the "prince of this world," that is, he is the *legal ruler* of the world. How did this happen? It happened when Adam sinned, for in sinning, Adam gave his God-given authority and dominion over the earth to Satan. One of the results of Adam's fall is Satan became the legal ruler of Earth. This is further affirmed when Satan tempts Jesus in the desert:

> The devil led him up to a high place and showed him in an instant *all the kingdoms of the world*. And he said to him, '*I will give you all their authority* and splendor; it has been *given* to me, and *I can give it to anyone I want to*. If you worship me, it will all be yours.' (Luke 4:5–7 NIV)

Satan here shows Jesus all the kingdoms of the world, and he clearly says he, Satan, has *authority* over these kingdoms, because that *authority* has been *given* to him. As a result he can do whatever he wants with these kingdoms. Jesus, in his reply, does not contest Satan's (lawfully) given authority over the kingdoms of the world; rather, he replies: "It is written: 'Worship the Lord your God and serve him only'" (Luke 4:8 NIV). Who *gave* Satan this authority over all the kingdoms of the world? It was given to him by Adam, at the time of Adam's fall.

Adam's Fall and Satan

When Adam gave the lordship and dominion of the earth to Satan, this had other immediate consequences as well. First, evil and violence entered into nature. Before Adam's fall there was no death, sin, or evil upon the earth—whether in nature or in animals. Animals did not kill each other for food; rather, *all* animals ate plants: "And to all the beasts of the earth and all the birds in the sky and all the creatures that move along the ground—everything that has the breath of life in it—*I give every green plant for food*" (Gen 1:30 NIV). That changed with Adam's fall. In giving dominion of the earth over to Satan, death and violence now entered into every aspect of nature—animals, who were originally subject to Adam, now became subject to the dominion of the devil. As a result, death and violence entered the world, entered into nature, animals started to kill and eat each other, and plants became poisonous, carrying death. This is not how God created it, but it is how Satan corrupted it. All of that was the result of Adam's fall, of Adam giving up his authority and dominion over the earth, over all of its creatures and its vegetation, to Satan.

The Imprisoned Fallen Angels in the Pit Released

The other immediate result of Adam's fall is it now allowed *all* of the fallen, rebellious angels to be let out of the pit, the place of their imprisonment inside the earth, so they also could take up residence with Satan upon the earth. In fact, we are told the habitation of Satan and his fallen angels is now in the air, in the earthly sky, or the "heaven" of the earth:

> ... in which you used to live when you followed the ways of this world and of the *ruler of the kingdom of the air,* the spirit who is now at work in those who are disobedient. (Eph 2:2 NIV)

> His intent was that now, through the church, the manifold wisdom of God should be made known to the *rulers and authorities* in the *heavenly realms.* (Eph 3:10 NIV)

> For our struggle is not against flesh and blood, but against the *rulers, against the authorities,* against the *powers of this dark world* and against the *spiritual forces of evil in the heavenly realms.* (Eph 6:12 NIV)

With the fall of Adam, Satan received authority over the earth, gaining the authority to live freely and act upon it (Job 1:7). With that authority also came the releasing of all the other fallen and rebellious angels—the rulers, authorities (angelic ranks)—from the pit to also live and act upon the earth, under Satan's authority, taking up residence in the earthly sky or "heavenly realms." This is why Satan is called the "ruler of the kingdom of the air" (Eph 2:2).

As a result of the fall of Adam, the pit has been emptied out. This is later referenced in Luke when the demon-possessed man comes to Jesus, and the possessing demons ask Jesus:

> "What do you want with me, Jesus, Son of the Most High God? I beg you, don't torture me!" For Jesus had commanded the impure spirit to come out of the man. Many times it had seized him, and though he was chained hand and foot and kept under guard, he had broken his chains and had been driven by the demon into solitary places. Jesus asked him, "What is your name?" "Legion," he replied, because many demons had gone into him. And they begged Jesus repeatedly not to order them to go into the abyss. (Luke 8:28–31 NIV)

The evil spirits possessing the man brought and threw the man to the ground before Jesus (this also represents the evil spirits falling and bowing before Jesus, for they recognized him as God, and they know their place before him—at his feet). The evil spirits begged Jesus repeatedly not to send them back to the abyss, which is another name for the pit. The begging of the demonic spirits in Luke 8 to not be cast back into the pit is an added affirmation of the fallen angels being previously in the pit and released from it.

With the fall of Adam, Satan now had legal authority over the earth, and the other fallen rebellious angels were released from their imprisonment within the pit and were allowed to also inhabit the earth, with Satan, and under his authority, taking up residence in the earthly sky—and so Satan became the "prince of this world."

God's Consequential Curse upon Adam

After Adam's fall, in the course of God's conversation with Adam and Eve, during the course of which Adam confessed his sin against God, and Eve confessed her disobedience to Adam, God pronounced the consequence of Adam's sin, which can be seen as a curse of consequence:

> To Adam he said, 'Because you listened to your wife and ate fruit from the tree about which I *commanded you*, "You must not eat from it," cursed is the ground because of you; through painful toil you will eat food from it all the days of your life. It will produce thorns and thistles for you, and you will eat the plants of the field. By the sweat of your brow you will eat your food until you return to the ground, since from it you were taken; for dust you are and to dust you will return.' (Gen 3:17–19 NIV)

In these verses, God again affirms the commandment he gave concerning eating the fruit of the forbidden tree was given to Adam (v. 17), and that it was Adam who sinned by eating the forbidden fruit.

God also here changed man's diet. Originally, God said to Adam, "Behold, I have given you every plant yielding seed that is on the surface of all the earth, and every tree which has fruit-yielding seed; it shall be food for you; and to every beast of the earth and to every bird of the sky and to everything that moves on the earth which has life, I have given every green plant [or plant of the field] for food" (Gen 1:29–30 NASB). Originally, man was to eat seed-bearing plants and fruit with seed in it, and the animals were given the plants of the field to eat. After Adam sinned, God changed man's diet so man would now *also* eat of the *plants of the field*—which was originally given only to the animals to eat. Why does God curse Adam in regard to *food*? At the very least, it is a response to the fact that Adam *ate* of the forbidden fruit, and so now all of Adam's ensuing *eating* will be a hardship, a struggle, a toil.

Sacrifice

One other result of the fall of Adam was sacrifice. When Adam fell, both he and Eve became aware of their nakedness and were ashamed, because the sinful nature had taken up residence within their physical bodies via their blood. In their shame they took fig leaves to try to cover their nakedness. After they had their conversation with God, we are told the following: "The Lord God made garments of skin for Adam and his wife and clothed them" (Gen 3:21 NIV). This illustrates two things. First, animals had to die in order for their skins to be taken, so this is in fact the very first instance in the Bible of a *sacrifice* being performed, the purpose of which was to *cover* Adam and Eve's nakedness. As part of this sacrifice, blood was shed, and the sacrifice resulted in a *covering* of nakedness, which in fact was also the covering of sin since the sinful nature physically resided in Adam and Eve, in their bodies, as it does in our bodies today. The covering of their nakedness acted as a covering of their sin. This is a foreshadowing of the role sacrifice was to play in God's unfolding plan. The second point illustrated here is God himself was the instigator of the sacrifice—it was God who got the skins, performed the sacrifice, and put the skins on Adam and Eve to clothe them. In every aspect, God was the initiator of the sacrifice.

Driven Out of Eden

> And the Lord God said, 'The man has now become like one of us, knowing good and evil. He must not be allowed to reach out his hand and take also from the tree of life and eat, and live forever.' So the Lord God banished him from the garden of Eden to work the ground from which he had been taken. After he drove the man out, he placed on the east side of the garden of

> Eden Cherubim and a flaming sword flashing back and forth to
> guard the way to the tree of life. (Gen 3:22–24 NIV)

After the fall of Adam, God drives Adam out of Eden, to keep him away from the tree of life. Notice how Genesis 3:22–24 talks specifically about the *man*, not the woman, being driven out of Eden. We are told "the *man* has now become like one of us," and "*he* must not be allowed to . . . take also from the tree of life and eat," and that God "drove the *man* out" of Eden for that reason. God never refers to the *woman* in any of this. Again, the reason for this is that Adam, not the woman, was to keep God's commandment, to obey or to fall.

Why does God drive Adam out of Eden? It is just as when *Adam* ate from the tree of the knowledge of good and evil, and *then* Eve fell and sin entered into her. Likewise, if *Adam* was to now eat from the tree of life, then *both* he and Eve would remain physically alive forever, remaining *eternally* in sin, without any hope of redemption.

This is why God drove Adam from Eden—not in wrath or anger, but solely because of his love and mercy. God drove Adam out of Eden so Adam would not eat from the tree of life, for if Adam was to now eat from the tree of life, he, and all of humanity, would remain forever in sin. By driving Adam out of Eden, and then putting the Cherubim around the tree of life to guard and protect that tree so no human being would find it and eat from it, God was making salvation possible, he was making it possible for man to be redeemed. Driving Adam out of Eden is the wonderful expression of God's love and mercy, ensuring man would not remain forever in his sin, but could be set free from it.

Adam's Blood and the Sin of the World

Adam is the father of all humanity, the literal first father of all mankind—we, all of us, are his direct physical descendants. When Adam ate of the forbidden fruit, sin entered his body, taking up physical residence within his blood. As the father of all humanity, Adam passed on his blood, with its sinful nature, to all of his descendants. All of us literally have *Adam's* blood now flowing through our veins, with the same sinful nature that came to inhabit it.

When we were born, we did not get some newly created blood given to us; rather, we inherited our blood from our parents, who in turn inherited their blood from their parents, and so on back in time to Adam himself. It is true to say *all* the blood of the *whole* of humanity throughout history is *only* the blood of Adam himself—we, all of us, literally have *Adam's* blood flowing in our veins, and all the blood of humanity is *only* the blood of the *one man*, Adam.

As a result, *Adam's* sinful nature, the one in *his* blood, the same blood which now flows through our veins, is the source of *all* the sin all people commit. As a result, it is literally true to say it is the *blood* of *Adam* that is responsible for *all* the sin of humanity, for it is the blood of the *one man* that has brought all sin into the world.

The aftermath of Adam's fall was that man was left in a state of sin, having the sinful nature physically residing within his body, in his flesh, in his blood, coexisting with the goodness of being made in God's image and likeness. This resulted in man personally and intimately knowing both good and evil. Upon his fall, Adam had given his dominion over the earth to Satan, who now became the legal prince of this world. This also allowed for the release of the imprisoned fallen angels from out of the pit, all of whom were released to live freely upon the earth under Satan's authority, taking up residence in the earthly sky. The first sacrifice was then performed, in Eden, at God's instigation, as a covering for sin. This first sacrifice was a foreshadowing of God's unfolding plan of redemption.

11

God's Unfolding Plan—
Sacrifice and the High Priest

THE FIRST SACRIFICE IN Eden was the instigation of God's plan of salvation. Sacrifice, with its shedding of sinless blood and the ensuing death, would be the singular means by which the power of sin would be destroyed. That first sacrifice in Eden was but a picture of the one sacrifice to come, and yet prior to the one sacrifice to come, God would first institute an entire system of sacrifice whose purpose would be to illustrate the fullness of what sacrifice would accomplish and how it was being accomplished. This system of sacrifice would provide a temporary forgiveness of sin, a temporary destroying of the power of sin, thereby being also a picture of the one sacrifice to come which would provide for the permanent forgiveness of all sin for all people.

Why Sacrifice?

The reason sacrifice would be essential for the forgiveness of sin is because sacrifice involved the two elements necessary for overcoming sin, for the breaking of its power—the shedding of blood and the bringing of sin to completion in death.

Before instituting the system of sacrifice, which would be but an illustration of the one sacrifice to come, God would first institute a priesthood which would perform the sacrifices on behalf of the people. That priesthood would be headed by a chosen high priest, and that high priest would represent all the people of Israel before God. In that position, the high priest would have authority to perform the sacrifices before God on behalf of all the people of Israel. The high priest would himself also be a picture of the one High Priest to come, the one who would perform the permanent sacrifice for the entire sin of humanity.

The Sacrifice of Eden

The very first sacrifice recorded in the Bible is mentioned in Genesis 3:21, and it was a model for all the sacrifices to come: "The Lord God made garments of skin for Adam and his wife and clothed them" (NASB). The first sacrifice, occurring in Eden, was instigated and provided by God himself so as to cover the nakedness and shame of Adam and Eve. The reason Adam and Eve were ashamed of their nakedness was because they were conscious of the physical habitation of sin that came to dwell within their flesh, within their blood, as a result of Adam eating of the forbidden fruit. It was because of their nakedness and shame, which was the result of their consciousness of the sin now within their flesh, that both Adam and Eve hid from God, because, upon Adam sinning, sin's power of fear and deception immediately took up residence within them. As a result, Adam and Eve were deceived and came to fear God.

But God loved them, and in his mercy God came to them and made garments of skin for them to wear so as to cover their nakedness and their shame, in effect to cover their sin, so they would not run and hide from him. In making those garments of skin, it is implicit that an animal, or animals, had to die in order to give up their skin. As a result, those animals were sacrificed as a covering for Adam and Eve, as a covering for their sin. The death of these animals would have been the first physical deaths on Earth, and their sacrifice involved the shedding of blood and the ensuing death.

Covering for Sin

The Bible does not say the animal skins God brought to Adam and Eve were to cover sin, it only says God clothed Adam and his wife. However, it is implicit that the clothing of Adam and Eve is related to them becoming aware, and then ashamed, of their nakedness. It is absolutely clear the skins were to cover their nakedness and their shame. Their shame resulted from the fact that sin had come to physically reside within their bodies, within their blood, within their flesh, as a result of Adam eating of the forbidden fruit. That sin, or sinful nature, came to coexist within Adam and his wife together with the image of God, an image they both retained within their nature. It was that holy image of God within their nature that acted as a living conscience, convicting them of sin. This resulted in Adam and his wife first seeing their nakedness and then being ashamed of it, becoming ashamed of their sinfulness. Sin came to physically reside within their flesh, and it was the image of God within them, which they retained fully and which now came to coexist within them together with sin, that convicted them of that presence of sin within their bodies. We are told in Genesis 3:7, "Then the eyes of both of them were opened, and they realized they were naked; so they sewed fig leaves together and made coverings for themselves" (NIV).

Adam and his wife attempted to cover their nakedness and their shame with fig leaves. When God took animal skins to clothe them, it is implied these animal skins were to replace the fig leaves Adam and Eve used in an attempt to cover their nakedness and their shame, for the fig leaves were not effective. God fashioned the skins into garments Adam and Eve could wear. By wearing those garments, their nakedness, their flesh, was covered, which is to say the sin residing within their flesh was hidden by virtue of being covered by the garments. Clothing Adam and Eve in skins was an act of covering up their nakedness and the shame of their sinfulness. As a result, God instigated and then provided the sacrifice that "covers" sin.

It is important to understand this first sacrifice had nothing to do with the payment of any price or penalty for sin. Rather, the sacrifice was an act of mercy whose sole purpose was to cover, or hide, sinfulness; it was a demonstration of coming forgiveness in that, by covering up sin and shame, it signified that God was no longer seeing that sin (Isa 1:18), thereby demonstrating his forgiveness. This is important because it would prove to be a model for all the sacrifices to come.

God Institutes a Priesthood

That first sacrifice in Eden was itself but a foreshadowing of the system of sacrifice God would later institute, a system of sacrifice that would result in the temporary forgiveness of sin. That system of sacrifice was instituted by God, many thousands of years after Adam's fall, in the nation of Israel.

In order to perform the sacrifices for sin, God would first institute a priesthood. The priesthood would represent the people to God and God to the people. It was that priesthood and only that priesthood that would perform the sacrifices for sin, performed on behalf of the people, so as to bring temporary forgiveness of sin for the people. That initial priesthood was the priesthood of Israel.

Birth of Israel

Israel was the nation God brought into being through which he would unfold his plan of salvation for the world. The birth of Israel began with one man, Abraham. Somewhere around 2200 BC, God called a man named Abram to follow him, promising Abram he would make him the father of a great nation (Gen 12:1). Abram lived in the Chaldean city of Ur, and was the son of Terah, a pagan (Gen 11:27–31; Josh 24:2). Abram listened to God and followed his direction. God promised Abram he would have a son through whom God would fulfill his promises to Abram (Gen 15:2–6), but Abram's wife Sarai was barren and could not have children (Gen 11:30). Sarai convinced Abram to have sex with her maidservant, Hagar, who conceived and bore a child to Abram, a son named Ishmael (Gen 16:1–4). But God told Abram Ishmael was not to be his heir; rather, he would have a son with Sarai, whom he was to name Isaac, and through Isaac God would fulfill his promises to Abram (Gen 17:19–21). At that point, God changed Abram's name to Abraham (Gen 17:5), and Sarai's name to Sarah (Gen 17:15). Abraham and Sarah did have a son, Isaac (Gen 21:1–3).

When Isaac became a man, he married Rebekah (Gen 24:67), and they had two sons—Esau and Jacob (Gen 25:19–26). Esau was the older son, and as such he was the heir to Isaac's birthright, heir to the promises of God, which Isaac received from his father Abraham. But Jacob manipulated his brother Esau into giving him the birthright (Gen 25:29–34), which Esau did. As a result, the promises of God that were given to Abraham, which were then passed on to Isaac, were passed on to Jacob as part of the birthright.

Later, after he was married, Jacob wrestled with a man through an entire night, and it turned out the "man" with whom Jacob wrestled was

God himself (Gen 32:22–28; 35:10). It was then God changed Jacob's name to "Israel," which means "he who struggles with God."

Israel went on to have twelve sons (Gen 35:22). Each son became the father of a tribe of Israel. Israel and his sons and all their children, seventy people in total, later went to Egypt to escape a famine that had gripped the land (Gen 46:1–27). The people of Israel stayed in Egypt for 430 years (Exod 12:40), eventually becoming a nation. In the course of becoming a nation while in Egypt, they also became Egyptian slaves (Exod 1:8–14) until God delivered the nation Israel from Egypt through Moses (Exod 3:7–10). After God delivered Israel out of Egypt, he brought them to Mount Sinai where he gave them the Ten Commandments (Deut 5:1–22).

The purpose of the nation of Israel was to be the vehicle through which God would reveal to the world his plan for humanity, his plan of salvation. It would begin with God giving the Ten Commandments, would continue through the office of the high priest and then culminate in Jesus Christ. Everything about each of these points—the commandments and the high priest—is designed to lead to Jesus Christ.

Creation of the Priesthood

Moses and his brother Aaron were from the tribe of Levi (Exod 2:1–10), and after God brought Israel out of Egypt and gave them the Ten Commandments, God created a priesthood for Israel, from the tribe of Levi (Exod 28:1–3), the tribe of Moses and Aaron. All the priests of Israel were to come only from the tribe of Levi. Aaron was chosen by God to be the first high priest, or chief priest, of Israel.

Together with the institution of the priesthood, God also instituted a system of sacrifice for sin. The purpose of the sacrifices was to take the sin of the people away and to bring temporary forgiveness of sin. It was only the priesthood that was to perform the sacrifices on behalf of Israel for the forgiveness and atonement of sin.

The High Priest

Among the priesthood God instituted in Israel, one priest was chosen by God to be the chief priest, or high priest, of Israel. The unique purpose of the high priest was to represent God to all the people, to the entire nation, and to represent all the people of Israel to God.

At the time God instituted the priesthood of Israel, God also gave instructions to Israel to build the tabernacle. As Israel wandered in the desert for forty years, after they rebelled before God at Mount Sinai, the tabernacle would be the place in the wilderness where the high priest would come to meet with God and represent the nation of Israel before God, and where God would meet with the high priest. The part of the tabernacle where the high priest would come before God to meet with him was called the holy of holies, and only the high priest could enter the holy of holies. Eventually, the tabernacle was replaced by the temple, which was built later by Solomon. In the temple was also an area called the holy of holies, and, as with the tabernacle, only the high priest was ever allowed to enter, again as the representative of the nation of Israel before God. The high priest went into the holy of holies once a year and, while there, on that one occasion, he would make sacrifice, or atonement, for all the people of Israel (Lev 16), for the entire nation. The purpose of the high priest was to represent all of the people of Israel before God and make sacrifice for them, on their behalf, for their sins, so Israel could receive *forgiveness* of its sin (Lev 4:20, 26, 31, 35; 5:10, 13, 16, 18; 6:7; 19:22).

The High Priest and Adam

This role of the high priest was analogous to Adam's role as the first father of humanity. Just as Adam, in the truest sense, represented all humanity before God, since, as our father, all humanity was physically in Adam and came from him, likewise, the high priest represented all Israel before God, being a symbolic echo of Adam.

The high priest also foreshadowed Jesus Christ, the Second Adam, who would directly represent all humanity before God. The high priest was therefore a picture of both Adam, as the first father of humanity, and of Jesus Christ, the Second Father of humanity as well as the representative of humanity before God. As such, the high priest was a key part of the picture of sacrifice in God's plan of salvation and forgiveness, for the high priest alone had authority to perform the sacrifice on behalf of the people.

God Institutes a System of Sacrifice

After God gave the Ten Commandments, which came to be known as God's law, and at the same time as he established the priesthood and the office of high priest, God also instituted a system of animal sacrifice that was to be implemented by the priesthood and especially by the high priest. Those animal sacrifices were a way of addressing sin, temporarily, and were a picture of the sacrifice to come.

There were five sacrifices God instituted in Israel, three of which were voluntary and two of which were mandatory. The three voluntary sacrifices were the burnt offering (Lev 1), the grain offering (Lev 2), and the peace, or fellowship, offering (Lev 3). The two mandatory sacrifices were the sin offering (Lev 4) and the guilt offering (Lev 5:14–19).

The Day of Atonement

In addition to these five sacrifices, there was a special Day of Atonement (Lev 16). This special annual sacrifice could only be made by the high priest in the holy of holies, and was done on behalf of *all* the people of Israel, so as to make atonement for the sins of *all* the people.

The High Priest Makes Sacrifice for Himself

Before performing the Day of Atonement sacrifice, before even entering the tabernacle, the high priest was to bathe and put on special garments (Lev 16:4). He was then to sacrifice a bull as a sin offering for himself and his family (Lev 16:6, 11), so as to first *cleanse* himself of (not punish himself for) his own sin. Only when he was cleansed of his own sin could the high priest perform the sacrifice on behalf of all the people.

Why the High Priest Must Be Cleansed

In order for the high priest to perform the Day of Atonement sacrifice, he first had to bathe himself and then offer up a sacrifice for his and his family's sins. The reason this was necessary is because it illustrated the fact the one who was to make sacrifice on behalf of the nation, on behalf of all people, himself needed to be without sin, needed to be *sinless*. The high priest, of course, was not sinless, but God had allowed, by way of the high priest bathing himself and by way of offering up a sacrifice for his own sin, for the high priest to be *considered* as sinless. Being without sin was a necessary element of performing the atonement sacrifice, and the high priest's bathing and sacrifice for his own sin was an illustration of that fact.

God's Unfolding Plan—Sacrifice and the High Priest

By being considered sinless, this then allowed the high priest to be able to make sacrifice on behalf of the nation.

The Two Sacrifices

With his own sin cleansed and forgiven, which represented the high priest as sinless, the high priest could then make sacrifice for the people of Israel in the holy of holies. The blood of the sacrificed bull, which the high priest had sacrificed for his own sin, was to be sprinkled on the ark of the covenant, which was also situated in the holy of holies. The high priest was to then bring two goats to be sacrificed. The first goat was to be sacrificed for the uncleanness and rebellion of the Israelites (Lev 16:16), and the blood of that sacrifice was to also be sprinkled on the ark of the covenant.

The second goat was to be used to *take away* the sin of the people. The high priest would place his hands on the head of the second goat and confess over that goat the sin of Israel. The sin of the people would then pass through the high priest, through his hands, and come to lay on the second goat. The high priest would then send the goat out into the wilderness, alive, accompanied by an appointed man, who would release the goat into the wilderness (Lev 16:21). As the goat was released into the wilderness, it would run away, *taking away* the sins of the people. As a result, the sins of the people would be *forgiven* for one year (Lev 16:30).

The Two-Part Day of Atonement Sacrifice

The Day of Atonement sacrifice perfectly illustrates the full scope of the sacrifice for sin. The Day of Atonement sacrifice is a more involved sacrifice than a regular sin sacrifice as it is a sacrifice for the sin of the entire nation. As a result, in order to perfectly illustrate what the Day of Atonement sacrifice is accomplishing, God has broken up that Atonement sacrifice into two sacrifices. These two sacrifices *together* are a *full illustration* of what the Day of Atonement sacrifice is accomplishing and of what the coming permanent sacrifice for the sin of humanity will accomplish.

First, the high priest must bathe himself and make a sacrifice for his own sin, which is an illustration of the need for the high priest to be sinless in order to be able to exercise his high priestly authority. Once the high priest has bathed and made a sacrifice for himself, then the high priest lays his hands onto the head of the first sacrifice. By his laying on of hands onto the first sacrifice, the sin of the people is transferred through the high priest and onto the sacrifice, coming to inhabit the sacrifice's sinless blood. That *first sacrifice* is then slaughtered as the sin offering for the nation, shedding its blood and fulfilling that sin's demand for death (Lev 16:9). The first sacrifice involves the *shedding of blood* and bringing the sin of the people to *fulfillment* in *death*.

Second, the high priest then lays his hands onto the *second* sacrifice, onto the head of the goat, and over *that* goat there is *confession* (by the high priest) of the sins of the people. The sin of the people is transferred through the high priest onto that second sacrifice, onto the head of the goat, and the goat is then *released* into the wilderness, accompanied by a man. The goat then *runs away*, taking with it the sin of the people that was laid upon it, resulting in forgiveness of sin for the nation (Lev 16:30). The second sacrifice does *not* involve the shedding of blood.

The two-part sacrifice of the Day of Atonement shows the full picture of what the sacrifice is accomplishing. First, with the slaughter of the first sacrifice and the shedding of its blood, it shows the necessity for blood to be shed for there to be forgiveness of sin, showing the necessity of bringing the sin laid upon the sacrifice to completion in the death of the sacrifice. Sin is completed, has its fulfillment in death, and the first sacrifice provides the death that fulfills the sin of the people.

Second, with the goat being released into the wilderness and taking with it the sin of the people, it illustrates the *purpose* of the sacrifice, which was to *take away the sin of the people* so as to bring *forgiveness*. These two sacrifices taken *together* illustrate the *full* picture of what the Day of Atonement sacrifice was accomplishing—blood from a sinless sacrifice is shed, the people's sin is brought to completion in death, and this results in the *taking away*, or the breaking of the power, of the sin of the people, bringing *forgiveness* for that sin. There is *nothing* in the Day of Atonement sacrifice that in any way is connected with punishment for sin.

Together, the two parts of the Day of Atonement sacrifice reflect the *entire* picture of what was happening on behalf of the nation on the Day of Atonement—sin was being *both* taken away *and* forgiven by the shedding of innocent blood. This two-part Day of Atonement sacrifice, as performed by the high priest, was an illustration of what the coming permanent sacrifice for the sin of humanity would accomplish, and how it would be accomplished.

God's Unfolding Plan—Sacrifice and the High Priest

The Authority of the High Priest

Only the high priest had the authority to perform the rituals and sacrifices for the nation on the Day of Atonement. As high priest, only he had the authority to enter the holy of holies. As high priest, only he had the ordained and anointed authority to represent the entire nation of Israel before God. As high priest, he alone had the authority to take all the sin of *all the people* and transfer it, in full, onto the head of the sacrifice, so as to take away *all* the sin of Israel. That sin of the people was literally placed onto the goat, onto the sacrifice, not in a metaphorical or symbolic way, but literally so. All of this was by God-given *authority*, and only the high priest was given that authority, which he had by virtue of his office. The result of all of this is the sins of all the people, of the entire nation, were forgiven, temporarily, for one year, after which the Day of Atonement rituals and sacrifices needed to be repeated annually.

This office and authority of the high priest was an illustration of the office and authority of the High Priest to come, the one who would exercise that same authority of transferring the sin of the people onto the sacrifice for that sin, but in the case of that High Priest to come, it would be on behalf of all humanity.

The Sin Offering

In addition to the yearly Day of Atonement sacrifice, there was a mandatory sin offering to be performed throughout the year as necessary. The sin offering was a mandatory offering that could happen at any time, could be performed by *any* priest, and it was required in the following situations—if the anointed priest sinned, bringing guilt on the people (Lev 4:3); if the whole Israelite community sinned unintentionally (Lev 4:13); when a leader sinned unintentionally (Lev 4:22); or if any member of the community sinned unintentionally (Lev 4:27). In each and every case of making a sin offering, it was *required* that there be a *physical* laying on of hands onto the sacrifice. Just as when the high priest made the Day of Atonement sacrifice for the nation of Israel, and laid his hands onto the sacrifice so the sin of Israel passed through the high priest and onto the sacrifice, likewise the priest of the sin offering would lay his hands onto the sacrifice for the sin offering so the sin of that person would similarly pass through the priest to lay upon the sacrifice. As a result, when that sacrifice was slaughtered and its blood was shed, that sin was then taken away by the sacrifice, taken away by its shed blood, brought to completion in its death, and the sin was forgiven. Because the sin offering was for individuals rather than being for the nation, it was not necessary that it be the high priest who performed the sacrifice; rather, any priest could perform the sacrifice. The result of the sin offering was the same as with the Day of Atonement sacrifice—the sin was taken away and forgiven (Lev 4:26, 31, 35).

The Physical Laying on of Hands

It is important to understand that, for the Day of Atonement sacrifice and for all the sacrifices of the sin offerings, there was a *physical* laying on of hands, and *through* that laying on of hands the sin was *transferred* from the people onto the sacrifice (Lev 16:21). Then, with the shedding of the sacrifice's blood, and with the *death* of the sacrifice, that same sin was *taken away* and forgiven. Again, in all of this, there is not even the concept of punishment for sin—the concept of a sacrifice being punished for sin does not exist in the Bible. In fact, we know specifically that *none* of the sacrifices in the Old Testament had *anything* to do with *punishment*, for we are specifically told in Romans 3:25:

> God presented Christ as a sacrifice of atonement, through the shedding of his blood—to be received by faith. He did this to demonstrate his righteousness, *because in his forbearance he had left the sins committed beforehand unpunished.* (NIV)

Paul clearly tells us *none* of the Old Testament sacrifices—none of the sin offerings and none of the Day of Atonement sacrifices—had *anything* to do with *punishment*; they were *all* solely and exclusively about sin being *taken away* and *forgiven*. To *forbear* means to refrain, desist, withhold—it does *not* mean to delay; rather, it means to completely overlook and to let go.

Why Only One Sacrifice?

The sacrifices for the Day of Atonement, as well as the sin offering sacrifices, only required *one* animal to be sacrificed. How can this be just? The sin offering could be for the entire community, while the Day of Atonement sacrifice was for the entire nation, for millions of people. Why were there not millions of animals sacrificed for each person of the nation? Why was only *one* sacrifice sufficient to take away the sin of *all* the people?

It comes down to blood and the sinful nature. As we have seen, our sinful nature is a physical thing that resides in our blood. That one sinful nature is the source of all the sin we, humanity in its entirety, have ever committed or ever will commit.

We also must remember the blood which flows through our human veins is literally the blood of Adam. When we were born, we did not receive some newly created blood; rather, we inherited our blood from our human parents, who in turn inherited their blood from their human parents, and so on back through time to Adam. *All* the blood that flows through human veins is *only* the blood of Adam, the blood of the *one* man. Adam's *one blood,* is distributed throughout all of humanity.

As a result, the sinful nature that resides in our blood is the same *one* sinful nature that took up residence in *Adam's blood* upon him eating the fruit of the forbidden tree. Therefore, it is just for *one* sacrifice, and the blood of that *one* sacrifice, to cover the *entirety* of human sin, since the *totality* of all human sin is, in effect, all from the blood of the *one* man, Adam, whose blood and whose sinful nature resides in us all.

Since all the sin of humanity is the result of the blood of the one man, Adam, then it is not necessary to have individual sacrifices for every person in Israel, or for every human being on the planet, since it is only Adam's blood flowing in all of us. Therefore, since we all have the blood of Adam, we also have only the one, original, sinful nature inhabiting our blood. Therefore the *one* animal sacrifice is taking away the sin of the *one man* Adam, whose *one* sinful nature, by way of his blood, is within each of us. Adam's *blood* is the *source* of *all* the sin humanity would ever commit. As a result, the blood of the one sacrifice, and the death of the one sacrifice, is made for the blood of the one man Adam, father of us all.

Again, just to make it very clear, *none* of this had *anything* to do with *punishment*—the concept of *punishment* being visited upon a sacrifice for *payment* of sins is a concept that does not exist in the Bible. Romans 3:25 blatantly tells us there was *no* punishment visited upon *any* of the sin offerings or Day of Atonement offerings and sacrifices of the Old Testament—rather, the sacrifices would *take* away the sin, or break its power, which would result in *forgiveness* of sin.

Taken together, the daily sin offerings and guilt offerings, along with the special Day of Atonement sacrifice, paint a picture of the sins of individuals and of the entire nation being forgiven by God as a result of the shedding of sinless blood and by the death of the sacrifice. The two-part Day of Atonement sacrifice, with the first sacrifice being slaughtered and its blood being shed, together with the second sacrifice, the goat which ran into the wilderness with the sin of the nation upon itself, thereby taking that sin away, is a clear illustration that, by the shedding of innocent blood and by the death of the sacrifice, the sin of the people is *taken away*, resulting in forgiveness of sin for the nation.

The Taking Away of Sin

What does it mean for sin to be "taken away?" Even after the Day of Atonement or sin sacrifices were performed, the sinful nature would still remain within the people, within their blood, and the people would still continue to sin. What then was accomplished?

To "take away" sin means to "break its power" (John 1:29; Heb 2:14), to break its power of death (separation from God), fear, and deception. In the case of animal sacrifices for human sin, this was only a temporary accomplishment. By temporarily breaking this power of sin, it allowed people to have some capacity to *receive* the forgiveness of God for their sins, a forgiveness freely given by God. The sinful nature would still remain within the people, and it would still, overall, retain its power within them, but its power would be broken temporarily. This is why the Day of Atonement sacrifice had to be performed annually. This "breaking the power of sin" is described as "taking sin away."

Atonement

The sacrifice for the sin of the nation was performed by the high priest on the Day of Atonement. What does the word "atonement" mean? Atonement does *not* mean "making a payment for"; rather, to atone means "to reconcile," or simply to "make things right." The Day of Atonement can be understood as the Day of Reconciliation between God and his people. In the case of the Day of Atonement sacrifice, or the sin offerings, that reconciliation was made by God forgiving sin—the reconciliation was *not* made by making *payment* for sin, but rather, that reconciliation was made by God *forgiving* sin. Once the sins were forgiven, there was reconciliation between God and his people, for it was the *forgiveness* of sin that "makes things right" between the people and God.

Why Animal Sacrifice?

The Bible tells us: "... without shedding of blood there is no *forgiveness*" (Heb 9:22 NASB). First, it is again important to note the shedding of blood does not result in any payment for sin; rather, it results in *forgiveness* of sin. As Romans 3:25 specifically tells us, none of the millions of Old Testament sacrifices performed over a period of over 1,500 years ever had anything to do with punishment. The animal sacrifices of the Old Testament had nothing to do with punishment, they were all and only about forgiveness.

Why is the shedding of blood *required* for the forgiveness of sin? As we have seen, God himself performed the first sacrifice in Genesis 3, providing skins of animals to cover Adam and Eve's nakedness, to cover the shame that resulted from the physical sinful nature taking up residence in their flesh, within their blood.

As a result, since the sinful nature resides in our blood, it is true to say if a human being were to completely shed their blood, they would be rid of their sinful nature. It is for this reason the Bible tells us without the shedding of blood there is no forgiveness of sin, for our sinful nature *resides in our blood*. To shed one's blood, in effect, would be to shed one's sinful nature.

However, if one did shed their blood, not only would they shed their sinful nature, but they would also be dead, since it's that very same blood that gives us physical, *mortal* life. This is a problem. God wants us to live, he does not want us to die—so what is the solution? The temporary solution was God's institution of the animal sacrifices of the Old Testament as the first unfolding, or illustration, of his coming plan of salvation, also acting as a sort of "temporary fix" for sin.

When Adam ate of the forbidden fruit, physical sin, the physical sinful nature, entered into him, and then immediately into Eve, to reside in their blood. Our human blood is where our sinful nature physically resides. Adam was also the lord over the earth and over all of its creatures—all creatures, animals, and plants were under Adam's dominion (Gen 1:26). When Adam ate of the forbidden fruit, not only did sin enter into his flesh, into his blood, but he also gave up his *authority* over the earth, and over its creatures, to Satan, and Satan then became the ruler of the world. It is at that point animals started to kill and eat each other, that plants became poisonous, that death and decay entered the world, because now the earth was under Satan's dominion, a dominion freely and legally given to him by Adam when he sinned.

The animals of the earth, although they were under Adam's authority and under his dominion, were *not* born of Adam's flesh and, as a result, did *not* have Adam's blood flowing through their veins. As a result, animals did *not* have the sinful nature in their blood.

Also, because animals were not made in the image of God, animals are not moral creatures. Since animals are not moral creatures, they are incapable of committing sin. Therefore it is true to say animals are without sin, they are without the sinful nature and the blood of animals is sinless, free of sin. As a result, all the animals used in the Old Testament sacrifices were sinless. This sinlessness of the animal sacrifices was further illustrated by the need for the sacrificial animals to outwardly be "without blemish," (Lev 5:15; 6:6; 9:2) which is to say the animals used for sacrifice needed to be physically pure and without defect. The outward purity of the sacrifice was only an illustration of the inward purity, or sinlessness, of the sacrifice. As with the high priest first bathing himself and then offering up sacrifice for his own sin, it was necessary that the sin sacrifice *itself* be without sin. The requirement for the sacrifice to be without sin was essential to the mechanism of sacrifice, and that mechanism of sacrifice was made effective by the laying on of hands.

Why the Laying on of Hands

In the Day of Atonement sacrifices and most of the sin sacrifices of the Old Testament, it was *required* that the priest lay his hands onto the head of the sacrifice. Why? By the laying on of hands onto the head of the sacrifice, the sin of the people was being *transferred* onto the sacrifice (Lev 16:21). But what kind of transference was this? Was it the individual sinful *acts* that were being transferred onto the sacrifice, *or* was it the sinful-*ness* of the people, or the sinful *nature* that breeds the sinful acts, that was being transferred onto the sacrifice? Or was it the *power* of sin that was being transferred onto the sacrifice?

In every case where the sin offering is made, there is no reference to any sinful *acts* being transferred onto the sacrifice, that is, there is no *confession* of sinful *acts* spoken over the sacrifice. Rather, when a person or the community realizes they have sinned, hands are laid onto the head of the sacrifice as a *general transference* of the sin onto the head of the sacrifice.

God's Unfolding Plan—Sacrifice and the High Priest 175

The sacrifice is then killed, its innocent, sinless blood is *shed,* and the sin is taken away and forgiven. As a result, it is *not* the individual sinful acts that are being transferred onto the sacrifice; rather, it is the actual sinfulness, or the *power* of the sinful *nature* that bred the sinful acts, that is being transferred onto the sacrifice.

Why was the *physicality* of the laying on of hands necessary? The fact remains there is an actual *physical transference* of sin happening during the sacrifice. This is why God instituted *animal* sacrifice. The sacrifice of an animal resulted in the shedding of innocent, or *sinless,* blood, resulting in the death of the sacrifice. The high priest had the authority to *transfer* the sin of the people onto the animal sacrifice so the sacrifice could take away the sin of the people, temporarily break the power of the people's sin, and so allow the people to *accept* God's forgiveness.

The Mechanism of Sacrifice

There is an actual mechanism of sacrifice that makes the sacrifice effective for breaking the power of sin. The sinful nature that resides within our blood is an actual, physical thing; it is not some sort of spiritual state. The blood of the animals used in the sacrifices was *innocent* blood in that it did *not* have *any* sinful nature residing within it, because animals are not physical descendants of Adam and so do not have Adam's blood or his sinful nature. The blood of animals is therefore pure, innocent of sin.

When the priest lays his hands *physically* onto the sacrifice, the sinfulness of the people, the *power* of their sin, is *imputed* or *transferred* not only onto the head of the sacrifice, but also, as a result of the laying on of hands, *into the creature's innocent, sinless blood.* The sin of the people is coming to physically *inhabit* the sinless blood of the sacrifice. As the sacrifice sheds its blood, the sinfulness imputed into its sinless blood by the physical laying on of hands is also shed, taken away, brought to completion in death.

It is for this reason the sacrifice must itself be free of sin, having no sin within its own blood. By not having sin within its own blood, this allows for the sin of the people being transferred onto the sacrifice to come to inhabit that sinless blood. If sin was already within the blood of the sacrifice, then the sin being transferred onto the sacrifice would be unable to inhabit that blood since sin would already be residing within that blood. This is why it was necessary for the sacrifice itself to be without sin, and why animals were used for the sacrifices—animals have no sin, they do not have the sinful nature, and they are not capable of committing sin. As a result, the blood of animals is sinless and pure.

This is the mechanism of sacrifice, the means by which a sacrifice is made effective. The sin of the people is transferred onto the sacrifice, and then that sin *enters into* the *sinless blood* of the sacrifice. As the sacrifice sheds its blood, that sin is "taken away," meaning the power of the sin imputed into the sacrifice is broken and the people are then able to receive God's forgiveness of their sin. The way the power of sin is broken is the sin is brought to completion in death.

The Requirement of Death

It is the nature of sin to seek death, for sin is concluded, or has its completion, in death.

> For the *wages of sin is death*. (Rom 6:23 NASB)

> For we have already made the charge that Jews and Gentiles alike are all under the *power of sin*. (Rom 3:9 NIV)

> Therefore, since the children share in flesh and blood, he himself likewise also partook of the same, that *through death* he might *render powerless* him who had *the power of death*, that is, the devil. (Heb 2:14 NASB)

Death is the natural outcome of sin. When sin inhabits any physical creature, that sin is *fulfilled* in physical death, physical death is the *completion* of that sin, it is the full *conclusion* of that sin. Sin *demands* death—until sin has concluded in death, sin is active and relentless. Death is the culmination and fulfillment of sin. Once sin results in death, that same sin is then finished, done, broken of its power. This is key to understanding the mechanism of sacrifice and why a sacrifice must itself be sinless in order to take away sin and bring forgiveness.

If a sacrifice were itself to have sin, it could not serve as a sacrifice. If a sacrifice had sin, then the sin that would already be residing within the sacrifice, within its blood, would already be *demanding* the *death of that creature*, its host, as the fruit of that very *same* sin. Once that creature would die, then it would satisfy *only* the demand of its *own* sin, of the sin *already within itself*, the demand of the sin that was *already resident* in its blood. As a result, a creature which already has sin within itself, within its blood, cannot take upon itself anyone else's sin, for, by having sin itself, its death could only satisfy the demand of its *own* sin.

However, when a sacrifice is sinless, and others' sin is laid upon that sacrifice, then the sin laid upon it can now inhabit the *sinless blood of that sacrifice*. Once that sin inhabits the blood of the sacrifice, that sin will demand physical death, for physical death is the full conclusion and completion of sin. When the sacrifice sheds its blood and *dies*, then the *death of that sacrifice* has *fulfilled* the natural *demand* of the sin placed upon it, fulfilling the demand of the sin that came to dwell within its blood—the death of the sinless sacrifice has brought that very same sin to *completion*, to *conclusion*, brought it to *fulfillment*. Therefore, as a result, the sin that was laid upon the sacrifice has now been satisfied, fulfilled *in death*, and it *no longer has any power* for it has been made complete in death—its power *has been broken* by the death of the sinless sacrifice. As a result, the people whose sin was laid upon the sacrifice can now receive forgiveness of their sin. This could only be accomplished if the sacrifice itself had no sin.

This is why animals could be used as the sacrifice for sin, because the animal itself had no sin within its blood, it had no sinful nature, its blood was sinless since it was not a descendant of Adam. When the animal sacrifice died, as a sinless creature, dying with the sin of the people coming to inhabit its sinless blood, it satisfied that sin's demand for death. As a result of the sacrifice satisfying that sin's demand for death, the sin of the people was brought to completion, to fulfillment, to conclusion. As a result of the sacrifice's death, the sin of the people was taken away, which is to say its power was, *temporarily*, broken. It was the death of the sacrifice that broke the power of that sin.

Why were the Animal Sacrifices Not Resurrected?

Since the animal sacrifice itself had no sin, we would expect the animal, after its death, could then be resurrected as a creature who had conquered death, conquered it by never sinning and by having no sin of its own within itself. But this would be impossible. Why?

Sin and death were brought into the world by one man, by Adam, and Adam was lord of the earth. Even though the sacrificial animal had no sin, the animal was not made in the image of God and was therefore *not* a moral creature, and, as a result, the animal was not *capable* of committing sin. Since the animal was incapable of committing sin, the animal could not *conquer* sin, for the *conquest of sin* can only be made by a moral being who is capable of committing sin, but who chooses not to sin and has never sinned. By never sinning, such a moral being would conquer, or take authority over, sin. In the case of the sacrificial animal, since the creature was not capable of committing sin, it could never *conquer* sin. As a result of not being able to conquer sin, it could not conquer *death*, and since it could not conquer death, it remained dead. This is why the animal sacrifices were not resurrected upon their sacrificial death—although those animals themselves were without sin, those animals were not moral creatures, and as such they were incapable of conquering sin or death.

If Animals Have No Sin, Then Why Do Animals Die?

The wages of sin is death, but animals do not have sin; they are sinless, and yet all animals die. How is that possible? Even though animals do not have sin, they were fully *subject* to Adam's *authority*, for Adam was their lord and ruler (Gen 1:26). When Adam sinned, physical sin literally entered into *him*, taking up residence in his blood, but it did *not* enter into the blood of animals, since they were not made from Adam nor did they have his blood. But the animals *were* subject to Adam's *authority* and *dominion,* and when Adam sinned he *gave up that authority* over the earth and everything on it, including his authority over animals and plants, to Satan. As a result, all of nature—animals and plants—became subject to Satan, to *his* dominion. Satan himself came to hold the power of death (Heb 2:14). Since Satan held the power of death, then by coming under *Satan's dominion,* the animals and plants came under the dominion of *death*, and death now came to *all* living things, to all nature—to all animals and plants—even though those animals and plants did not themselves have sin within them. As a result, even though animals remain sinless, and have no sinful nature within their blood, they still die, for they are subject to the authority of Satan, who himself has the power of death.

A Temporary Solution

Animals, however, could only provide a temporary taking away of sin, a temporary satisfaction of sin's requirement for death, since the sin that was laid upon the animal was human sin. Even though the death of the animal sacrifice did fulfill sin's demand for death, it resulted only in a temporary breaking of the power of sin since the *full* demand of the human sin placed upon the sacrificial animal was a demand for *human* death. The only way any *permanent* taking away of human sin could occur, the only way human sin could reach its *permanent* completion and fulfillment in death, was if the sin of humanity was laid upon a sinless *human being*, someone who himself had no sinful nature within himself and who had never committed sin. Such a sinless human being could take upon himself the sin of the world, which would then come to inhabit his sinless blood. By giving his life to satisfy that sin's demand for human death, the entirety of the sin laid upon him would reach its fulfillment, its completion, in his death. As a result of the sacrifice of such a sinless human being, the full power of human sin would be broken. The breaking of that power of sin is described as the sin being taken away.

In all of this, there is *nothing* about punishment for sin, for such a concept is foreign to the Bible. Throughout the Bible, a sacrifice for sin *never* has punishment poured upon it, *never* pays a penalty for sin; rather, the sacrifice dies, and *with its death* it *satisfies* that sin's demand for death, and with the sacrifice's death, that sin has reached its conclusion, its completion, its fulfillment. That sin is *taken away*, meaning its *power is broken*, allowing the people to receive forgiveness of sin.

The Sacrifice of a Moral Being—The Permanent Sacrifice

The very thing which allowed for animals to be suitable as a sacrifice for sin—the fact that the blood of animals is sinless, being without the sinful nature—was also the very thing which prevented the sacrifices from being truly, permanently effective. The animal sacrifices for sin achieved only a *temporary* forgiveness of sin, not a *permanent* forgiveness. The main reason why the animal sacrifices resulted in only temporary forgiveness was because animals are not moral beings.

An animal is not a moral creature and is therefore incapable of committing or conquering sin, and as a result the animal cannot permanently reverse what Adam had done. In order for a sacrifice to accomplish *permanent* forgiveness of Adam's sin, to bring Adam's sin to *permanent* fulfillment and completion in death, that sacrifice itself must be *capable* of committing sin. It is not enough to just be "without sin," as the sacrificial animals were, but in order to accomplish *permanent* forgiveness, that sacrifice must also be able to commit sin, but must never actually commit sin.

This was the exact position of Adam in Eden. He was the son of God, made in God's image, created perfect and sinless, a moral creature who knew right from wrong. As a moral creature made in God's image, Adam was *capable* of choosing to sin, and in Adam's case, he chose to sin. Therefore the sacrifice that could permanently reverse Adam's fall would likewise have to be in that exact same position as was Adam in Eden—it would need to be a being bearing God's image, a being with Adam's full created humanity; it would need to be a moral being, perfect and sinless, as Adam originally was, and yet still be capable of choosing to sin. The only sacrifice that could be in this position was a sacrifice that was a descendant of Adam, a fully human sacrifice who, like Adam, was without sin, but who could choose to sin. If such a sinless human sacrifice could be found, and if that human sacrifice would choose to not commit sin, choosing instead to remain obedient and faithful to God, then that sacrifice would overcome sin, would *conquer* sin, by never sinning. By conquering sin, that sacrifice would then take *authority* over sin. As a result, that sacrifice would have power and authority over both sin and death.

God's Unfolding Plan—The Sacrifice to Come

God's institution of the high priest and the sacrificial system was an illustration of God's unfolding plan of salvation and redemption. With the institution of the high priest of Israel, the high priest had the authority to represent the nation before God, to make sacrifice on behalf of the people for the sin of the people. The high priest had the authority to take the sin of the people and place it upon the sin sacrifice for the sin of the people, so as to have that sin brought to completion in death and to have its power broken, albeit temporarily, thereby allowing the people to receive forgiveness for their sin. In this way, the office of the high priest was an echo of the First Adam, who himself was the first father of all humanity and who, in that capacity, brought sin into the world and to all people, his descendants.

But the high priest was also a foreshadowing, or an illustration, of the Second Adam to come, who would be both a Second Father of humanity and the representative of humanity before God, and who also would have the authority to take the sin of the world, the sin of all people, and lay it upon the sacrifice for that sin, thereby taking that sin away, breaking its power, and making forgiveness of sin available to all humanity.

God would manifest his plan of salvation, his plan of redemption, with the birth of a Second Adam. This Second Adam would be a descendant of Adam's blood—fully human, yet, like the First Adam, he would be without sin and without the sinful nature. Like the First Adam, the Second Adam would be a son of God, a moral person who would know right from wrong and who would be capable of choosing to sin. If the Second Adam would choose not to sin, choosing instead to remain obedient and faithful to God, then the Second Adam would conquer sin, would take authority over it, and sin would have no power over him. The Second Adam would be the high priest of all humanity and, in that position, would have the authority to take the sin of all humanity and lay it upon the sacrifice for that sin. The Second Adam himself would then also be the sacrifice for that sin who, by the shedding of his blood, by the giving of his life, would satisfy that same sin's demand for death. In so doing, the Second Adam, by the shedding of his blood and by his death, would take away the sin of the world, which was brought into the world by the blood of the First Adam—the Second Adam would break the power of that sin by bringing it to full conclusion, completion, and fulfillment in his death.

This salvation of humanity and the redemption of all things would be accomplished by the Second Adam upon the cross. It is only by the profound love and grace of God that there would be a Second Adam. Just as the First Adam was the son of God (Luke 3:38), so the Second Adam would be the Son of God, Jesus Christ.

PART II

The Cross

12

God the Son

THE SECOND ADAM WAS the culmination of God's unfolding plan of salvation and redemption and would be the means through which that salvation and redemption would be accomplished. The Second Adam would be a man, a son of God, just as the First Adam was a son of God, but whereas the First Adam was the created son of God, the Second Adam would be the begotten son of God, born of a human woman. The Second Adam would be God himself taking on human flesh, marrying his uncreated self to Adam's created humanity forever—the Second Adam would be God Incarnate. The Second Adam would redeem and reverse the fall of the First Adam, breaking the power of the sin of humanity by the shedding of his own blood and by his own death, making forgiveness of sin, and salvation, available to all. The Second Adam would be God the Son, Jesus Christ.

Who is God the Son? What is his nature? What was he like before his incarnation? The nature and person of God the Son is vividly made clear throughout the entire Bible, throughout both the Old and New Testaments, for the entirety of Scripture testifies and bears witness to him (John 5:39).

The Trinity—God's Very Nature

God is a Trinity, and being a Trinity is the very essence of God's nature. No human mind can truly grasp the nature of the Trinity, but to describe it in limited human language we can describe the Trinity as three distinct persons who, together, make up the one God.

Each of the three persons of the Trinity—God the Father, God the Son, God the Holy Spirit—is described and talked about throughout the Bible. It is important to understand each of the three members of the Trinity is three distinct persons, and yet, together, the three persons of the Trinity are the one God.

The Trinity is alluded to right in the beginning of the Bible:

> Then God said, "Let *us* make mankind in *our* image, in *our* likeness, so that they may rule over the fish in the sea and the birds in the sky, over the livestock and all the wild animals and over all the creatures that move along the ground." (Gen 1:26 NASB)

The "us" and "our" in this passage is an expression of the Trinity. From this passage we can understand each person of the Trinity shares the same divine nature, so that, when God says "let *us* make mankind in *our* image, in *our* likeness," it is a testament to the fact that Father, Son, and Holy Spirit all have, and share, the same divine image, nature, and likeness.

The Lord is One

In fact, this is how we are to understand when Scripture tells us the LORD is one: "Hear, O Israel: The Lord our God, the Lord is one" (Deut 6:4 NKJV). Why are we told "the LORD is one?" Even though Israel would not have understood it at the time, to declare "the LORD is one" is in fact an affirmation of the Trinity, an affirmation of the three distinct persons of the Trinity together being the *one* God. Though the one LORD God is three distinct persons, the three persons of the Trinity together is the one God—so, the LORD is one.

Kiss the Son

Another clear affirmation of the Trinity in the Old Testament is in Psalm 2. Psalm 2 is a prophetic psalm which refers to the day of wrath that is to come upon the earth, a time also referred to as the last days. We are told the following:

> Therefore, you kings, be wise; be warned, you rulers of the earth.
> Serve the Lord with fear and celebrate his rule with trembling.
> Kiss his son, or he will be angry and your way will lead to your
> destruction, for his wrath can flare up in a moment. Blessed are
> all who take refuge in him. (Ps 2:10–12 NIV)

In verse 12, we are clearly told the LORD has a son and that we are to kiss his son or he will be angry. Though Israel would not have understood it at the time, this Son is a reference to God the Son, to Jesus Christ, and is therefore also an affirmation of the Trinity.

The Divine Nature of the Trinity—The Father is God

In Genesis 1:26, the Trinity is affirmed. Throughout the rest of Scripture, God's trinitarian nature continues to be affirmed, and specifically so. There is no question the Father is God, for this is clearly and repeatedly affirmed throughout the Bible (Matt 11:25; 18:14; Mark 8:38; Luke 10:21; John 1:1–14; 4:23; 1 Cor 1:3; etc.). The Father is God.

The Son is God

The Bible also clearly and repeatedly affirms Jesus Christ the Son is God (John 1:1–14; 10:30; Heb 1:1–12; Titus 2:13). It is interesting to note John 10:30, when Jesus says "I and the Father are one," seems to echo almost exactly Deuteronomy 6:4 ("Hear, O Israel: The Lord our God, the Lord is one"). Scripture clearly shows the Son is God.

The Holy Spirit is God

The Holy Spirit, though not explicitly called God in Scripture, is clearly affirmed throughout Scripture as being God, and the church has always understood it so (Acts 5:3–4; Matt 28:19; all of John and the New Testament, where the Holy Spirit is referred to as "he"). Acts 5:3–4 in particular makes this clear when Peter says to Ananias and Sapphira "you have lied to the Holy Spirit . . . you have not lied just to human beings but to God" (NIV). With that statement, Peter equates the Holy Spirit with God and so clearly affirms the Holy Spirit is God.

Another very clear affirmation of the Holy Spirit as God is in the fathering of Jesus Christ through the Virgin Mary. Normally, when we think of Mary's pregnancy, we think of God the Father as the one who specifically fathered, or begot, Jesus. But the Bible clearly tells us it was the person of the Holy Spirit who came upon Mary and who made her pregnant with God's Son: "The Holy Spirit will come upon you, and the power of the Highest will overshadow you; therefore, also, that holy One who is to be born will be called the Son of God" (Luke 1:35 NKJV).

We know very clearly Jesus is the Son of God. Therefore, if Jesus is fathered by the person of the Holy Spirit, and if Jesus is the Son of God, this affirms the Holy Spirit is God. Furthermore, Jesus himself clearly affirms the Holy Spirit as part of the Trinity. He does this clearly when he tells his apostles: "Go therefore and make disciples of all the nations, baptizing them in the name of the Father and of the Son and of the Holy Spirit" (Matt 28:19 NKJV).

By telling his apostles to go and baptize believers in the name of the Father, the Son, and the Holy Spirit, this is inarguable confirmation the Holy Spirit is as much God as is the Father or the Son. It is clear from Scripture that each person of the Trinity—the Father, the Son, the Holy Spirit—is God, and together these three persons, this Trinity, are the one God.

The Role of Each Person of the Trinity—The Holy Spirit

Although the three persons of the Trinity together constitute the one God, it also seems clear each person of the Trinity has defined specific roles for himself. For example, the Holy Spirit is called the Advocate (John 14:26), because he advocates for, or helps, believers. He is also called the Guide who will guide us in all truth (John 16:13). He is called the Teacher, who will teach us what we are to say (Luke 12:12). He is described as living in us, indwelling all believers, sealing believers for salvation (Rom 8:11; Eph 1:13–14; 2:22). We are also told the Holy Spirit intercedes, or prays, for us when we don't know how to pray (Rom 8:26–27). These are some of the very clear and specific roles that describe the Holy Spirit's work.

The Role of God the Son—He is the Judge

Likewise, the Bible clearly outlines some specific roles God the Son has defined for himself. For example, the Bible tells us God will "judge all things," for we are told,

> The Lord shall judge the peoples. (Ps 7:8 NKJV)
>
> For he is coming to judge the earth. He shall judge the world with righteousness, and the peoples with his truth. (Ps 96:13 NKJV)
>
> Before the Lord, for he is coming to judge the earth. With righteousness he shall judge the world, and the peoples with equity. (Ps 98:9 NKJV)

The Bible clearly affirms God will judge all things. Yet we are also very clearly told the *Father* judges no one; rather, *all* judgment has been entrusted to the *Son* (John 5:22 NKJV). When the Bible talks about God judging the earth, judging the people, judging for the sake of justice, or judging for any reason, it is *not* the Father who will judge; rather, it will be the God *the Son* who will judge. God the Son is the Judge of all things.

The Role of God the Son—He is the Creator

Scripture also clearly outlines it is the person of the Son who *executed* the creation, that is to say, it is the Son who brought all things into being—God the Son is the creator:

> In the beginning was the Word, and the Word was with God, and the Word was God. He was with God in the beginning. *Through him all things were made; without him nothing was made that has been made.* (John 1:1–3 NIV)
>
> The Son is the image of the invisible God, the firstborn over all creation. *For in him all things were created: things in heaven and on earth, visible and invisible, whether thrones or powers or rulers or authorities; all things have been created through him and for him.* He is before all things, and in him all things hold together. (Col 1:15–17 NIV)

In Hebrews 1:10, God the Father is speaking of the Son when he says: "He also says, 'In the beginning, Lord, *you laid the foundations of the earth, and the heavens are the work of your hands*'" (NIV). In these verses, God the Son is described as being the one who brought all things into being, the one who laid the foundations of the earth, the one who made the heavens, the one in whom, and through whom, all things were created, and in whom all things hold together. It is true God is a Trinity, and that the Trinity is one, yet it seems the actual making of the creation was brought forth by God the Son. God the Son is the creator of all things.

The Role of God the Son—He is the Word of God

In Scripture, Jesus, God the Son, is clearly called the Word of God (John 1:1–14). The Word of God is described as being the creator of all things:

> In the beginning was the Word, and the Word was with God, and the Word was God. He was with God in the beginning. *Through him all things were made; without him nothing was made that has been made.* (John 1:1–3)

The Word is the creator of all things. It is interesting to note that in Genesis 1, when God first restores the cursed earth and then creates life upon it, he does so each time by *speaking* both the restoration and the creation into being—he didn't just *think* it into existence; rather, he *spoke* it into existence. As described in John 1:3, whose very opening words harken back to Genesis 1:1, this speaking creation into existence was accomplished by God's Word.

What does it mean for God the Son to be the Word of God? We can understand the Word of God as being the *speaking* of God, as being the one who *speaks*, or enunciates, God's will upon creation, the one who brings God's will into existence. This is in complete alignment with the *speaking* of creation into being, in Genesis 1, as being done specifically by the Word of God, by God the Son, as is affirmed in John 1:1–3—God the Son, as the *speaking* of God, spoke God's will into being. As a result, one of the roles of God the Son, the Word of God, is he brings the will of God into being by speaking it into existence.

The Son Equal to the Father

The Bible also teaches us very clearly that God the Son, in his person and in his nature, was equal to God the Father.

> Who, although he existed in the form of God, did not regard *equality with God a thing to be grasped*, but emptied himself, taking the form of a bond-servant, and being made in the likeness of men. (Phil 2:6–7 NASB)

> But about the Son he says, 'Your throne, O God, will last forever and ever; a scepter of justice will be the scepter of your kingdom. You have loved righteousness and hated wickedness; *therefore God*, your God, has set you above your companions by anointing you with the oil of joy.' (Heb 1:8-9 NIV)

> And now, Father, glorify me in your presence with *the glory I had with you before the world began*. (John 17:5 NIV)

These verses very clearly affirm God the Son, before his incarnation, was equal with the Father. Yet consider John 14:28:

> You have heard Me say to you, 'I am going away and coming back to you.' If you loved Me, you would rejoice because I said, 'I am going to the Father,' for my Father is greater than I. (John 14:28 NKJV)

If God the Son is equal to God the Father, then how can Jesus say *the Father is greater* than the Son? God the Son *was* equal with the Father, but he did not *remain* equal with the Father. As Philippians 2:6-7 tells us, the Son became *human*, and by becoming human the Son let go of his equality with God the Father, so that, since the incarnation, the Son is now no longer equal with the Father. The Son became human, the Father never did. The Son, prior to his incarnation, was equal with God the Father, but after his incarnation, the Father is now greater than the Son

The Role of God the Son—He is the Bridegroom

In creating humanity, God is creating a bride for himself, creating his own companion, his own Eve. But the actual union between God and man is to be accomplished specifically through the person of God the Son. It is the role of God the Son to *marry* humanity, to *unite* man with God, to be the bridegroom:

> Jesus answered, 'How can the guests of the *bridegroom* mourn while he is with them? The time will come when the *bridegroom* will be taken from them; then they will fast.' (Matt 9:15 NIV)

> Let us rejoice and be glad and give him glory! For the *wedding of the Lamb* has come, and *his bride* has made herself ready. (Rev 19:7 NIV)

> One of the seven angels who had the seven bowls full of the seven last plagues came and said to me, 'Come, *I will show you the bride, the wife of the Lamb*.' (Rev 21:9 NIV)

> For this reason a man will leave his father and mother and be united to his wife, and the two will become one flesh.' This is a profound mystery—but *I am talking about Christ and the church*. (Eph 5:31–32 NIV)

This union between God and man, this marriage of God with humanity, with his companion, is to be accomplished through the person of the Son—it is the role of the Son to unite humanity with God.

The Likeness of God and the Divine Form

The Bible tells us very clearly Adam was created in both the image and likeness of God:

> Then God said, "Let Us make man in Our image, according to Our likeness." (Gen 1:26 NASB)

To be made in God's *likeness* means we, humanity, *physically look like God*. There are some who say to be made in God's likeness means only that we have his nature—that we have will, personality, emotion, and a moral character—but the Bible is very clear that to be made in someone's *likeness* means to physically look like that person:

> ... God did by sending his own Son *in the likeness* of *sinful flesh*. (Rom 8:3 NIV)

The Bible tells us specifically Jesus was sent in the *likeness* of sinful flesh. If likeness meant Jesus shared our nature, then that would mean Jesus Christ was a sinner. But we know Jesus Christ had no sin:

> For he made him who knew no sin to be sin for us. (2 Cor 5:21 NKJV)

Jesus Christ had no sin, and yet he came in the likeness of sinful flesh. Only human beings have sinful flesh—animals do not have sinful flesh, and neither do angels, only human beings (the term "sinful flesh" is itself a further affirmation the sinful nature is a physical thing that resides physically in our flesh, within our blood). For Jesus to be in the "likeness of sinful flesh," to be in our human likeness, means Jesus Christ physically *looked* human—he looked like us, he looked like an ordinary man. Likewise, to be created in God's *likeness* means we, humanity, physically *look* like God.

How can we physically look like God? We are flesh and bone and spirit, and yet is not God all spirit, and not flesh and bone? Jesus tells us the following: "God is spirit, and his worshipers must worship in the Spirit and in truth" (John 4:24 NIV). If God is spirit, then how can we physically look like him? Here, in John 4:24, Jesus seems to be referring *specifically* to God the *Father*, for in the previous verse he tells us: "Yet a time is coming and has now come when the true worshipers will worship the Father in the Spirit and in truth, for they are the kind of worshipers the Father seeks" (John 4:23 NIV). It is clear in John 4:23 Jesus is referring specifically to God the Father, telling us God the Father is Spirit.

Yet throughout the Old Testament, God is often described as having a hand (Exod 6:1, 8; 13:14; 24:11; Ps 10:12; 17:14; 110:1), a face (Exod 33:11; Num 12:8; 2 Sam 21:1; Ps 34:16), an arm (Ps 89:13; Isa 62:8), a back (Exod 33:23), eyes (Gen 6:8; Deut 11:12; 12:28; 21:9; 2 Chr 16:9, etc.). If God is Spirit, then how can he have a hand, an arm, a face, eyes, and a back? Of course some will say this is only a metaphorical description of God, but it does not read that way, especially when Moses is described specifically as talking with God "face to face," and also when Moses is allowed to specifically *see* God's back. It is the clear meaning in these verses that God has a hand, an arm, a face, eyes, and back.

Again, how can this be if God is Spirit? The Father may be Spirit, but that does not necessarily mean the Son is similarly only spirit. Scripture seems to make clear the Son in fact has a divine form that is part of his uncreated divine nature. Therefore, it is the *Son* who has eyes, who has a face, a hand, an arm, etc.—this divine form is part of the Son's uncreated divine nature. This is why we are told in Genesis: "Then God said, 'Let us make mankind in our image, in our *likeness* . . .'" (1:26 NIV). To be made in God's *likeness* means we physically *look* like God. Since Jesus tells us the Father is spirit, and since the Bible clearly tells us God the Son was the agent of creation, we can conclude humanity is made specifically in the likeness of *God the Son*—we physically *look* like *him*, like his divine form.

It is very important to understand the uncreated, divine form of God the Son is *not* our humanity, it is *not* flesh and bone, and it is *not*, in any way, subject to time and space. Rather, it would be his original, *uncreated divine* form, the uncreated original divine form in whose likeness humanity was made.

The Right Hand of the Father

When Jesus ascended to heaven after his resurrection, he took his seat at the right *hand* of the Father" (Matt 22:44; Rom 8:34; Eph 1:20). Also, in Genesis 1:26, at the creation of man, God says man will be made in "*our* likeness." Does this not mean God the Father also has a divine form, since he is clearly described as having a right hand and seemingly sharing the *likeness* in which humanity was made?

We know the Father is spirit (John 4:24), and it is possible the divine form is a form of eternal, uncreated spirit, in which case it is very possible the Father shares the same eternal, uncreated divine form as the Son. It is also possible that to sit at the Father's "right hand" is just an expression of exaltation, however there is no question the resurrected Jesus Christ is literally seated on an actual throne, in heaven, at the right "hand" of the Father, so it is unlikely the expression of being seated at the Father's right hand is only a statement of exaltation.

It is possible God the Father does not have a divine form such as the Son had, but rather, by virtue of the nature of the Trinity, where the LORD is one, the divine form of the Son imbues the whole nature of the Trinity. We cannot say whether the Father has a divine form such as the Son had, but we can say with certainty the Son, without question, did have an eternal, uncreated divine form, the form in whose likeness Adam was made.

The Uncreated Divine Form of God the Son

God the Son had an original uncreated divine form as part of his eternal divine nature, and that original uncreated form was the likeness in which humanity was made. If we were to *see* the divine form of the Son, that divine form would have had the *appearance* of a human form since the human form was made in the likeness of that divine form, but that original divine form was not human in that it was not a form of flesh and bone, it was not comprised of any created substance; rather, it was an eternal, uncreated form, not in any way subject to time and space—the uncreated and eternal divine form was part of the very essence of the Son and his divinity.

The Bible repeatedly affirms this divine form of God the Son as it describes humanity's interactions with God. As a result, it is clear it was God the Son with whom humanity was interacting throughout the Old Testament.

God the Son Throughout the Old Testament

Since it will be the Son who will be uniting humanity with God by marrying humanity, it is specifically the role of the Son to engage with humanity, his future bride, throughout humanity's history. This is seen throughout the Old Testament, God interacting with human beings, and right from the beginning, in Eden. It is clear from the Bible that, throughout those interactions of God with humanity, it is usually, perhaps always, God the Son, *not God the Father*, with whom humanity is interacting. It is God the Son who called and interacted with Abraham, God the Son who wrestled with Jacob, God the Son who walked in Eden, God the Son who gave Moses the Ten Commandments, God the Son who speaks with Job. How do we know this? The Bible clearly tells us:

> *No one has seen the Father* except the one who is from God; only he has seen the Father. (John 6:46 NIV)

> *No one has ever seen God*, but *the one and only Son*, who is himself God and is in closest relationship with the Father, has made him known. (John 1:18 NIV)

> And the Father who sent me has himself testified concerning me. *You have never heard his* voice nor seen his form. (John 5:37 NIV)

The Bible clearly tells us *no human being* has ever *seen the Father*. And yet throughout the Old Testament there are many times when a human being is specifically described as *seeing* God *with their eyes*.

Moses Sees God, and Talks with Him Face to Face

> Now Moses used to take a tent and pitch it outside the camp some distance away, calling it the "tent of meeting." Anyone inquiring of the Lord would go to the tent of meeting outside the camp. And whenever Moses went out to the tent, all the people rose and stood at the entrances to their tents, watching Moses until he entered the tent. As Moses went into the tent, the pillar of cloud would come down and stay at the entrance, while the Lord spoke with Moses. Whenever the people saw the pillar of cloud standing at the entrance to the tent, they all stood and worshiped, each at the entrance to their tent. *The Lord would speak to Moses face to*

face, as one speaks to a friend. Then Moses would return to the camp, but his young aide Joshua son of Nun did not leave the tent.

Moses said to the Lord, "You have been telling me, 'Lead these people, but you have not let me know whom you will send with me. You have said, 'I know you by name and you have found favor with me.' If you are pleased with me, teach me your ways so I may know you and continue to find favor with you. Remember that this nation is your people."

The Lord replied, "My presence will go with you, and I will give you rest."

Then Moses said to him, "If your presence does not go with us, do not send us up from here. How will anyone know that you are pleased with me and with your people unless you go with us? What else will distinguish me and your people from all the other people on the face of the earth?"

And the Lord said to Moses, "I will do the very thing you have asked, because I am pleased with you and I know you by name."

Then Moses said, "Now show me your glory."

And the Lord said, "I will cause all my goodness to pass in front of you, and I will proclaim my name, the Lord, in your presence. I will have mercy on whom I will have mercy, and I will have compassion on whom I will have compassion. But," he said, "*you cannot see my face*, for no one may see me and live."

Then the Lord said, "There is a place near me where you may stand on a rock. *When my glory passes by, I will put you in a cleft in the rock and cover you with my hand until I have passed by. Then I will remove my hand and you will see my back*; but my face must not be seen." (Exod 33:7–23 NIV)

Jacob Sees God Face to Face

That night Jacob got up and took his two wives, his two female servants and his eleven sons and crossed the ford of the Jabbok. After he had sent them across the stream, he sent over all his possessions. So Jacob was left alone, and a man wrestled with him till daybreak. When the man saw that he could not overpower him, he touched the socket of Jacob's hip so that his hip was wrenched as he wrestled with the man. Then the man said, "Let me go, for it is daybreak." But Jacob replied, "I will not let you go unless you bless me." The man asked him, "What is your name?"

"Jacob," he answered.

Then the man said, "Your name will no longer be Jacob, but Israel, because you have struggled with God and with humans and have overcome."

Jacob said, "Please tell me your name."

But he replied, "Why do you ask my name?" Then he blessed him there.

So Jacob called the place Peniel, saying, "*It is because I saw God face to face*, and yet my life was spared." (Gen 32:22–30 NIV)

Job Sees God with His Eyes

My ears had heard of you, but now *my eyes have seen you*. (Job 42:5 NIV)

God Walks and Talks with Adam and Eve in the Garden

Then the man and his wife heard the sound of the Lord God *as he was walking in the garden* in the cool of the day. (Gen 3:8 NIV)

Abraham Sees God and Talks with Him

The Lord appeared to Abraham near the great trees of Mamre while he was sitting at the entrance to his tent in the heat of the day. *Abraham looked up and saw* three men standing nearby. *When he saw them,* he hurried from the entrance of his tent to meet them and bowed low to the ground.

He said, "If I have found favor in your eyes, my lord, do not pass your servant by. Let a little water be brought, and then you may all wash your feet and rest under this tree. Let me get you something to eat, so you can be refreshed and then go on your way—now that you have come to your servant."

"Very well," they answered, "do as you say."

So Abraham hurried into the tent to Sarah. "Quick," he said, "get three seahs of the finest flour and knead it and bake some bread."

Then he ran to the herd and selected a choice, tender calf and gave it to a servant, who hurried to prepare it. He then brought some curds and milk and the calf that had been prepared, and set these before them. While they ate, he stood near them under a tree.

"Where is your wife Sarah?" they asked him.

"There, in the tent," he said.

Then one of them said, "I will surely return to you about this time next year, and Sarah your wife will have a son."

Now Sarah was listening at the entrance to the tent, which was behind him. Abraham and Sarah were already very old, and Sarah was past the age of childbearing. So Sarah laughed to herself as she thought, "After I am worn out and my lord is old, will I now have this pleasure?"

Then *the Lord said to Abraham,* "Why did Sarah laugh and say, 'Will I really have a child, now that I am old?' Is anything too hard for the Lord? I will return to you at the appointed time next year, and Sarah will have a son."

Sarah was afraid, so she lied and said, "I did not laugh."

But he said, "Yes, you did laugh."

When the men got up to leave, they looked down toward Sodom, and Abraham walked along with them to see them on their way. Then *the Lord said,* "Shall I hide from Abraham what I am about to do? Abraham will surely become a great and powerful nation, and all nations on earth will be blessed through him. For I have chosen him, so that he will direct his children and his household after him to keep the way of the Lord by doing what is right and just, so that the Lord will bring about for Abraham what he has promised him."

Then the Lord said, "The outcry against Sodom and Gomorrah is so great and their sin so grievous that I will go down and see if what they have done is as bad as the outcry that has reached me. If not, I will know."

The men turned away and went toward Sodom, but Abraham remained standing before the Lord. *Then Abraham approached him* and said: "Will you sweep away the righteous with the wicked? What if there are fifty righteous people in the city? Will you really sweep it away and not spare the place for the sake of the fifty righteous people in it? Far be it from you to do such a thing—to kill the righteous with the wicked, treating the righteous and the wicked alike. Far be it from you! Will not the Judge of all the earth do right?"

The Lord said, "If I find fifty righteous people in the city of Sodom, I will spare the whole place for their sake."

Then Abraham spoke up again: "Now that I have been so bold as to speak to the Lord, though I am nothing but dust and ashes, what if the number of the righteous is five less than fifty? Will you destroy the whole city for lack of five people?"

"If I find forty-five there," he said, "I will not destroy it."

Once again he spoke to him, "What if only forty are found there?" he said.

"For the sake of forty, I will not do it."

Then he said, "May the Lord not be angry, but let me speak. What if only thirty can be found there?"

He answered, "I will not do it if I find thirty there."

Abraham said, "Now that I have been so bold as to speak to the Lord, what if only twenty can be found there?"

He said, "For the sake of twenty, I will not destroy it."

Then he said, "May the Lord not be angry, but let me speak just once more. What if only ten can be found there?"

He answered, "For the sake of ten, I will not destroy it."

When the Lord had finished speaking with Abraham, he left, and Abraham returned home. (Gen 18:1–33 NIV)

In this passage, it is clear one of the three men who were with Abraham was the LORD, and he was there *physically*. This passage repeatedly tells us Abraham *saw* the LORD, as one of the three men; Abraham *approached* him when the other two men went away—those other two men who went away to Sodom are the two angels Lot encounters at the gates of Sodom and invites into his home (Gen 19:1). The third "man" that remained with Abraham was the LORD, God himself, who was *physically* there, whom Abraham *sees* and *talks* with, and whom Abraham *approaches*.

No Human Being Has Seen the Father

The Bible clearly tells us no human being has ever seen the Father (John 1:18; 5:37; 6:46), and yet, in each of the above instances, human beings specifically and physically saw God with their eyes: Moses saw God with his eyes, and talked with him face to face; Jacob saw God with his eyes, and wrestled with him; Job saw God with his eyes; Adam and Eve both physically walked and talked with God in Eden; Abraham saw, talked, and interacted with God.

How can this be, since no human being has ever seen the Father? It is because in each of these cases it was not the Father with whom they were interacting, or whom they were seeing. In each and every one of these cases, it was God the Son with whom they were interacting, God the Son whom they were seeing.

What did Moses, Jacob, Job, Adam, Eve, and Abraham see when they saw God? Their eyes would have seen his form, a form which would have had the appearance of a human form, having the appearance of a face, a back, a hand, eyes, and so forth. In each case, they would have seen the divine form of God the Son, the form in whose likeness Adam was created.

The great majority, or possibly even all, of the times a human being in the Old Testament meets with, speaks with, or encounters God, they are meeting, speaking with, or encountering God the Son, not God the Father—no human being has ever seen the Father (John 6:46), but they have seen the Son.

Other Descriptions of Seeing God in the Old Testament

There are also other instances in Scripture where a man *sees* God and gives a physical description of him:

> In my vision at night I looked, and there before me was one *like a son of man*, coming with the clouds of heaven. He approached *the Ancient of Days* and was led into his presence. (Dan 7:13 NIV)

> As I looked, "thrones were set in place, and the *Ancient of Days* took his seat. His clothing was as white as snow; *the hair of his head was white like wool*. His throne was flaming with fire, and its wheels were all ablaze." (Dan 7:9 NIV).

> And among the lampstands was someone *like a son of man*, dressed in a robe reaching down to his feet and with a golden sash around his chest. *The hair on his head was white like wool, as white as snow.* (Rev 1:13–14 NIV).

In these passages, Daniel sees God and describes him as looking like a "son of man," that is, he describes God as looking like a human being, appearing as having a human form.

Revelation further describes that same being of Daniel's vision in a similar way as does Daniel, describing him as one "like a son of man" and with hair "white as wool." In Revelation, though, it is made clear the being who looks "like a son of man," whose hair is white as wool, is in fact Jesus Christ, God the Son. Therefore, Revelation 1:13–14 affirms the person whom Daniel describes in Daniel 7 as being "like a son of man," as looking *human*, is the same person as described in Revelation 1:13–14—it is Jesus Christ, God the Son. In Daniel 7:13 and 7:9, Daniel is *seeing* the preincarnate Jesus Christ, God the Son, and is accurately describing what he sees. When Daniel sees and describes the pre-Incarnate God the Son as someone "like a son of man," as *looking* human, this would in fact be an accurate description of the *pre-Incarnate* divine form of God the Son. This is a further affirmation of God the Son having an uncreated divine form as part of his divine nature.

Since the Bible clearly tells us no man has seen the Father, and since we know Moses, Abraham, Jacob, Adam, Eve and Job specifically and physically *saw* God *with their eyes*, we therefore know with certainty it was Jesus whom they were seeing. As a result, throughout the Old Testament, when a human being meets with, speaks with, or sees God, they are meeting with, speaking with, or seeing God the Son, and *not* God the Father, and the form which they saw with their eyes was the uncreated divine form of God the Son, the divine form in whose likeness Adam, and all humanity, was created.

Why is it God the Son Who Interacts with Humanity?

God is a Trinity, three distinct persons who together are the one God, and God has determined it would be through the person of the Son that God would unite himself with his bride, his companion: mankind.

Jesus, God the Son, is the creator of all things—the entire Trinity was involved in all of the creation, but it seems it was specifically through the person of the Son that the creation was executed and brought into being, called forth by the Word of God, the *speaking* of God, who *spoke* all things into being. Likewise, it was God the Son who spoke man into creation, creating him in both the image *and likeness* of himself.

Why was it God the Son who executed the creation? Why was it God the Son who thereafter is the one who was regularly engaging with humanity? The reason for this is it would be God the Son, not God the Father, who would be marrying humanity, who would be uniting God with his companion, with his bride. That uniting of God with man is one of the specific roles defined for God the Son—it is God the Son who would become Incarnate God, who would become man and God forever and inseparably united within his own incarnate nature, uniting man and God within himself. It is therefore the role of God the Son, from the beginning, to be the one to engage and interact with humanity throughout history. It is the bridegroom making preparation for his bride.

God the Son, the Second Adam

Throughout the Bible, the nature and person of God the Son are made clear. We see from the Bible God the Son is one of the three persons of the Trinity who, in his divine nature, was equal with the God the Father. God the Son was the person of the Trinity who executed the creation, bringing it into being, speaking it into existence as the eternal Word of God. It is God the Son who is the Judge of all things, of the entire creation. We see it was specifically God the Son who was regularly engaging and interacting with humanity from the beginning, the bridegroom interacting with his future bride.

God had destined this for himself, that it would be through the person of God the Son that the union of God and man, the union of God with his companion, with his bride, would be accomplished. This union between God and man would require the redemption of fallen humanity. The redemption of humanity would begin with the incarnation, for it is with the incarnation that God the Son would be born the Second Adam.

13

The Incarnation

"The Word became flesh and made his dwelling among us."
(John 1:14 NIV)

THE INCARNATION OF JESUS Christ, God the Son, together with the cross and the resurrection, is the greatest of all events in the history of creation. With the incarnation, God the Son united himself with Adam's created humanity, being born a son of Adam, becoming fully human forever, coming to have the exact same created humanity as us. The incarnation was the birth of the Second Adam. But what did it mean for God the Son to become incarnate? What did it mean for him to take on human flesh? And why did he do it?

Begotten Not Created

To become incarnate means to "take on human flesh," and the incarnation of Jesus Christ was the Son of God taking on human flesh. Adam was the son of God (Luke 3:38; Gen 1:26), but he was the *created* son of God, whereas Jesus Christ, the Second Adam, was the *begotten* son of God:

> I will declare the decree: The Lord has said to Me, 'You are My Son, today I have begotten You.' (Ps 2:7 NKJV).

> And the Word became flesh and dwelt among us, and we beheld his glory, the glory as of the only begotten of the Father, full of grace and truth. (John 1:14 NKJV)

> He who believes in him is not condemned; but he who does not believe is condemned already, because he has not believed in the name of the only begotten Son of God. (John 3:18 NKJV)

> For to which of the angels did he ever say: 'You are My Son, Today I have begotten You'? And again: 'I will be to him a Father, And he shall be to Me a Son'? (Heb 1:5 NKJV)

> In this the love of God was manifested toward us, that God has sent his only begotten Son into the world, that we might live through him. (1 John 4:9 NKJV)

To be *begotten* and to be *created* are two very different things. To be *created* means to be made by God *outside of* and *apart from* himself. Adam was *created* by God, just as a tree was created by God, created outside of God as a separate thing from God. Adam was created in the image and likeness of God (Gen 1:26), whereas trees, animals, and plants were not, and so Adam was unique among all of God's creation. But Adam was nonetheless a created being, a being who had a beginning.

To be *begotten*, on the other hand, means God physically *reproduced himself* in his own *offspring*, generating a son from his own divine nature, so that his Son is the reproduction of himself. A begotten Son is not *created outside of* or *apart from* God, but rather, is a Son who is *born of* God, born of *the same essence* as is God, born of the same *divine nature* as is God, having the same divine nature as his Father. As a result, like God, the *begotten* Son, in his nature, is himself eternal, without beginning and without end (Heb 7:3); he is exactly as much God as is God the Father (Heb 1:8–9). By begetting a Son with a human woman, God's begotten Son would be the union of the two natures, the union of God's uncreated divine nature with the created human flesh of the woman, a Son who would be both fully human and fully divine, with the two natures becoming united within himself as one new nature. This is the incarnation—the physical union of divinity with humanity, an eternal and inseparable union, in the person of the begotten Son of God. Where Adam was the created son of God, Jesus, the Second Adam, was the *only begotten* son of God, fully human and fully divine.

The Incarnation—Impregnating a Human Woman

The act of God begetting Jesus Christ was the result of God impregnating a human woman. How was this impregnation accomplished? The Gospel of Luke gives us a detailed account:

> The angel went to her and said, 'Greetings, you who are highly favored! The Lord is with you.'
> Mary was greatly troubled at his words and wondered what kind of greeting this might be. But the angel said to her, 'Do not be afraid, Mary; you have found favor with God. You will conceive and give birth to a son, and you are to call him Jesus. He will be great and will be called the Son of the Most High. The Lord God will give him the throne of his father David, and he will reign over Jacob's descendants forever; his kingdom will never end.'
> 'How will this be,' Mary asked the angel, 'since I am a virgin?'
> The angel answered, 'The Holy Spirit will come on you, and the power of the Most High will overshadow you. So the holy one to be born will be called the Son of God' (Luke 1:28–35 NIV)

God the Holy Spirit *came upon* Mary, a virgin, and impregnated her with himself, reproducing himself in union with her flesh, within her womb. This impregnation resulted in the physical conception of God's begotten Son within Mary's womb. Mary's Son would be the literal, physical, human, and divine Son of God, as well as the son of man, the offspring of man and God, begotten of God.

The Incarnation—Fully Human and Fully God

As a result of being the begotten offspring of God and of the woman, Jesus Christ is both *fully* human and *fully* God:

> While we wait for the blessed hope—the appearing of the glory of our great *God* and Savior, *Jesus Christ*. (Titus 2:13 NIV)

> For if the many died by the trespass of the one man, how much more did God's grace and the gift that came by the grace of *the one man, Jesus Christ*, overflow to the many! (Rom 5:15 NIV)

> How much more will those who receive God's abundant provision of grace and of the gift of righteousness reign in life through *the one man, Jesus Christ!* (Rom 5:17 NIV)

> For there is one *God* and one mediator between *God* and mankind, *the man Christ Jesus*. (1 Tim 2:5 NIV)

The Bible is very clear—the Incarnate Jesus Christ is *both* God *and* man. He is not 50 percent God and 50 percent man; rather, he is *fully* 100 percent God and *fully* 100 percent man. His full divinity and his full humanity are completely, inextricably, and eternally united, a new inseparable, unbreakable nature of 100 percent God/man. This God/man nature belongs uniquely to Jesus Christ, and it is now and forever his eternal nature. The Second Adam is fully God and fully man, joined forever as one.

The Incarnation—Letting Go of His Equality with God the Father

Prior to his incarnation, God the Son was equal with God the Father, for the Son was the creator of all things, the Word who spoke all things into being (John 1:3; Col 1:16–17).

> Though he was God, he did not think of equality with God as something to cling to. (Phil 2:6 NLT)

> He also says to the Son, 'In the beginning, Lord, you laid the foundation of the earth and made the heavens with your hands.' (Heb 1:10 NLT)

> Now, Father, bring me into the glory *we shared* before the world began. (John 17:5 NLT)

God the Son *was* equal with the Father, but when Jesus became incarnate, taking on Adam's humanity, he *let go* of his equality with the Father so that, once he became incarnate, Jesus was *no longer equal with the Father*.

> Though he was God, he did not think of equality with God as something to cling to. Instead, he gave up his divine privileges; he took the humble position of a slave and was born as a human being. When he appeared in human form, he humbled himself in obedience to God and died a criminal's death on a cross. (Phil 2:6–8 NLT)

> You heard me say, 'I am going away and I am coming back to you.' If you loved me, you would be glad that I am going to the Father, for *the Father is greater than I*.' (John 14:28 NIV)

> But about that day or hour *no one knows,* not even the angels in heaven, *nor the Son,* but only the Father. (Matt 24:36 NIV)

Even though God the Son was equal with the Father, by letting go of his equality with the Father upon his incarnation, the Father is now greater than the Son, because the Father never became man. Jesus is eternally Incarnate God/man, and, as a result, Jesus will never again be equal with the Father. In becoming incarnate, Jesus let go of his equality with the Father *forever.* This was the true and unfathomable cost of our salvation.

The Incarnation—The Original Form of Divinity Versus Adam's Humanity

We know with certainty the original uncreated divine form of the Son was *not* a human form, *not* a human physicality, *not* a form of flesh and bone. We know this as a certainty since Adam's *human form* was a *created* form, created from the dust of the earth. The very Earth whose dust formed Adam's physical substance was itself created by God (Gen 1:1). Since Adam's form was a created humanity made from the dust of the earth, it is therefore impossible that the original *uncreated* divine form of the Son could be of the same *created* substance as was Adam's created humanity. The original divine form of the Son, the form in whose *likeness* Adam was created, was not the same flesh-and-bone humanity of Adam, was not a form made from the dust of the earth, nor was it in any way a created form—rather, it was an eternal, *uncreated* divine form, a form that was in every way the very essence and nature of God the Son.

We also know with certainty the substance of the original divine form of the Son was *not* a form of flesh in any way whatsoever, since we are told specifically that, at the incarnation, "the Word *became* flesh" (John 1:14). This clearly tells us the original divine form was not a form whose substance was flesh, since flesh is what the original divine form *took on* at the incarnation. As a result, we can know the original divine form of the Son was of a different essence than was the created human form of Adam, for our human form is a *created* form, made from earthly dust, a form of flesh and bone.

It may be the essence and substance of the Son's original divine form was an essence of Spirit, but even if it was a form whose essence and substance was Spirit, it was still certainly a *definable* form, a form with the appearance of a head, arms, legs, hands, face, mouth, eyes, ears—this is inarguable, for it was the divine form in whose likeness Adam was made.

The Divine Form Subsumed into Adam's Created Humanity

If God the Son had an original uncreated divine form, then what happened to that divine form upon the incarnation? In becoming incarnate, God the Son, in his original and uncreated divine form, took on, or *wedded himself* to, Adam's *created* humanity. God the Son *subsumed* his own eternal, uncreated divine form and his full divinity *into* Adam's created human flesh.

When God the Holy Spirit impregnated Mary (Matt 1:18), God's Son was begotten, reproduced, conceived in Mary's womb. In that moment of conception, it was the Son who made alive the conception within Mary's womb, and he did so by simultaneously and inextricably wedding himself with Adam's humanity within Mary. At his conception, at the moment of his incarnation within Mary's womb, he came to fully inhabit the entirety of humanity, fully inhabiting it with his full-begotten divinity, not just inhabiting it as a sort of "coming to live inside" kind of thing, as if it was a core of divinity with an outer shell of humanity, but rather, he inextricably married and united his divine self utterly and totally, in every essence, to Adam's created humanity and to its every essence. At the incarnation, Jesus did not become two natures coexisting side by side within his human form; rather, he became *one completely new nature*, a nature that is *only* his, a *single nature* that is the complete, total, absolute, and inseparable union of divinity and humanity.

It is exactly as when a man and a woman have a child. A child is not half its mother and half its father, in some sort of divisible way; rather, the child is wholly and uniquely a new being, an indivisible union of mother and father—impossible to separate apart, with mother and father forever and permanently entwined and made one in the person of their child. It is the same with the incarnation—Jesus Christ is wholly and uniquely the indivisible union of mother and Father—the inseparable union of created humanity with uncreated divinity, forever and permanently entwined as one new nature in the person of Jesus Christ. This union happened at the moment of his conception, his incarnation.

From the incarnation onward, upon subsuming his own uncreated divine self into Adam's created humanity, Jesus' eternal form became, now and forevermore, a form of *created flesh and bone*. Since the incarnation, Jesus' form is now the form of a *human body* (Luke 24:39), it is the form and substance of created humanity made one with divinity, a physical form whose substance is of the dust of Earth. Jesus' incarnation, his union with created humanity, humanity and divinity made one within his own body, is forever.

The Son of Man

Throughout the Gospels, Jesus refers to himself, more than any other way, as "the Son of man." The Aramaic and Hebrew word for "man" is similar to the name "Adam," so when Jesus refers to himself as the "Son of man," he is in fact affirming he is the "son of Adam." In calling himself the "son of man," Jesus is affirming he is both fully the Son of God and fully the son of Adam, an affirmation of humanity and divinity united forever and inseparably as one

The Humanity of Jesus Christ—Did He Have the Sinful Nature?

The Bible clearly tells us Jesus, the incarnate Son of God, had no sin (2 Cor 5:21; Heb 4:15; 1 John 3:5). But if Jesus was born fully human, having the exact same humanity as Adam, then how could Jesus be born without sin? The sinful nature resides within Adam's blood, and Adam's blood flowed through Jesus' veins—how then could Jesus have Adam's blood flowing through his veins and yet still be born without sin?

To understand how Jesus could be fully human, with Adam's blood flowing through his veins, and yet still be born without sin, we need to understand sin and death came into the world, and to all people, through one *man*:

> Therefore, just as *sin entered the world through one man*, and *death through sin*, and in this way *death came to all people*, because all sinned—To be sure, sin was in the world before the law was given, but sin is not charged against anyone's account where there is no law. Nevertheless, death reigned from the time of Adam to the time of Moses, even over those who did not sin by breaking a command, as did Adam, who is a pattern of the one to come. But the gift is not like the trespass. For if *the many died by the trespass of the one man*, how much more did God's grace and the gift that came by the grace of the one man, Jesus Christ,

overflow to the many! Nor can the gift of God be compared with the result of one man's sin: The judgment followed one sin and brought condemnation, but the gift followed many trespasses and brought justification. For if, by *the trespass of the one man, death reigned through that one man*, how much more will those who receive God's abundant provision of grace and of the gift of righteousness reign in life through the one man, Jesus Christ! (Rom 5:12–17 NIV)

Sin did not enter the world through one man and one woman, it entered the world *only* through one *man*—through *Adam*. It was Adam *alone* who was commanded not to eat from the forbidden fruit, receiving that commandment from God before Eve was even created; it was Adam *alone* who caused the fall by eating that fruit—when Eve ate from that fruit, nothing happened, but when Adam ate from that fruit, then Eve, and everything else, fell. It was Adam and Adam a*lone*—our *father*, not our mother Eve—who brought sin and death into the world.

We are clearly told all people die only because of the trespass of the *one man*, Adam, not by the trespass of the one woman, Eve. We are told by the sin of that *one man*, Adam, death reigns *through* that *man* and, in that way, death comes to all people, to all humanity. The clear conclusion is this: the sinful nature is passed on through humanity by the *man*, not by the woman. We, humanity, have the sinful nature passed on to us by our human *fathers* and not by our human mothers. Just as sin and death were passed on to all humanity by Adam, passed on to us through his blood, so the sinful nature continues to be passed on to us by our human *fathers*, never through our human mothers—*only the father* passes on the sinful nature to his children, through his blood.

How then can Jesus be born fully human, with the exact same humanity as Adam, having Adam's blood flowing through his veins, and yet *not* be born with the sinful nature? It is because Jesus did not have a human father. Even though Jesus' mother, Mary, was fully human and had the sinful nature within her, his Father was not human; his Father was God. Since the sinful nature is passed on to the children only by their human father, and not by their human mother, and since Jesus' Father was not human, Jesus did not receive the sinful nature. And so Jesus was born fully human, yet he was born without the sinful nature—he had no sinful nature residing in his blood. This is clearly affirmed when Jesus' *blood* is described as being *precious*, and as being *without blemish or defect*:

> For you know that it was not with perishable things such as silver or gold that you were redeemed from the empty way of life handed down to you from your ancestors, but with the *precious blood of Christ,* a lamb without blemish or defect. (1 Pet 1:18–19 NIV)

Jesus Christ was fully human and yet was born *without* the sinful nature, and so his blood is precious, pure, and *sinless.*

The Sinful Nature—Women are Saved through Childbearing

An additional affirmation of the fact that the woman does not pass on the sinful nature to her children is found in 1 Timothy 2:15: "But women will be saved through childbearing" (NIV). How will women be saved through childbearing? Does this verse mean women are breeding machines and the more children a woman has the more likely she will be saved? No, certainly not; rather, it is an affirmation that a woman does not pass on the sinful nature to her children.

Salvation is made possible specifically as a result of the woman not passing on the sinful nature to her children. By not passing on the sinful nature to her children, it is the woman who makes possible the eventual birth of the Second Adam, a man who would be born without sin. Since the woman, the mother, would be fully human, her offspring would have her full humanity, having Adam's full, created humanity. But in having an offspring whose Father is God, and because the woman does not pass on the sinful nature to her children, then the human offspring of the woman would *not* be born with the sinful nature, for the mother cannot pass the sinful nature on to her children. Therefore, because the woman cannot pass the sinful nature on to her children, it is the woman who makes possible the birth of a sinless Savior, a Savior who would be fully and completely human, but who would be born with no sin residing within him. By not passing on the sinful nature to her children, it is the woman, and her childbearing, who makes salvation possible.

The Incarnation—Adam, Round Two

The incarnation was the full and unbreakable union of divinity with humanity, whereby God the Son became fully human and yet remained fully God, becoming an eternally inseparable union of divinity and humanity intertwined forever. Although Jesus had a human mother, he did not have a human father, and as a result he was born without the sinful nature. The sinful nature resides in our blood, and since Jesus had no sin his blood is described as precious, without blemish or defect. As a result, the Incarnate Jesus had the exact same perfect, sinless humanity as did Adam before the fall. The Second Adam, Jesus Christ, would be Adam, Round Two.

Like the First Adam, the Second Adam was perfect man. Like the First Adam, he was morally, spiritually, and intellectually perfect, fully indwelt by the Holy Spirit. Like the First Adam, he was a moral being, capable of sin, but also capable of choosing not to sin. Like the First Adam, he would be the father of a new humanity. As the Second Adam, he would represent all humanity before God in regards to sin.

In that capacity of representing all humanity before God in regards to sin, the Second Adam would be the high priest of humanity. As the high priest of humanity he would have the authority to take the sin of all humanity and lay it upon the sacrifice for that sin, the sacrifice that would take away, or break the power of, the entirety of that sin. The Second Adam, Jesus Christ, would himself *be* that sacrifice for the sin of humanity. His sacrifice would be the one sacrifice that would bring a permanent breaking of the power of sin over humanity, accomplished by bringing the entire sin of humanity to completion and conclusion in death. By bringing that sin to full completion and conclusion in his death, the Second Adam would reverse and redeem the fall of the First Adam—the blood of the Second Adam would take away all the sin brought into the world by the blood of the First Adam. This would be the accomplishment of the Second man, the Last Adam, the high priest of humanity.

14

The Second Man, the Last Adam, the High Priest

IT IS ESTIMATED THE population of the world at the time of the flood (ca. 3,800–3,700 BC) ranged from 7 to 15 billion people. From the time of the flood to the time of Jesus Christ it is estimated that there would have lived another 3-plus billion people, giving a total of anywhere from 10 to 18 billion people having lived from the time of Adam to the time of Jesus Christ. And yet we are told the following: "'The first man Adam became a living being'; the last Adam, a life-giving spirit. The spiritual did not come first, but the natural, and after that the spiritual. The first man was of the dust of the earth; the second man is of heaven" (1 Cor 15:45–47 NIV). How can Jesus be called the *second* man if billions of people had lived between the time of Adam and the time of Jesus Christ? Wouldn't Jesus be the 10 billionth man or so? How are we to understand this?

Man as Man was Meant to Be

Adam was the created son of God (Luke 3:38), created perfect and sinless—perfect in his mind, emotions, and will, spiritually and physically perfect, completely without sin, fully indwelt by the Holy Spirit, and with a perfect relationship with God. Jesus was the begotten Son of God (Heb 1:5 NKJV), begotten as perfect and sinless—perfect in his mind, emotions, and will, perfect spiritually, completely without sin, fully indwelt by the Holy Spirit, and with a perfect relationship with God.

Throughout humanity, only Adam and Jesus Christ were human sons of God—between Adam and Jesus Christ, no other human being was a son of God. All human beings are created by God, and God is the creator of all mankind, but God is not the *father* of all human beings. Human beings are sons of God only if they were *created* sons of God, as was Adam, or *begotten* sons of God, as was Jesus Christ, or *adopted* sons of God, as are Christians (Rom 8:15; Gal 4:5; Eph 1:5). Throughout the entirety of human history, only the created Adam, the begotten Jesus Christ, and the adopted Christians are sons of God. Every other use of the term "sons of God" in the Old Testament is solely and exclusively in reference to angels (Job 1:6; 2:1; 38:7; Gen 6:2). No human being in the Old Testament ever calls God "Father."

By being created as perfect and sinless, being in perfect union and fellowship with God, Adam, the son of God, was man as man was meant to be. By being begotten as perfect and sinless, being in perfect union and fellowship with God, Jesus Christ, the Son of God, was also man as man was meant to be. As a result, even though there would have lived many billions of people between Adam and Jesus Christ, Jesus Christ was in fact the Second Man, the second human son of God, the Second Man who was man as man was meant to be—perfect and sinless, in perfect union and fellowship with God. Adam was the First Man, and Jesus Christ was the Second Man.

The Last Adam

In addition to being called the Second Man, Jesus Christ is also called the Last Adam. What does it mean for Jesus to be the Last Adam? To be an "Adam" is to be a father of humanity. Adam was the physical first father of all humanity, all human beings are his children and his descendants: "Your *first father* sinned; those I sent to teach you rebelled against me" (Isa 43:27 NIV). Just as Adam was the physical father of all humanity, so Jesus Christ would father a new humanity by his Spirit: 'The first man Adam became a living being'; the last Adam, a life-giving spirit" (1 Cor 15:45).

Adam was our physical father, our father by way of his body, but Jesus Christ would be a life-giving spirit, fathering a new humanity, giving that new humanity birth and life, by way of his Spirit. How do we become born of Jesus Christ, born of his Spirit? We become born of his Spirit by *believing* in him. When we believe in him, his Spirit comes and births new life in us. It is when we believe in Jesus Christ we are born sons of God: "For you are all sons of God through faith in Christ Jesus" (Gal 3:26 NKJV). It is in this way, by way of his Spirit, Jesus Christ would father a new humanity. By being the father of a new humanity, Jesus Christ is an "Adam." Though Jesus would in fact be the Second Adam, he is not referred to as the Second Adam; rather, he is specifically called the *Last* Adam. Why?

To be the *Last* Adam means Jesus Christ would be the *Final* Adam. In being the Final Adam, it means after Jesus Christ there would never again be another Adam who would father a new humanity—Jesus Christ would be the final chance at birthing a new humanity. The new humanity Jesus Christ would father would be a redeemed humanity, and, as the Last Adam, Jesus would be the last and final means through which a new and redeemed humanity could be born (Eph 1:7). Jesus Christ is therefore both the Second Man, being man as man was intended to be, and also the Last Adam, the last and final father of a new humanity.

Heirs of Our Father's Actions

As Adam's children, we inherit our human natures and our blood from Adam—the blood that flows through human veins, together with the sinful nature contained therein, is Adam's blood. Our flesh and blood, God's image and likeness, and our sinful nature, is our physical inheritance from Adam, our first father. Also, as Adam's physical descendants, we are heirs of Adam's *choice* and *actions*. Adam sinned in Eden and as a result we are heirs to his sin, inheriting the sinful nature and inheriting death from him: "For as in Adam all die . . ." (1 Cor 15:22 NASB).

Likewise, just Adam, our first father, determined the fate of the entire human race by his actions, by his choices and ultimately by his sin, so Jesus Christ, the new Adam, would determine the fate of the entire human race by his actions, by his choices and, ultimately, by his sinless life. As a result, by being born of Jesus Christ, we would then become heirs of *his* choices, of his actions and accomplishments. If Jesus Christ, the Second Adam, would defeat sin and death, then we, by being born of him and by being his heirs, would also have that same victory over sin and death, for that victory over sin and death would be our inheritance, an inheritance that would be ours once we believe in him and become born as his children by way of his Spirit. This victory over sin and death the Bible describes as eternal life:

> For God so loved the world that he gave his only begotten Son, that whoever believes in him should not perish but have everlasting life. (John 3:16 NKJV)

> Heirs of God and joint heirs with Christ, if indeed we suffer with *him,* that we may also be glorified together. (Rom 8:17 NKJV)

> Having been justified by his grace we should become heirs according to the hope of eternal life. (Titus 3:7 NKJV)

The Last Adam, Jesus Christ, would make a new inheritance available to his children, an inheritance of eternal life, so those who would believe in him would be heirs to his life, his choices, his actions, and his conquest of sin and death.

As a result, we see Jesus Christ and Adam were in the exact same position of perfection and sinlessness in regards to both God and man, with each being the father of humanity—Adam being our physical father, and Jesus Christ fathering a new humanity by way of his Spirit—and with the actions and choices of each coming to define future humanity. Ultimately it is the life, choices, and actions of the Last Adam that would redeem the life, choices, and actions of the First Adam.

Adam—The Pattern of the One to Come

In addition to being described as our first father, the Bible describes Adam as a *pattern* of the Second Adam to come: "Nevertheless, death reigned from the time of Adam to the time of Moses, even over those who did not sin by breaking a command, as did Adam, who *is a pattern of the one to come*" (Rom 5:14 NIV). This verse specifically connects Adam with Jesus Christ, for in being a pattern of the one to come, Adam is a pattern for Jesus Christ. To be the "pattern of the one to come" means everything Adam was—the father of humanity, the one whose choice and actions would define humanity—is a *pattern* of what Jesus Christ would also be, meaning Jesus Christ would also be the father of a new humanity, would also be one whose choice and actions would define humanity. Adam and Jesus Christ are interchangeable fathers of humanity—interchangeable in that as the actions and choices of Adam brought ruin to humanity, so the actions and choices of Jesus Christ could bring redemption to humanity.

The High Priest

In addition to being the Second man and the Last Adam, Jesus Christ is also described as the high priest of humanity:

> Therefore, in all things he had to be made like his brethren, that he might be a merciful and faithful High Priest in things pertaining to God, to make propitiation for the sins of the people. (Heb 2:17 NKJV).

> Therefore, holy brethren, partakers of the heavenly calling, consider the apostle and High Priest of our confession, Christ Jesus. (Heb 3:1 NKJV)

> Seeing then that we have a great High Priest who has passed through the heavens, Jesus the Son of God, let us hold fast our confession. For we do not have a High Priest who cannot sympathize with our weaknesses, but was in all points tempted as we are, yet without sin." (Heb 4:14–15 NKJV)

> So also Christ did not glorify himself to become high priest, but it was he who said to him:
> "You are My Son, Today I have begotten You." As he also says in another place: "You are a priest forever according to the order of Melchizedek"; who, in the days of his flesh, when he had offered up prayers and supplications, with vehement cries and tears to him who was able to save him from death, and was heard because of his godly fear, though he was a Son, yet he learned obedience by the things which he suffered. And having been perfected, he became the author of eternal salvation to all who obey him, called by God as High Priest "according to the order of Melchizedek," of whom we have much to say, and hard to explain, since you have become dull of hearing." (Heb 5:5–11 NKJV)

> This hope we have as an anchor of the soul, both sure and steadfast, and which enters the presence behind the veil, where the forerunner has entered for us, even Jesus, having become High Priest forever according to the order of Melchizedek. (Heb 6:19–20 NKJV)

Jesus Christ is described as the high priest of humanity, described as a high priest forever, in the order of Melchizedek. What does it mean for Jesus to be a high priest?

The High Priest—Our Representative

To be a high priest of humanity is not the same as being an Adam. As an Adam, Jesus Christ would father a new humanity, but as high priest, he would also *represent* humanity before God and God to all humanity. Adam was *not* our *representative*, he was our *father*. It is because Adam was not our representative that Adam was incapable of taking the sin of humanity and laying it onto a sacrifice for that sin. The reason Adam was incapable of taking the sin of humanity and laying it onto a sacrifice for that sin is because Adam himself had sin; only by being without sin can one be a representative of humanity and have the authority to take the sin of humanity and lay it onto the sacrifice for that sin. Adam was our father, but he was not our representative.

Jesus Christ, though, in addition to being the Last Adam, the final Father of a new humanity, would *also* be our representative, being so by virtue of his office as high priest, for it is the entire purpose of a high priest to represent humanity before God. This office of being the high priest of humanity is clearly illustrated by the Levitical priesthood of the Old Testament and the office of the high priest of Israel.

The High Priest of Israel

The role of the high priest of Israel was to represent all Israel before God and to represent God to all Israel. It was the role of the high priest to perform the annual sin sacrifice for the whole nation of Israel on the Day of Atonement (Lev 16) so the sins of Israel would be *taken away* and Israel could receive *forgiveness* (not punishment) for its sins. In this role, the high priest of Israel represented Israel to God, and God to Israel. This representation is an illustration of the role Jesus would fulfill as the high priest of *humanity*, representing all *humanity* to God and representing God to all humanity.

Most importantly, however, the high priest of Israel had the *authority* to take the sin of the people, the sin of all the nation, and *place that sin upon the sin sacrifice* so as to make atonement for the sin of the people. The high priest had that authority by virtue of his position as high priest.

The Levitical Priesthood—Sinlessness and the Laying on of Hands

In order to be able to perform the Day of Atonement sacrifice for the sin of the nation of Israel, the high priest *first* had to make sacrifice for *himself*. This was a necessity and represented the fact the high priest who was to make the sacrifice on behalf of the nation must himself be without sin. This picture of the high priest being without sin was an illustration of the coming Jesus Christ and of his position as high priest of humanity, for Jesus himself would *actually* be without sin, and by being without sin he would have the authority to take the sin of humanity and lay it upon the sacrifice for that sin.

Also, the Old Testament high priest would physically transfer the sin of the people onto the sacrifice by the laying on of his hands onto the sacrifice. With that laying on of hands, the sin of the people would be physically transferred through the high priest and come to rest upon the sacrifice, coming to inhabit that sacrifice's sinless blood. This laying on of hands demonstrated the necessity of a physical connection between the high priest and the sacrifice in order for the transfer of sin to be accomplished.

This laying on of hands by the high priest was an illustration of the coming Jesus Christ who, as the high priest of humanity, would also have the authority to physically transfer and lay the sin of humanity upon the sacrifice for that sin, with that transfer of sin being accomplished by his physical connection to that sacrifice.

In the case of Jesus Christ, though, it was not necessary for him to lay hands upon the sacrifice in order to transfer that sin onto the sacrifice, for Jesus himself, in his own person, would *be* that very same sacrifice. Jesus Christ would be *both* the high priest of humanity *and* the sacrifice for that sin of humanity—he would lay the sin of humanity upon *himself*. As a result, the physical connection between the high priest and the sacrifice for sin would be already preexisting in his own person since the high priest and the sacrifice would be one and the same.

The office of the high priest of Israel therefore serves as a graphic illustration of Jesus Christ as high priest of all humanity. Just as the Old Testament high priest had the authority to take the sin of the nation and lay it upon the sacrifice for that sin, likewise Jesus Christ, as the high priest and representative of *humanity*, would have the authority to take the sin of humanity and lay it on the sacrifice for that sin—he would have that authority by virtue of his office as high priest of humanity. Just as the high priest of Israel had to be without sin in order to perform the Day of Atonement sacrifice for the nation, likewise Jesus Christ must be without sin in order to perform the sin sacrifice for all humanity. Just as the high priest of Israel had to have a physical connection to the sin sacrifice in order to transfer the sin of the nation onto the sacrifice for that sin, likewise Jesus Christ as high priest of humanity must also have that physical connection with the sin sacrifice so as to lay upon that sacrifice the full sin of humanity. The authority for all of this would belong to Jesus Christ by virtue of his being the high priest of humanity, a High Priest in the order of Melchizedek.

A High Priest in the Order of Melchizedek

Jesus is not described as a high priest in the order of Levi; rather, he is described as a High Priest in the order of *Melchizedek*. To understand the nature of Melchizedek's high priesthood, we must first understand Melchizedek. Who is Melchizedek? He appears in the Bible out of nowhere, in Genesis 14:18: "Then Melchizedek king of Salem brought out bread and wine; he was the priest of God Most High" (NKJV). Melchizedek is described as a priest of God Most High, and yet this was centuries before the Levitical priesthood of Israel was instituted. Since this was not the Levitical priesthood of Israel which God would institute centuries later, then what kind of priesthood was Melchizedek's, and who instituted it?

The Eternal Priesthood

From the Bible's description of Melchizedek, it is clear Melchizedek is not a human being, for Melchizedek is described as having an *eternal* priesthood (Heb 6:20; 7:17, 21).

> For this Melchizedek, king of Salem, priest of the Most High God, who met Abraham returning from the slaughter of the kings and blessed him, to whom also Abraham gave a tenth part of all, first being translated "king of righteousness," and then also king of Salem, meaning "king of peace," *without father, without mother, without genealogy, having neither beginning of*

> days nor end of life, but *made like the Son of God, remains a priest continually.* (Heb 7:1–3 NKJV)

Melchizedek is described as someone who himself is eternal, as someone who was without father and without mother. He is also described as being without genealogy, which means he was without human ancestry. He is also described as having neither beginning of days nor end of life, that is, Melchizedek is described as being eternal. From this we can understand Melchizedek cannot be human, for all human beings, apart from Adam and Eve, have a mother, a father, and human ancestry, and all human beings have a beginning and an end of life. Therefore if Melchizedek is without father or mother or human ancestry, is without beginning of days or end of life, he cannot be human. If Melchizedek is not human, then who is he? This passage specifically and directly references Melchizedek as being made "like the Son of God," Jesus Christ. As a result, the Bible makes a clear and direct connection between Melchizedek and Jesus Christ.

In fact, since the high priest Melchizedek is not human, being without father and without mother, being without genealogy, having neither beginning of days nor end of life, and since Jesus Christ is directly referenced in connection to Melchizedek, most understand Melchizedek as being an appearance of the preincarnate Jesus Christ. It is Jesus Christ, God the Son, who himself *is* Melchizedek, being without human father or mother, being without genealogy, having neither beginning of days nor end of life, remaining a priest continually. The priesthood of Melchizedek is an eternal priesthood. Therefore, as a high priest "in the order of Melchizedek," Jesus Christ would have that same eternal priesthood, a priesthood without beginning or end, a priesthood whose scope was not merely Israel, but rather a priesthood whose scope would be *all humanity*, a priesthood which transcends all time.

Melchizedek and Bread and Wine

This synonymous connection between Melchizedek and Jesus Christ is further affirmed and reinforced when we look at what Melchizedek did when he met with Abraham in Genesis 14:

> Then Melchizedek king of Salem brought out bread and wine; he was the priest of God Most High. (Gen 14:18)

Upon Abraham's victory over Chedorlaomer, Melchizedek appears out of nowhere specifically to have fellowship with Abraham, to celebrate Abraham's victory over Chedorlaomer, and to bless him. This celebration was a special time of fellowship union between Melchizedek and Abraham, and it was a fellowship union which was celebrated by means of . . . bread and wine!

Bread and wine are the same elements as used in communion, instituted later by Jesus Christ before his crucifixion. In fact, we can understand Genesis 14:18 and the fellowship celebration between the high priest Melchizedek and Abraham through the means of bread and wine as being a foreshadowing of the communion of Jesus Christ, which is the special fellowship union between the believer and Jesus Christ through the means of bread and wine (1 Cor 10:14–22). As such, this direct connection between Melchizedek's fellowship celebration with communion further affirms the identification of Melchizedek with Jesus Christ (Heb 5:6).

Melchizedek—King of Salem

Another affirmation of Melchizedek as Jesus Christ is found in Melchizedek's title as "king of Salem." In Genesis 14:18, Melchizedek is specifically described as the king of Salem ("Salem" is the root of Jeru-Salem). The name Salem is also rooted in the Hebrew word *shalom*, which means "peace." When Melchizedek is described as the "king of Salem" he is in fact being described as the "king of peace." The description of Melchizedek as the king of peace echoes one of the titles of Jesus Christ listed in Isaiah: "For unto us a Child is born, unto us a Son is given; And the government will be upon his shoulder. And his name will be called Wonderful, Counselor, Mighty God, Everlasting Father, Prince of Peace" (Isa 9:6 NKJV). The description of Melchizedek as the "king of peace" is synonymous with the description of Jesus Christ as the "Prince of Peace." This synonymous identification of "king of peace" with "Prince of Peace" further affirms the identification of Melchizedek with Jesus Christ.

Melchizedek and Jesus Christ

There is much affirmation within Scripture that Melchizedek is Jesus Christ. By understanding that Melchizedek is Jesus Christ, we can then understand the high priesthood of Jesus by understanding the high priesthood of Melchizedek as it is outlined for us in Scripture. When Jesus is described as a High Priest in the order of Melchizedek, the priesthood of Melchizedek is in fact a description of Jesus' own priesthood. Just as Melchizedek's priesthood is an eternal priesthood, so the priesthood of Jesus Christ is a preexisting, eternal priesthood, a divine priesthood rather than a human priesthood. As such, by being a preexisting, eternal priesthood, the scope of that priesthood is not just Israel, but rather its scope is all humanity. Whereas the Levitical priesthood was for Israel only, Melchizedek's priesthood is for all people. As a result, we can understand that to be a High Priest in the order of Melchizedek is to be the eternal high priest of all humanity.

The Authority of the High Priest of Humanity

It is by being the high priest of all humanity that Jesus Christ would make salvation possible. By being the high priest of humanity, by being the *representative* of all humanity before God, Jesus Christ would have the intrinsic *authority* to take the sin of *all humanity* and transfer it onto the sacrifice for that sin so the sacrifice could then take away the sin of humanity and make forgiveness available to all people.

This authority Jesus would have as high priest of humanity is a different authority than Jesus would have as the Last Adam. In being the Last Adam, Jesus would father a new humanity, but the position of Last Adam does not give him the authority to take the sin of humanity and transfer it upon the sacrifice for that sin. It is only in his role as the high priest of humanity, which role he would have simultaneously with being the Last Adam, that Jesus would have the authority to take the sin of humanity and lay it upon the sacrifice for that sin. Taken together, by being both the Last Adam as well as the high priest of all humanity, Jesus Christ would be able to lay the sin of humanity upon the sacrifice for that sin and also be the father of a new humanity.

The Position of Jesus Christ

The position of Jesus Christ in regards to God and man was as follows—Jesus was the Second Man, the Last Adam, the high priest of all humanity. As the Second Man, Jesus was only the second man ever to be as man was meant to be. As the Last Adam, Jesus would father a new humanity. As high priest of humanity, Jesus would have the authority to take the sin of all humanity and lay it onto the sacrifice for that sin.

The First Adam was a pattern of the one to come, meaning Adam was a pattern of the coming Jesus Christ. Adam was the created son of God, Jesus was the begotten Son of God; Adam was the First Man, Jesus was the Second Man; Adam was perfect and sinless and in perfect union and fellowship with God, Jesus was perfect and sinless and in perfect union and fellowship with God; Adam was the father of humanity, Jesus would become the father of a new humanity; Adam brought sin into the world and to all people through his blood, Jesus would take away the sin of the world through the shedding of his blood; Adam brought death to all people, Jesus would bring life to all who believe in him; Adam gave away the dominion of the earth, Jesus Christ would take back the dominion of the earth. The parallels between Adam and Jesus Christ, between the First Adam and the Last Adam, are exact.

The Sacrifice—The Requirement of Sinlessness

In addition to being the high priest of humanity, having the authority to take the sin of humanity and lay it upon the sacrifice for that sin, Jesus Christ would himself *be* the sacrifice for that sin. In order for Jesus to be the sacrifice for that sin, Jesus would have to be sinless. Jesus was in fact born without sin. Adam, however, was also originally without sin, being created perfect and holy, the sinless son of God (Luke 3:38). But Adam did not remain sinless; Adam sinned. If Jesus was to be the sacrifice for the sin of humanity, then Jesus must not only be born without sin but he must *remain* without sin throughout his entire life, remaining sinless by never committing sin in his life. It is only by remaining sinless throughout his life that Jesus would *conquer* sin, and in conquering sin Jesus would then have *all authority* and *power* over sin.

It was paramount for Jesus to conquer sin by never sinning. As the Second Adam, he would have to be put in a place of testing whereby he would face specific temptation to sin. It is a testing that would echo Adam's testing in Eden. Just as Adam was put in a place of testing to choose whether or not he would sin, so Jesus Christ, the Second Adam, must be put in a place of testing to choose whether or not he would sin. In each case that testing would come by way of Satan. For Adam, that testing took place in the paradise of Eden, for Jesus that testing would take place in the desert wilderness. It would be in the desert wilderness Jesus Christ would face Satan's direct temptation, and would either conquer sin and take authority over it or would commit sin and fail. Without Jesus' victory over sin, there could be no salvation. The fate of humanity would depend on the outcome in the desert.

15

The Temptation in the Desert

JUST AS ADAM WAS tested by facing temptation to sin, so Jesus Christ, the Second Adam, would be tested by facing temptation to sin. It was important the Second Adam be tested just like the First Adam, tested by Satan so he could choose if he would remain obedient to God or if he would sin. It is also important to understand Jesus Christ was capable of choosing to sin, just as was Adam—his temptation to sin was a real temptation, no less real than the temptations all human beings face throughout their lives, and no less real than the temptation Adam faced in Eden.

Eden was the place of testing for the First Adam. In Eden, God placed two trees—the tree of life and the tree of the knowledge of good and evil—in the center of Eden. After God had planted Eden, and after he had placed the two trees in the center of Eden, God then took Adam and placed him in Eden, and gave him one command: to not eat from the fruit of the tree of the knowledge of good and evil. After God gave this one command to Adam, he caused Adam to fall into a deep sleep and then, from Adam, he created the woman, Eve, flesh of Adam's flesh and bone of his bones. The commandment to not eat from the fruit of the tree of the knowledge of good and evil was given by God to Adam, and only to Adam, before Eve was even created. It was Adam and Adam alone who was responsible to keep that one commandment, and it was Adam alone who could break the commandment and commit sin.

The temptation to eat from the tree of the knowledge of good and evil would come from Satan, who was allowed out of the pit, the place of imprisonment for the fallen angels, cast there after their rebellion against God. Satan was allowed out of the pit so he could tempt Adam in Eden, the purpose of which, at the very least, was to answer Satan's accusation against God that Satan did nothing wrong in rebelling against God, but rather that he, Satan, was only acting according to the nature with which God created him. In effect, such an argument blames God for Satan's actions, making God at fault for Satan's rebellion. Trying to cause the fall of man was of immense importance to Satan, as it was his way of justifying his own rebellion. If Adam would sin, Satan could say to God, and to the entire angelic realm, "See, anyone you create will naturally sin against you. It's the natural result of your creation, so I did nothing wrong. I was only acting according to the nature with which you made me."

In Eden, only Adam was given the one commandment to not eat of the fruit of the tree of knowledge of good and evil, and only Adam had to be seduced to eat of the fruit of that tree. Satan had only one chance to try and engender the fall of Adam—he would either succeed or fail, and if he failed, he would have no second chance to tempt Adam, for with his failure to seduce Adam to sin, Satan would have been fully defeated. The fall of man was of extreme importance to Satan, and he put all his mind and intellect into devising a strategy by which he could entice Adam to sin.

In the course of planning this strategy, Satan would have spent considerable time watching, observing, and studying Adam. Satan would have concluded that if he was to approach Adam directly, and tempt him to sin directly, Adam would resist him and Satan would be defeated. In the course of his strategizing, Satan came to know and understand Adam, at one time, had been alone, being without Eve. He would have come to understand it was not good for Adam to be alone, that Adam did not want to be alone again. It was upon this fact that Satan devised his strategy to tempt Adam.

Instead of approaching Adam directly, tempting him to sin directly, Satan devised a strategy whereby he would tempt Adam through Eve, created a situation where Adam would be put in the position of fearing the loss of Eve, fearing he would once again be alone. Satan's gamble was if Adam was put in the position of fearing he would lose Eve, Adam would choose Eve rather than risk losing her and being alone.

This is exactly the scenario that played out in Eden. Eve took the fruit from the tree of the knowledge of good and evil, and ate it. When she ate it, nothing happened, for she did not sin, because she was not the one to whom the commandment was given. In fact, after eating from the fruit of that tree, Eve thought the fruit was good, since nothing happened upon eating it and it tasted good. She then, on her own, went to Adam, and offered him the fruit. When Eve approached Adam with the fruit, fruit from which she had already eaten, that was exactly the moment Satan had tried to set up. Adam was now faced with his wife Eve, the only other human being in all creation, having eaten from the fruit of the forbidden tree. He knew God had said whoever eats of that fruit will die, and Adam would have known clearly what Eve had done, and so he would have feared the *possibility* of losing Eve. There would have been great war in Adam's soul. He had a choice to make—either trust God in this situation, trust that somehow he would redeem Eve's actions, or he also could eat of that fruit and join with Eve in whatever fate she would suffer, and in so doing, he would not again be alone. Perfect, sinless, unfallen Adam chose to eat. The moment Adam ate, Eve fell and became a sinner, by way of Adam (1 Tim 2:14), and Adam himself fell because he committed the sin (Isa 43:27).

When Adam ate, not only did he and Eve fall, experiencing instant death before God, being made dead in their spirit and so having their relationship with God broken, but at that same time, Adam, in eating of that fruit and in sinning against God, gave the authority over the entire Earth, and of the world, to Satan. Authority had been given to Adam to rule over the earth and over everything on it, for God had given him dominion over all the earth (Gen 1:28). When Adam sinned, he gave that dominion up to Satan. When Adam gave that dominion up to Satan, then the entire fallen angelic host were released permanently from their imprisonment within the pit, being made free to be upon the earth, ultimately taking residence in the earthly sky (Eph 2:2; 6:12). This entire transfer of dominion occurred in Eden, the place of Adam's testing, and this is how it all played out.

The First Adam and the Second Adam, as men, are interchangeable; in fact we are told the First Adam is a pattern of the one to come: "Nevertheless, death reigned from the time of Adam to the time of Moses, even over those who did not sin by breaking a command, as did Adam, who is a pattern of the one to come" (Rom 5:14 NIV).

To be a pattern of the one to come means the one to come would be exactly like Adam, and so he was. Just as the First Adam was put in a place of testing, so the Second Adam needed also to be put in a place of testing, where he, like the First Adam, would have the choice of being obedient to God or of committing sin. The First Adam was tested in the paradise of Eden, the Second Adam would be tested in the desert.

The Testing of the First Adam and the Second Adam

Both the First and Second Adams had to endure a test at the hands of Satan, who wished to cause their fall and once again justify his own rebellion against God. Also, if Satan could succeed in causing the fall of the Second Adam, Satan would forever retain the authority and lordship to the earth the First Adam had given him.

However, there was one immensely important difference between the two testing scenarios. With the First Adam, Satan had found a way to bring temptation to Adam without approaching him directly, instead devising an extremely calculated scenario that began with Eve, thereby bringing temptation to Adam *indirectly*. However, with the Second Adam, Jesus Christ, this would not be an option; with the Second Adam, Satan would be forced to tempt him *directly*.

Satan's Argument of Fairness

We know from what ensued, and from comparing the testing of Jesus Christ to the testing of the First Adam, there is no question Satan would have certainly argued to God—just as he did in the book of Job—that these two testing scenarios were not comparable. He would argue that forcing him to tempt the Second Adam, Jesus Christ, directly, was not a fair scenario since it was not the same situation as it was with the First Adam in Eden. As a result, and we know this very clearly from what ensued, God accommodated this difference between the two scenarios. Satan was forced to tempt the Second Adam directly, but, to accommodate the different scenarios and make the testing situation of Jesus Christ comparable to that of the First Adam, God allowed the following.

Eden Versus the Desert

For his testing, Jesus Christ, the Second Adam, would first be put in a position of extreme physical weakness. The First Adam was in a paradise garden, surrounded by food of all kinds, both tasty and pleasing to the eye; the Second Adam would starve for forty days and nights before his temptation would begin. Furthermore, he would starve himself not in the luxurious comfort of a garden paradise; rather, he would starve himself in the barren wasteland of a desert wilderness. Also, not only would he starve himself for forty days and forty nights, but he would do so while living outside, in the wilderness, enduring its extreme heat by day and its frigid cold by night, having nothing but a rock upon which to lay his head. After starving himself for forty days and nights, and doing so alone in the extremes of the desert wilderness, he would be in a place of extreme physical weakness, and only *then* would his temptation begin.

One Commandment Versus Anything

In Eden, Adam was given only *one* commandment to obey—to not eat the fruit of the tree of the knowledge of good and evil—and that one commandment was the *only* avenue Satan had to try to entice Adam to sin. With the Second Adam, Jesus Christ, there were to be *no restrictions* as to how he could sin. Satan would be allowed to tempt him with anything which might induce Jesus Christ to fall.

One Chance Versus Three Chances

In Eden, Satan had only *one* chance to try and engender the fall of Adam, and if Satan failed in that one attempt, then it would have been all over for Satan—he would have been defeated and Adam would have won.

With the Second Adam, Jesus Christ, Satan would be allowed to tempt him *three* times, and he could do it according to his own timeframe, that is to say, Satan could tempt him once, and then go away, and come back later to try again, thereby extending the time of starvation and wilderness hardship for Jesus beyond the initial forty days and nights.

This is what God allowed so as to make an equivalence between the temptation of the First Adam and the Second Adam—the Second Adam would be tempted only after being put in a position of extreme physical weakness. He could be tempted with anything—no restrictions—and Satan would have three chances to tempt him. All of this God allowed in exchange for the fact that Satan *must* tempt the Second Adam *directly*.

The First Temptation

After Jesus was baptized, he went into the desert wilderness and lived there, in the outdoors, living with the wild animals, unsheltered and completely exposed to the elements, for forty days and nights (Mark 1:13). During those forty days and nights he ate no food—he fasted the entire time. As a result, after those forty days and nights, he was in a place of extreme physical weakness:

> Then Jesus was led by the Spirit into the wilderness to be tempted by the devil. *After* fasting forty days and forty nights, he was hungry. The tempter came to him and said, "If you are the Son of God, tell these stones to become bread." (Matt 4:1–3 NIV)

This first temptation is a brilliant temptation, showing both strategy and planning. As in Eden, it is a masterful, well-conceived temptation that is working on many levels simultaneously. On the one hand, Satan is appealing to the fact that Jesus is physically starving and utterly weak, so this first temptation is aimed at his physical needs and bodily cravings.

However, even more so, on another level, Satan is *also* appealing to righteous pride. Not only is he tempting the starving Jesus with food, but he is simultaneously asking him to *prove* he is in fact the Son of God. It is an appeal to pride, and not only is it an appeal to Jesus' own pride and identity, but it is also, by extension, tempting Jesus to defend his Father. If Jesus changes the stones to bread, not only would he satisfy his great physical need, not only would he show himself to be the Son of God, but in doing so he would also be defending his Father by saying "Yes, God is My Father." It is a masterful and subtle appeal to defending the Father. *All* of this is going on in Satan's first temptation of Jesus Christ. But the starving Jesus answers Satan's temptation: "Jesus answered, 'It is written: man shall not live on bread alone, but on every word that comes from the mouth of God'" (Matt 4:4 NIV). Even in his great weakness, Jesus resisted the devil and did not sin.

The Second Temptation

After this, Satan came a second time to tempt Jesus:

> "Then the devil took him to the holy city and had him stand on the highest point of the temple. 'If you are the Son of God,' he said, 'throw yourself down. For it is written:
> He will command his angels concerning you,
> and they will lift you up in their hands,
> so that you will not strike your foot against a stone.'" (Matt 4:5–6 NIV)

This temptation, like the first, is a masterpiece of seduction. It is an extremely powerful, calculated, well-thought-out, strategic temptation. Satan takes the starving and physically broken Jesus to the top of the Temple Mount, standing him on the very highest point of the temple. Here, once again, Satan begins by appealing to Jesus' pride by asking him to prove his identity, that he is the Son of God, and, by extension, tempt him to defend God as his Father.

In addition, in this second temptation, Satan himself quotes Scripture. This now adds yet another layer of temptation. In addition to still being in an incredibly weak physical state, and being tempted to prove he is the Son of God while defending his Father, now he is also being tempted to prove the truth of Scripture. If Jesus will only throw himself off the Temple Mount, off the highest point of the temple, then, according to Satan, he will not only prove he is the Son of God and God is his Father, but he will also prove God's Scripture is true, accurate, and can be trusted. The second temptation is working simultaneously on all of these levels. Jesus, physically broken and utterly weak, answers Satan's temptation: "Jesus answered him, 'It is also written: "Do not put the Lord your God to the test"'" (Matt 4:7 NIV). Once again, Jesus resisted the devil and did not sin.

The Third Temptation

The third temptation is the final chance Satan has to cause the fall of the Second Adam. So far, he has tried twice to tempt Jesus to sin, and both times Jesus Christ has resisted him and has not sinned. The first two temptations were brilliantly conceived, being masterpieces of thought, deception, and manipulation, with each of the two temptations simultaneously working powerfully on multiple levels. The third and final temptation is as follows:

> The devil led him up to a high place and showed him in an instant all the kingdoms of the world. And he said to him, 'I will give you all their authority and splendor; it has been given to me, and I can give it to anyone I want to. If you worship me, it will all be yours.' (Luke 4:5–7 NIV)

This temptation is very different than the first and second temptations. Whereas the first and second temptations were brilliantly conceived, being powerfully strategic and working on multiple levels simultaneously, this third temptation has the tone of desperation. Satan knows this is his final chance. In this third temptation, there is nothing brilliant or strategic going on, there are no multiple levels on which the temptation is working. Rather, it is a temptation of desperation—this third temptation is nothing more than Satan showing Jesus the kingdoms of the world and saying that he, Satan, will give them to Jesus if Jesus worships him. The tone of desperation here is tangible—there is no strategy, no plan, only a final grasping at straws. And Jesus answers Satan: "Jesus said to him, 'Away from me, Satan! For it is written: "Worship the Lord your God, and serve him only"'" (Matt 4:10 NIV).

Once again, in his broken and starving state, Jesus resisted the devil and did not sin. At this point, Satan's temptations were over: "Then the devil left him, and angels came and attended him" (Matt 4:11 NIV). It is also important to note that here, in this third temptation, when Satan shows to Jesus all the kingdoms of the world, and says of them "*I will give you all their authority and splendor; it has been given to me, and I can give it to anyone I want to,*" Jesus does not contest the fact that Satan had indeed been given all the kingdoms of the world and all their authority, and had the right to give them to whomever he wanted. With these words Satan was affirming Adam had given him this dominion—it is an affirmation of the fact that when Adam sinned, not only did man fall, but all the authority and dominion over the earth that God gave to Adam (Gen 1:28) had been given to Satan, given to him by Adam when Adam sinned.

Satan Defeated, Sin Conquered

Satan was defeated not on the cross, but there in the desert—that is where the Second Adam, Jesus Christ, overcame the devil, resisted his temptations, and did not sin. Jesus remained permanently sinless, and, in so doing, showed rebellion and sin are *not* the natural results of being made by God, showed God is *not* the cause or the author of sin or rebellion, showed sin and rebellion are completely the result of the free-will choice made by each individual. Jesus' victory in the desert was the doom of Satan.

After defeating Satan, Jesus remained completely sinless *throughout his entire life*—he never sinned in word, thought, or action. By never sinning, not only did Jesus defeat Satan, but he also *conquered sin itself*, showing sin did not have power over him. By conquering sin, Jesus now took *authority* over sin, for sin now had no power over him; rather, Jesus now had all power over sin. Sin was defeated by Jesus. Jesus, just like Adam, could have sinned, his temptations were real, and he could have, like Adam, chosen to be faithless to God, but he did not; rather, he chose to be obedient to God, to remain faithful to him, by never sinning. This obedience is affirmed in Philippians 2:8: "And being found in appearance as a man, he humbled himself by becoming *obedient* to death—even death on a cross!" (NIV).

This obedience that is spoken of in Philippians 2:8 includes not only the willingness to go to the cross, but also, more specifically, being obedient to God throughout his life by *never sinning*—and so Philippians 2:8 affirms for us that Jesus *remained* obedient to God even up to his death upon the cross. Jesus never sinned, and in never sinning he fully conquered sin and thereby took authority over sin. By taking authority over sin, Jesus had the authority, the right, to break the power of sin—to break its power of fear, deception, and death. If Jesus had sinned, he would not have had that authority, but he did not sin, and so that authority over sin was now his.

In addition to being the Second Adam, Jesus was also the high priest of humanity, and as high priest of humanity he had the authority to take the sin of humanity and lay it upon the sacrifice for that sin. The sacrifice for that sin would be a sinless sacrifice born of Adam's blood, the sacrifice of a fully human, sinless man. Jesus Christ himself would be that sacrifice, the sacrifice who would accomplish the permanent taking away of sin, the permanent breaking of its power, making forgiveness of sin available to all. He would accomplish this on the cross by the shedding of his sinless blood and by his death.

16

The Crucifixion

JESUS CHRIST ACCOMPLISHED REDEMPTION and salvation for all humanity upon the cross. It was upon the cross Jesus broke the power of sin, brought the sin of humanity to completion, conclusion, and fulfillment in his death, making forgiveness of sins available to all who would believe in him, thereby becoming the Father of a new humanity. Also, it was upon the cross Jesus Christ took back the dominion of the earth that Adam had given away when he sinned in Eden. But *how* was this all accomplished? What was the *mechanism* by which Jesus accomplished these things upon the cross? In the 1500s, a new teaching arose that tried to give an explanation of how salvation was accomplished upon the cross, and it is the new teaching known as penal substitution.

Penal Substitution

The basic idea of the penal substitution teaching is this—while Jesus Christ was hanging on the cross, God the Father *punished* Jesus for all the sins of humanity. It teaches that because God is a just God, his justice *must* be satisfied. When sin is committed, there *must* be a *penalty* paid for that sin in order for there to be *justice*. If sin is not *punished*, then God is not just. Since humanity has sinned, all of us owe a *debt* to God. God, however, loves us and wants us to have fellowship with him, so instead of having *us* pay the required debt, or penalty, for our own sin, which we are incapable of doing, God sent his Son Jesus Christ *to take our punishment* upon himself, on our behalf, and by so doing *pay the penalty* we owed for our sin. In the penal substitution teaching, Jesus is our substitute for receiving our punishment, taking our punishment for us, and, as such, paying the price each of us owe to God's justice as a result of us having sinned. As a result, God's justice is satisfied, his law is fulfilled, and we can now have fellowship with God. In this teaching, it was while Jesus was on the cross that God the Father poured out his divine wrath upon Jesus, punishing him for our sins. Penal substitution teaches that once we believe in Jesus Christ, we then become participants in his sacrifice on the cross, join with him in his payment of our penalty, and are therefore individually justified before God.

For 75 percent of the 2,000-year history of the church, the penal substitution teaching did not exist. During the Reformation, certain Dutch Reformers (i.e., Calvin) became some of its prime proponents. Those who promote this teaching attempt to make it look like this teaching has been around from the start of the church. They do this primarily by trying to find one sentence, or phrase, in an ancient Christian letter, or an ancient Christian book, that could be construed in a penal substitution sort of way. However, the fact is the church never used, believed, or taught such a teaching, and such a teaching did not even come into existence until the Reformation. What then gave rise to it?

The Requirement of the Law

The penal substitution teaching arose primarily from certain reformers being fixated on God's law. Here is how their argument goes: God's justice is equated with God's law. God's law is holy, and therefore it cannot be ignored. If God's law is broken, then his justice demands there be a penalty, or a punishment, for the breaking of his law. If God's law is broken and there is no punishment for that transgression, then God is not just. As a result, they say this is what Jesus did on the cross: by being punished on the cross by God the Father for the sins of humanity, Jesus paid the penalty that was *required* by the *law*, and in so doing he satisfied the justice of God's *law*, satisfied the *requirement of the law*, thereby allowing for us to be saved and to have fellowship with God.

This teaching also says while Jesus hung on the cross, God the Father *turned away* from Jesus because Jesus became sin, for this teaching also says God cannot look upon sin (even though God interacts directly with Satan, face to face, in Job 1:6–12 and 2:1–7). It is while God the

Father was turned away from Jesus on the cross the Father poured out his divine wrath and punishment upon Jesus Christ, and so satisfied his justice and the requirements of the law. Ultimately, penal substitution teaches we are *justified by the law*, since we can only be justified before God if the *requirement of the law* is met and *satisfied*. Yet the Bible clearly tells us no one is ever justified by the law (Rom 3:20, 28).

Every aspect of the penal substitution teaching is false and unbiblical, based on misguided human philosophy and not on biblical truth, and in fact it contradicts the very clear teaching of Scripture as to what actually happened on the cross and of how salvation was accomplished. There is nothing in the Bible that ever equates or connects any sin sacrifice with punishment for sin, ever. All the Old Testament sacrifices were but a picture of the one sacrifice which was to come, the sacrifice of the Second Adam, the sacrifice of Jesus Christ. Romans 3:25 specifically tells us *none* of the Old Testament sacrifices had *anything* to do with punishment. Therefore, since all the Old Testament sacrifices were a picture of the one sacrifice to come, and if none of the Old Testament sacrifices ever had anything to do whatsoever with punishment for sin, as a result we can know the one sacrifice to come itself would have no connection whatsoever with punishment of sins. This being true, and if Jesus Christ was *not* punished upon the cross for the sins of humanity, then *how* did Jesus Christ accomplish salvation upon the cross?

The Second Adam

The key to understanding how salvation was accomplished upon the cross is to understand that Jesus Christ is the Second Adam. To be an Adam is to be a father of humanity, and as the Second Adam Jesus would be the Second Father of a new humanity, a redeemed humanity. In addition to being the Second Adam, the Second Father of a new humanity, Jesus Christ also represented humanity before God as the High Priest of all humanity, a High Priest in the order of Melchizedek. Adam, on the other hand, did *not* represent humanity before God; rather, Adam was only the physical *father* of humanity, not the representative of humanity before God—the representation of humanity before God is fulfilled solely by the office of High Priest of humanity, and Adam was not the high priest of humanity. It was by virtue of being the High Priest of humanity Jesus Christ had the authority to take the sin of humanity and lay it upon the sacrifice for those sins. That sacrifice would then *break the power* of that sin, breaking its power of death, fear, and deception. With the breaking of this power of sin, forgiveness of sin would be *made available* to all humanity, and the fall of the First Adam would be redeemed.

In addition to being the Second Adam, and in addition to being the High Priest of humanity, Jesus himself would also be the sacrifice for the sins of humanity, sacrificing his perfect, sinless self for the sin of the world. Jesus Christ, the Second Adam, would take the full sin of humanity, which was the sin of the one man Adam, and lay that sin, with all of its power, upon himself as he sacrificed himself for that sin. That sacrifice would happen upon the cross and would be the accomplishment of God's plan of redemption and salvation, the full flowering of the first sacrifice as performed by God himself in Eden, resulting in the reversal of the fall of the First Adam.

The Cross—The Culmination of All Previous Sacrifices

All the previous sacrifices, from Eden right up to the time of Jesus Christ, would culminate in the one sacrifice of Jesus Christ upon the cross. Just as none of the previous sacrifices as instituted by God ever had any connection whatsoever with punishment for sins (Rom 3:25), likewise the one sacrifice of Jesus Christ upon the cross would also not in any way involve any punishment for sins. Rather, the sacrifice of Jesus Christ would be the taking away of sin, which is the breaking of the power of sin, making the forgiveness of sin available to all, exactly as did the Day of Atonement and sin sacrifices throughout the Old Testament, albeit only temporarily. All of the Old Testament sacrifices were but a picture and a foreshadowing of this one sacrifice to come.

The Old Testament Sacrifices

It is understood by virtually everyone, throughout the 2,000-year history of the church, that the animal sacrifices of the Old Testament were a picture and illustration of the one sacrifice which was to come, the sacrifice of Jesus Christ. As a result, the nature of the animal sacrifices of the Old Testament reveals the nature of the upcoming sacrifice of Jesus Christ, and so we are told in Romans 3:25: "God presented Christ as a sacrifice of atonement, through the shedding of his blood—to be received by faith. He did this to demonstrate his righteousness, because in his forbearance *he had left the sins committed beforehand unpunished*" (NIV).

The exodus would have happened around 1550–1450 BC (almost certainly under Pharaoh Dudimose II), which means sin sacrifices and the Atonement sacrifices for Israel took place over a period of approximately 1,500-plus years, resulting in millions of animals being sacrificed as sin offerings over that period. This included the sacrifices for individual sin, as well the Day of Atonement sacrifices for the nation, performed by the high priest. Romans 3:25 tells us very clearly *none* of the Old Testament sin sacrifices had *anything* to do with *punishment*—all of those sins, all of which were laid upon the animal sacrifices for those sins, were left *unpunished*.

If the Old Testament sacrifices had nothing to do with punishment, why then were there sacrifices? The Bible tells us very clearly—the purpose of the animal sacrifices was so the sin of the people would be laid upon the sacrifice, which was then either killed or it ran away (as did the second goat in the Day of Atonement sacrifice). In both cases the sacrifice is described as *taking away* the sin of the people, and bringing *forgiveness* of sin for the people (Lev 16:21–22). This is the *only* picture and meaning of sacrifice for sin in the Bible—sin sacrifice in the Bible is *never* connected with punishment, it is *always* and *only* the taking away of sin and the bringing of *forgiveness*.

These Old Testament sacrifices in every way illustrate and foreshadow the sacrifice of Jesus Christ. Like all the sin sacrifices of the Old Testament, Jesus, on the cross, would take upon himself the sin of the world, the sin of all humanity. Once that sin of the world was upon him, that sin would then come to enter into and inhabit his sinless blood, which is the mechanism of sacrifice. With the shedding of his blood, resulting in his death, Jesus would bring that sin of the world to completion, and in so doing would break the power of that sin—breaking its power of death (separation from God), fear (to run away from God), and deception (to think God wants to condemn and hurt you). The breaking of the power of sin was accomplished by Jesus giving the sin of the world the death it was seeking, desiring, and striving for. In so doing, by bringing the sin of humanity to completion and conclusion in his death, Jesus Christ would make it possible for humanity to *receive* God's forgiveness.

In all of this, as with all the Old Testament sacrifices throughout the entire 1,500-plus years of sacrifices, there was *no punishment whatsoever* poured upon Jesus Christ as he hung on the cross. The Bible never describes Jesus as the "Lamb of God who pays the price for the sin of the world," rather, he is described as "the Lamb of God, who *takes away* the sin of the world!" (John 1:29). In doing so, Jesus brought *forgiveness* of sin, not payment for it: "In him we have redemption through his blood, the *forgiveness* of sins" (Eph 1:7 NKJV). *How* was it that *one man* could accomplish this for all humanity?

The Justice of Salvation—One Man Responsible for Sin

Adam was the created son of God, perfect and without sin. Adam and Adam alone was given a commandment to not eat of the fruit of the tree of the knowledge of good and evil. But Adam *did* eat, and when he ate of it, Adam sinned (Isa 43:27) and Eve, upon Adam's eating, became a sinner (1 Tim 2:14). The result of Adam's sin was he and Eve immediately died to God, which is to say their spirits became dead to God, separated from him, their fellowship with God broken, with fear and deception coming to rule over them.

The power of sin—its power of death, fear, and deception—was immediately evident in Adam and Eve upon Adam eating of the forbidden fruit. This is shown by the fact that Adam and Eve, immediately upon the fall, went to hide themselves when they heard God walking in Eden. They hid themselves because they were now scared of God, they feared his condemnation, feared his judgment, feared God would "get them." Adam almost immediately was willing to offer up Eve to destruction in order to save himself (Gen 3:12). All of this was the immediate result of Adam eating from the tree—when Eve ate the fruit of the tree, nothing happened, as she was not the one given the commandment, but when Adam ate, everything changed—man fell and sin was now residing in humanity, and Adam had given away the authority and dominion of the earth to Satan.

The sinful nature that resulted from Adam's sin was not some nebulous spiritual state—it was absolutely and unequivocally a *physical* thing that took up *physical residence* in Adam's *blood*. This is why Paul constantly, throughout his letters, refers to the sinful nature as "the flesh." It is called the flesh because every cell of our bodies is imbued with our blood, and it is in our blood the sinful nature resides. This is also why there is no *forgiveness* of sins without the shedding of *blood*. Sin and blood, forgiveness and blood, go hand in hand.

The sinful nature is passed on to all human beings *only* by our human fathers, *not* through our mothers (1 Cor 15:22; Rom 5:12). This is also why we are told women will be saved through childbearing:

> But women will be saved through childbearing—if they continue in faith, love and holiness with propriety. (1 Tim 2:15 NIV)

How is a woman saved by childbearing? First Timothy 2:15 is in fact an affirmation the woman does not pass on the sinful nature to her children. Since the woman does not pass on the sinful nature to her children, she (and everyone) will be saved through the woman's childbearing because one day her childbearing will ultimately result in one offspring to come from the woman, an offspring who would be born without the sinful nature, an offspring who would not have a human father. It is only because the woman does not pass on the sinful nature to her children that a sinless offspring, and therefore salvation, is made possible, for it is the woman who makes possible the birth of a sinless Savior. Therefore, all humanity is saved by the woman's childbearing. (It is also a beautiful picture of the equivalence of man and woman—the first woman, Eve, came from Adam, while the Second Adam, Jesus Christ, came from the woman).

One Blood—Adam's Blood

The sinful nature of all human beings resides in our blood, which sinful nature we inherit only from our human fathers. But here is the extremely important point to remember—the blood that is now flowing, and has always flowed, through human veins is solely and exclusively the *one blood* of *Adam himself*.

When we were born, God did not create new blood to inhabit our bodies; rather, we *inherited* the blood of our parents, who in turn *inherited* their blood from their parents, and so on, all the way back to Adam. The only human blood in existence is the blood of our first father—Adam. It is *Adam's* blood that is flowing in each one of us, it is through *Adam's* blood we have the sinful nature residing within us, the same one sinful nature that came to inhabit Adam's blood after he ate of the forbidden fruit. All human sin is therefore born out of that one sinful nature, of *Adam's* sinful nature, of that *one man's* blood now residing in us.

As a result, it is true to say all the sin ever committed by any and all human beings has its *source* in the *blood of Adam*, our first father. It is solely and exclusively *Adam's blood* that has brought *all sin* into the world and to *all* humanity—it is the blood of the *one man* that is responsible for *all* of this.

One Man for One Man

Adam was the first father of humanity as well as the father of the fall, but God provided a Second Adam, Jesus Christ. This Second Adam, like the first, was the son of God, but unlike the First Adam, who was the created son of God, the Second Adam was the *begotten* son of God. To be begotten means Jesus Christ was the offspring of both a human woman and God himself. By being begotten through a human woman, Jesus Christ was totally, fully, completely human, with exactly the same humanity as the First Adam. However, since Jesus Christ, the Second Adam, did not have a human father, he did not receive the sinful nature in his blood. Jesus Christ, the Second Adam, was born without sin.

Therefore, the Second Adam was in exactly the same position before God as was the First Adam *before his fall*—totally and completely human, a moral being completely free of sin and having no sinful nature. This is why Jesus' blood is described as "precious" (1 Pet 1:19)—it is precious because it is pure and holy, it is pure and holy because there is no sinful nature within it, and there is no sinful nature within it because Jesus Christ did not have a human father. Therefore, the Second Adam, Jesus Christ, is of the exact same pattern of man as was Adam before his fall: "Nevertheless, death reigned from the time of Adam to the time of Moses, even over those who did not sin by breaking a command, as did *Adam, who is a pattern of the one to come*" (Rom 5:14 NIV).

The Sacrifice of a Moral Being and a Descendant of Adam

For a sacrifice to accomplish the permanent reversal of the fall of Adam, that sacrifice must be a moral being, and must be a *descendant of Adam*, being exactly and fully human as was Adam. As the begotten Son of God, Jesus Christ was fully human, yet also fully God. He was a descendant of Adam, born with Adam's full and complete humanity, but he did not have the sinful nature. Although he was without sin, as was Adam originally,

The Crucifixion

Jesus Christ, like Adam, was a moral being who *was capable* of committing sin. Like Adam, Jesus could have sinned, but, unlike Adam, he chose not to sin. By never sinning, by living a life of complete obedience and faithfulness to God, Jesus Christ conquered sin. In conquering sin, Jesus took authority over sin. As a result, sin and all of its power became subject to Jesus Christ. By gaining authority over sin, only Jesus Christ had the power and the authority to *break* the *power* of sin—he could break its power because he himself never sinned and so took authority over sin, had power over it (Matt 9:6; Mark 2:10; Luke 5:24)—by having power over sin, Jesus could make sin powerless.

Jesus Christ—The Permanent Sacrifice

The animal sacrifices of the Old Testament would only *temporarily* take away sin by the shedding of their sinless animal blood, and by their death. The reason it was only temporary is because those animals were not moral beings, and, as such, by not being moral creatures, the animals were incapable of committing sin. Since an animal is incapable of committing sin, the animals used in the sacrifices could never *conquer* sin, for the only way to conquer sin was to be a moral being capable of committing sin but choosing not to sin. By not being able to *conquer* sin, an animal could therefore never *take authority* over sin. By not being able to take authority over sin, an animal could never permanently break the power of sin. Only a moral creature, a moral being, who was capable of sin but who chose to never sin, could conquer sin and thereby take authority over sin. Jesus Christ was that moral being who was capable of sin but who never sinned.

Also, the animals were not descendants of Adam and, since they were not descendants of Adam, their death could never give the sin of humanity the *human* death sin was seeking and striving for, for the sin of Adam was seeking its satisfaction in *human* death. As a result, the animal sacrifices of the Old Testament could only accomplish a temporary reprieve from sin.

As such, the sacrifice, or death, of a moral being, a descendant of Adam, who conquered sin by never sinning, *would* break the power of the sin of all humanity *permanently* since that sinless sacrifice would give the sin of humanity the *human* death for which it was striving. The sacrifice of Jesus Christ, the Second Adam, would permanently accomplish this.

Only Jesus Christ Could Redeem the Fall

As a result, as the Second Adam, Jesus Christ was the only one who could redeem the fall of the First Adam, break the power of sin over humanity, bring that sin to conclusion and completion in his death, bring freedom to all people from sin, and become the Father of a new humanity. It would be the Second Adam redeeming what the First Adam had done, the shed blood of the Second Adam redeeming what the blood of the First Adam had brought into the world. It would be one man for one man.

The sin of the First Adam, which resulted in the sinful nature which now resides in all people, *must* meet its fulfillment, conclusion, and completion in *human death* for it is the nature of sin to seek death (Rom 6:23). Sin is restless, imbued with *power* until it is *satisfied* with the death of its host. When sin meets death in the *death of its host* that sin is then *fulfilled*, made complete, brought to full conclusion.

When Jesus Christ took the full sin of the world upon himself, he became Host to the full sin of humanity, and then by dying with that sin upon him and within his blood, his death *satisfied* that entire sin of humanity. In his death, the sin of *all humanity* was brought to *conclusion* and *completion*. Once sin is concluded, once it is made complete, it no longer has any power—its power of death, fear, and deception is broken. The Bible describes this breaking of the power of sin as "taking away" the sin of the world (John 1:29).

The Sinless Blood of the Sacrifice

Jesus himself had no sin within himself, being born without the sinful nature as a result of not having a human father. As a result, Jesus' own human blood was sinless. Since Jesus' blood was sinless, then, upon the sacrifice of himself, and upon taking the sin of humanity upon himself, his sinless blood would allow for the sin of the world to come to *enter into* and *inhabit* his own sinless blood, thereby fulfilling the mechanism of sacrifice, for it is the mechanism of sacrifice that the sin laid upon the sacrifice comes to enter into, or inhabit, the sinless blood of the sacrifice. As a result, Jesus would break the power of the sin of the world by the *shedding* of his *blood*, for the shedding of his blood would result in his death, and it was by his death that he would give the sin of humanity the completion and fulfillment it was seeking.

The Authority of the High Priest of Humanity

In addition to being the Second Adam, the Second Father of a new humanity, and in addition to being the sacrifice for the sin of the world, Jesus Christ was also the High Priest of humanity, a High Priest in the order of Melchizedek. It was not enough to be the Second Adam or the Second Father of a new humanity, for in order for the sacrifice to be accomplished, the sin of the world first needed to *be laid upon* that sacrifice. By being the High Priest of humanity, Jesus Christ represented all humanity before God, and represented God to all humanity in regards to *sin*. As a result, by virtue of his office as High Priest of humanity, as the representative of all humanity in regards to sin, Jesus Christ had the power and the authority to take the entire sin of all humanity and lay that sin upon the sacrifice for that sin. Since Jesus Christ would himself be that sacrifice, he would in fact lay the sin of humanity upon himself. He had that authority solely by his office of High Priest of humanity.

How Salvation was Accomplished—Jesus the High Priest

It was specifically by virtue of being the High Priest of all humanity, a High Priest in the order of Melchizedek, that Jesus had the authority to take the sin of humanity and lay it upon himself as the sacrifice for that sin, for that authority is intrinsic to the office of high priest (Heb 4:14–15; 5:5–10; 6:20; 7:26; 8:1; 9:11, 25; 10:21). Where the Levitical high priest was the high priest of Israel, and had the authority to take the sin of all Israel and lay it upon the sacrifice for the whole nation, likewise Jesus, by being the High Priest of *all humanity*, had the authority to take the sin of *all humanity* and lay it upon the sacrifice for *all humanity*.

This is illustrated throughout the Old Testament by the position of the high priest of Israel, who represented God to Israel and who represented Israel to God. The high priest of Israel had the authority, on the Day of Atonement, after purifying himself (which symbolized the need for the high priest to be sinless), to lay his hands on the head of the sacrifice for the nation and then, with that laying on of hands, the sin of the people, and the *power* of that sin passed *through* the high priest, *through his hands*, coming to lay upon the sacrifice. The first sacrifice was killed and the second sacrifice ran away, taking with it the sin of the people, and the people would have the forgiveness of sins.

This is an *exact representation* of the authority Jesus had as the High Priest of humanity. He, like the high priests of the Old Testament, had the authority to take the sin of the people and have it pass through him to sit upon the sacrifice for that sin. In the Old Testament, the high priest could do this only for the people of Israel, because he was high priest only of Israel, but in the case of Jesus Christ, he is the High Priest of *all humanity*. As a result, as the High Priest of all humanity, Jesus had the authority to take the sin of *all humanity*, the full sin of *Adam*, and lay it upon the sacrifice for that sin.

When Jesus was hanging on the cross, this is in fact exactly what he did. By his own authority as High Priest of humanity, Jesus took the sin of all humanity and laid it upon the sacrifice for that sin. In this case though, he himself was *also* the sacrifice. As a result, Jesus took the sin of humanity and laid it upon *himself*.

> And the Lord has laid on him the iniquity of us all. (Isa 53:6 NKJV)

> The next day John saw Jesus coming toward him and said, "Look, the Lamb of God, who takes away the sin of the world!" (John 1:29 NIV)

> Who himself bore our sins in his own body on the tree, that we, having died to sins, might live for righteousness—by whose stripes you were healed. (1 Pet 2:24 NKJV)

What Happened When the Sin of the World was on Jesus

In the Old Testament, once the high priest had placed the sin of the people upon the sacrifice, then the sacrifice would either run away (Day of Atonement) or would be killed and its blood would be shed (Sin sacrifices). Both of these *together* illustrate the *fullness* of what happened at the sacrifice for sin—blood was shed so as to *take away* sin. What was the *mechanism* by which this happened? *How* did the shedding of blood accomplish this?

In the Old Testament sacrifices, unblemished animals were used as sin sacrifices. To be unblemished represented purity and sinlessness. This sinlessness of the animal sacrifices, however, was not just symbolic or representational, but was in fact real—since the sacrificial animals were not descendants of Adam, their blood did not have Adam's sinful nature, and so their blood was *in fact* sinless. The sacrifice of animals in the Old Testament was in fact a sacrifice of *sinless* blood.

We can understand the mechanism of sacrifice as follows: when the sin of the people, which is the power of the sinful nature that resides in people's blood, is laid upon a sacrifice, a sacrifice whose blood has no sin, then the power of the sin that is laid upon that sacrifice *physically enters into*, or *comes to inhabit*, the *sinless blood* of the sacrifice. It is only because the sacrifice itself *has no sin* that its blood is capable of *receiving* the sin laid upon it—its sinless blood is *available* to be inhabited by the sin laid upon it—if the blood of the sacrifice already had sin within it, it could not receive into itself the sin that was laid upon it and as a result the sacrifice would be ineffective. As a result, it is the blood of the sacrifice being sinless that makes the sacrifice effective—this is the mechanism of sacrifice. Once the sin is laid upon the sinless sacrifice, and while the sacrifice is shedding its blood, and the sacrifice is dying, the sin of the people, now inhabiting the blood of the sacrifice, is literally *taken away* by the shedding of that sacrificial blood, being brought to a *temporary* conclusion in the death of the animal sacrifice.

This exact same mechanism of sacrifice occurs in Jesus' sacrifice upon the cross: "For he made him who knew no sin *to be sin* for us, that we might become the righteousness of God in him" (2 Cor 5:21 NKJV).

How Salvation was Accomplished—Jesus Made to Be Sin

Second Corinthians 5:21 is an affirmation of this same *mechanism* of sacrifice by which the sacrifice breaks the power of sin. The sin is laid upon the sacrifice—in the case of the cross, it was laid upon Jesus Christ. With the sin of the world laid upon him, Jesus' sinless blood *receives* the sin laid upon him so the sin comes to physically enter into, or comes to *inhabit*, his sinless blood.

There is a physicality to this description, but how are we to understand it? What does it mean that Jesus came to "be" sin? Did Jesus' face change? Did his body become some sort of black, vile substance? No; rather, in saying "For he made him who knew no sin *to be sin*" it is in fact describing the *mechanism* of sacrifice and blood. It is a description of the sin of the world, which Jesus took upon himself, coming to enter into, or *inhabit*, his own sinless blood. As a result, by the sin actually coming to *physically* inhabit Jesus' blood, Jesus was being *physically* made to actually *be* sin—the sinless blood within his body was actually *becoming inhabited* by the sin of the world. This is a physical event, and 2 Corinthians 5:21 is a description of that mechanism of sacrifice, the physical entering of the sin into the sinless blood of the sacrifice. This same mechanism of sacrifice is further affirmed: "Who himself bore our sins *in his own body* on the tree, that we, having died to sins, might live for righteousness—by whose stripes you were healed" (1 Pet 2:24 NKJV). Peter tells us Jesus did not just take our sin *upon* himself, but, like 2 Corinthians 5:21, he tells us Jesus bore our sins *in* his body.

Once again, there is a physicality here. To say Jesus bore our sins in his body is another way of saying the sin of the world came to *physically inhabit* Jesus' own sinless blood, coming to be *inside* him, to be *in* his blood. By coming to be in his blood, that sin came to be *in* his body. As a result, 1 Peter 2:24 affirms the exact same mechanism of sacrifice as does 2 Corinthians 5:21. Being made to *be sin* is the same meaning as bearing our sins in his body. Both 2 Corinthians 5:21 and 1 Peter 2:24 affirm while Jesus was hanging on the cross, the sin of the world came to *physically inhabit* his sinless blood, thus fulfilling the mechanism of sacrifice.

How Salvation was Accomplished—The Requirement for Death

When Jesus was on the cross, he laid upon himself the full sin of humanity, all of which was the sin of the one man—Adam. When that sin was upon him, it physically entered into and came to inhabit his sinless blood, which is why we are told Jesus was made to *be* sin. It is the nature of all sin to desire death (Rom 6:23), to seek death, to strive for the death of its host. In achieving the death of its host, that sin is then fulfilled, or brought to conclusion, having run its full course. The sin of the world that came to inhabit Jesus' blood was itself desiring, starving for, and seeking its fulfillment in human death. Sin is relentless until it is fulfilled in death—sin is not complete until it has culminated in death.

While Jesus was upon the cross, with the sin of the world upon him and inhabiting his sinless blood, he, in his body, was Host to the sin of the world. While the sin of the world was upon him and within his blood, he shed his blood and, with the shedding of his blood, he *died*. By *dying* on the cross, with the sin of the world upon him and *within* him, Jesus *satisfied* that same sin's *demand* for death, thereby bringing the entire sin of the world to *conclusion*, making the sin of all humanity, the entirety of the sin of the one man—Adam—fulfilled in his death.

It was by bringing that sin to full conclusion in his death that Jesus was able to utterly break the power of that sin, for by bringing the sin of humanity to full completion and fulfillment in his death the full sin of humanity had now run its course and was finished. By having run its course, by being brought to conclusion, completion, and fulfillment, the power of that sin—its power of death, fear, and deception—was now broken, destroyed, finished, for it too had now run its course and as a result was also finished. The entire sin of humanity would now forevermore be powerless because of Jesus' bringing it to fulfillment in his death upon the cross. As a result, one man, by his death, broke the power of the *entire* sin of humanity. The one man, Jesus Christ, by the shedding of his sinless blood, and by his death, broke the power of the sin brought into the world by the blood of the one man—Adam.

The Blood of Adam and the Blood of Christ

How is it just that the blood of one man—Jesus Christ—can take away the sin of all humanity? The perfect justice of it is this—the sin of all humanity is born from our sinful nature, and our sinful nature resides in our blood. The blood that flows through the veins of all people who have ever lived and who ever will live is only the blood of the *one man,* Adam, our first father. Adam brought sin into the world through *his blood* and we, as his children, have inherited his blood and his sinful nature. The Second Adam, Jesus Christ, breaks the power of, or takes away, that very same sin by the shedding of *his sinless blood*, by his *death*. In this way the Second Adam redeemed the fall of the First Adam, the blood of the Second Adam redeemed what the blood of the First Adam had caused.

The justice of the cross is not that Jesus Christ was hanging on the cross in place of all human beings, which he was not. Rather, he was hanging on the cross as a Second Adam to reverse what the First Adam had done. It was one Adam redeeming what the other Adam had caused, and this is the perfect justice and grace of God—it was "an Adam for an Adam," "one man for one man," for it is the grace of God that there even was a Second Adam. This full destruction of the power of sin was accomplished by the death of Jesus Christ upon the cross.

The Father Does Not Turn His Face Away

The teaching of penal substitution, which teaches justification and salvation by the law, teaches that Jesus Christ was punished by God the Father for our sins, being the recipient of God's wrath while he was hanging upon the cross, and this has led to some additional unbiblical ideas and teachings. One of the foremost of these is the teaching that while Jesus was hanging on the cross, God the Father turned his face away from Jesus. This teaching says that, because Jesus had become sin and God cannot look upon sin, God the Father turned away from the Son. The teaching then says it was at that moment, at the moment God the Father turned his face away from the Son, God the Father poured out his wrath, his punishment, upon Jesus. Matthew 27:46 is invoked as proof: "My God, My God, why have You forsaken Me?" (NKJV). When Jesus cried out these words, he was in fact hanging on the cross. Does not this cry of Jesus upon the cross affirm that God the Father turned his face away from Jesus while he was hanging on the cross, that God the Father had forsaken Jesus? It certainly does not, for the Bible *specifically* tells us God the Father did *not* turn his face away from Jesus while he was hanging on the cross.

Psalm 22

Psalm 22 was written approximately 1,000 years before Jesus' crucifixion, and yet it gives us the literal thoughts of Jesus as he was hanging on the cross. In fact, Psalm 22 begins with the exact same words that Jesus cried out in Matthew 27:46:

> My God, My God, why have You forsaken Me? (Ps 22:1 NKJV)

It continues:

> But I *am* a worm, and no man;
> A reproach of men, and despised by the people.
> All those who see Me ridicule Me;
> They shoot out the lip, they shake the head, *saying,*
> "He trusted in the Lord, let him rescue him;
> Let him deliver him, since he delights in him!"
> But You *are* he who took Me out of the womb;
> You made Me trust *while* on My mother's breasts.
> I was cast upon You from birth.
> From My mother's womb

The Crucifixion

You *have been* My God.
Be not far from Me,
For trouble *is* near;
For *there is* none to help.
Many bulls have surrounded Me;
Strong *bulls* of Bashan have encircled Me.
They gape at Me *with* their mouths,
Like a raging and roaring lion.
I am poured out like water,
And all My bones are out of joint;
My heart is like wax;
It has melted within Me.
My strength is dried up like a potsherd,
And My tongue clings to My jaws;
You have brought Me to the dust of death.
For dogs have surrounded Me;
The congregation of the wicked has enclosed Me.
They pierced My hands and My feet;
I can count all My bones.
They look and stare at Me.
They divide My garments among them,
And for My clothing they cast lots.
But You, O Lord, do not be far from Me;
O My Strength, hasten to help Me!
Deliver Me from the sword,
My precious *life* from the power of the dog.
Save Me from the lion's mouth
And from the horns of the wild oxen!
You have answered Me.
I will declare Your name to My brethren;
In the midst of the assembly I will praise You.
You who fear the Lord, praise him!
All you descendants of Jacob, glorify him,
And fear him, all you offspring of Israel!
For he has not despised nor abhorred the affliction of the afflicted;
Nor has he hidden his face from him;
But when he cried to him, he heard." (Ps 22:6–24 NKJV)

These are the thoughts of Jesus Christ as he was hanging on the cross, recorded 1,000 years before the event. In verses 14–18, Jesus says in his heart:

> *I am poured out like water,*
> *And all My bones are out of joint;*
> *My heart is like wax;*
> *It has melted within Me.*
> *My strength is dried up like a potsherd,*
> *And My tongue clings to My jaws;*
> *You have brought Me to the dust of death.*
> *For dogs have surrounded Me;*
> *The congregation of the wicked has enclosed Me.*
> *They pierced My hands and My feet;*
> *I can count all My bones.*
> *They look and stare at Me.*
> *They divide My garments among them,*
> *And for My clothing they cast lots.*

Here Jesus tells us how his hands and feet are pierced, nailed to the cross; tells us how he can count all of his bones, which are out of joint; tells us those who are surrounding him at the foot of the cross are casting lots for his clothes (see Matt 27:45). All of this is a description of what was going on while Jesus was crucified, *while* Jesus cries out "My God, My God, why have You forsaken Me?" But Psalm 22 continues, as it describes God the Father during this exact same time:

> For he has not despised nor abhorred the affliction of the afflicted,
> *Nor has he hidden his face from him,*
> But when he cried to him, he heard. (Ps 22:24)

Psalm 22:24 tells us very clearly while Jesus Christ was hanging on the cross, at the same time as he was crying out "My God, My God, why have You forsaken Me?," God the Father did *not* turn his face away from Jesus, did *not* hide his face from Jesus, did *not* despise or abhor Jesus; rather, God the Father was with Jesus fully, embracing him fully, being fully one with him in love and fellowship. As a result, to teach that God the Father turned his face away from Jesus as Jesus was hanging on the cross is a false teaching. Furthermore, it demeans the very nature and character of God, by robbing God of his love and mercy.

If this is true, and the Father did *not* turn his face away, then what does it mean when Jesus cried out "My God, My God, why have You forsaken Me?" If God the Father did not turn his face away from Jesus while Jesus was hanging on the cross, then was Jesus mistaken when he cried out that God had forsaken him? How are we to understand it, since we are clearly told in Psalm 22:24 that God the Father did *not* turn his face away from Jesus Christ while he hung on the cross?

The Wages of Sin—The Death of the World

While Jesus was hanging on the cross, he laid upon himself the sin of the world. This was not a metaphoric or symbolic act—he actually, really, and truly laid upon himself the full physical sin of the world, together with all of its power. But when Jesus took upon himself the sin of the world, he also took upon himself everything that *came with* that sin, including death: "For the wages of sin is death" (Rom 6:23 NKJV). Death goes hand in hand with sin—wherever there is sin, there is death, for death is the full conclusion of sin. But what is true death? The Bible describes true death as separation from God, the breaking of fellowship with him. This is why, when Adam ate of the fruit of the tree, both he and Eve instantly died a *true* death. Physically they continued to live for centuries, but in their spirit, that component of man that can have fellowship with God, they died instantly.

When Jesus took upon himself the sin of the world, he also, at that same time, took upon himself the full *death* of the world, since the *death* of the world *came together* with that sin. While the death of the world was upon him, Jesus fully *experienced* that full death of the world before God. That is to say, Jesus himself experienced that same full and complete *death before God*, the full *separation* from God, that *the world was experiencing*. The heart of that death, the heart of what Jesus experienced when the sin of the world was upon him, was the breaking of fellowship with the Father, a real and true separation from God. While he was hanging on the cross, Jesus experienced a complete death before God, a real separation from God the Father. He experienced this specifically as a result of having the sin of the world upon him, coming to reside within him, within his blood, as he hung on the cross, for with that sin of the world came the death of the world.

It was while Jesus was experiencing the death of the world and the resulting separation of the world from God, that he cried out in fear and separation, "My God, My God, why have You forsaken Me?" His cry of "My God, My God" in no way means God the Father had turned his face away from the Son, which, as Psalm 22:24 clearly and specifically tells us, we know the Father did not do. Rather, with that cry, Jesus is testifying, or bearing witness, to the fact that the sin of the world was *actually* upon him right then, and it was upon him *together* with the death of the world. His cry was a witness to the fact the full sin *and the full death* of the world were *actually upon him* and he was *experiencing this reality* as he hung on the cross. As Jesus cried out from the depths of his pain at experiencing that separation from the Father, God the Father was with him fully, loving him, embracing his beloved Son in whom he was well pleased, neither despising him nor abhorring him, neither punishing him and certainly not turning his face away from him.

To say while Jesus was hanging on the cross the Father turns his face away is a lie, a false teaching, and it is especially so as it demeans and insults the very nature of God, for it characterizes God as a God who requires and insists on vengeance, despises and abhors his own, is incapable of forgiveness, and is driven only out of a need to punish in order to balance the scales of justice. But in truth God is love, can forgive without any need of punishment or vengeance, and loves his Son, upon whom he did not pour out any punishment or wrath. The Father did *not* turn his face away.

Isaiah 53—Divine Punishment on the Cross?

But what about Isaiah 53? Here we are told the following about Jesus Christ:

> Surely he has borne our griefs
> And carried our sorrows;
> Yet we esteemed him stricken,
> Smitten by God, and afflicted.
> But he *was* wounded for our transgressions,
> *He was* bruised for our iniquities;
> *The chastisement for our peace was upon him,*
> And *by his stripes we are healed.*
> All we like sheep have gone astray;
> We have turned, every one, to his own way;
> And the Lord has laid on him the iniquity of us all.
> (Isa 53:4–6 NKJV)

Does this not say Jesus was *punished* (or *chastised*) for our sins? No, it does not. In these verses it is clear the punishment (chastisement) described is the *human* punishment inflicted upon Jesus by the Romans, and is *not* any sort of *divine* punishment or wrath poured out upon Jesus by God the Father for the punishment of sin. How do we know this? Because this verse clearly tells us: "By his stripes we are healed" (Isa 53:5). Here, the word "stripes" refers specifically to the human punishment of being flogged by the Romans, that is, it refers specifically to Jesus being *whipped* before his crucifixion (Matt 27:26; Mark 15:15; John 19:1). Each whip stroke would leave a stripe upon Jesus, a lash mark. To say "by his stripes we are healed" is to say "by his whipping we are healed." This is exclusively a reference to the human suffering inflicted upon Jesus by the Romans.

The phrase "by his stripes we are healed" is given in the same breath as the words "The chastisement for our peace was upon him." Together, these words all express the same, one thought—just as the meaning of "by his stripes we are healed" refers solely and exclusively to the *human* punishment inflicted upon Jesus by being whipped by the Romans, likewise the words "The chastisement [punishment] for our peace was upon him," refers solely and exclusively to the *human* punishment inflicted upon Jesus by being *crucified* by the Romans. "The chastisement [punishment] that brought us peace was on him" does *not* refer to *any* sort of divine wrath of God being poured out upon Jesus while he hung on the cross; rather, it refers *only* to the fact that Jesus was *crucified*. It means only that he was *sacrificed*—the crucifixion was the *sacrifice* that brought us peace. This is the clear meaning of this passage. While crucified, Jesus Christ took the sin of the world upon himself, brought that sin to completion in his death, bringing us *forgiveness* of sins through that sacrifice and thereby bringing us *peace* through that forgiveness. As a result of the Romans' punishment of crucifixion—of being sacrificed—our salvation was accomplished, which is to say the sacrifice of Jesus Christ brought us peace with God. The punishment referred to in Isaiah 53 is solely and exclusively the *human* punishment inflicted upon Jesus by the Romans, the punishment of being crucified, and in no way does it refer to *any* sort of divine wrath poured out upon Jesus by God.

If the Power of Sin was Broken, Why is Sin Still Here?

God the Father did not punish Jesus Christ for the sins of the world; rather, Jesus Christ took upon himself the sin of the world and, by the shedding of his blood, and by his resulting death, he broke the power of the sin of the world by bringing it to completion in his death, thereby giving us the freedom to receive forgiveness. "The next day John saw Jesus coming toward him, and said, "Behold! The Lamb of God who takes away the sin of the world!" (John 1:29 NKJV). But if the sin of the world was taken away and its power broken upon the cross, then does that mean people no longer have sin? Do not we, as Christians, still have sin, the sinful nature, residing within us, even after we believe? If so, then what actually was taken away? What was the power that was broken?

The fact is that yes, even after we believe in Jesus Christ and are born as God's children, the sinful nature continues residing within us. Even though Jesus Christ was crucified upon the cross, and broke the power of sin, bringing it to completion in his death, our sinful nature still resides within our blood, in our flesh, and we still sin. So what was actually accomplished by the taking away the sin of the world?

To take away the sin of the world, on the one hand, means the sin of the world literally entered into Jesus' sinless blood while he was sacrificing himself on the cross, and with that shedding of blood the Second Adam took away, or shed, what the First Adam had brought into the world. When his blood, inhabited by the sin of the world, was shed, that same sin of the world literally flowed out of him. But, even more so, to take away the sin of the world means Jesus Christ *broke the power* of the sin of the world.

The power of sin is the power of death, fear, and deception. The power of death is the power to kill our spirit so our fellowship with God is broken, leaving us separated from God, dead to God; the power of fear is to cause us to run away from God, to try and hide from him, for fear he will condemn and destroy us; the power of deception is to cause us to believe God is looking to condemn us, to punish us and harm us, making us unable to recognize God in fact loves us and forgives us. All of this is the power of sin, and all of this is what inhabits each of us in our sinful nature, just as it inhabited Adam himself almost immediately upon his fall.

It is this power of sin—death, fear, and deception—residing within us, in our sinful natures, in our blood, in our flesh, that *prevents* us from having fellowship with God, from understanding God loves us, from understanding God is not looking to destroy us but is, rather, looking to love and forgive us. This power of sin, residing within us in our sinful nature, enslaves us:

> We know that what we used to be was nailed to the cross with him. That happened so *our bodies* that were *ruled by sin* would *lose their power*. So we are no longer *slaves of sin*. (Rom 6:6 NIrV)

You used to be *slaves of sin*. (Rom 6:17 NIV)

Apart from Jesus Christ, we are *slaves* to this power of sin within us. Therefore, in order for us to come to have fellowship with God, to come to the *knowledge* of God's love for us, to be *able* to *recognize* God actually loves us and is looking to forgive us and not destroy us, that power of sin had to be *broken*, for the power of sin is the *obstacle* which prevents us from coming to God. This is exactly what Jesus did when he took away the sin of the world by the shedding of his blood—he *broke* that entire power of sin:

> It has now been made known through the coming of our Savior, Christ Jesus. *He has broken the power of death*. Because of the good news, he has brought life out into the light. That life never dies. (2 Tim 1:10 NIrV)

This is also what is meant by Luke 1:77:

> 'To give his people the *knowledge of salvation* through the *forgiveness of their sins*.' (NIV)

To say Jesus broke the power of death (2 Tim 1:10) is also to say he broke the power of sin, for death is the wage, or result, of sin. To break the power of death is to break the power of sin. By breaking the power of sin—its power of fear, deception, and death—Jesus allows us to be set free from that enslaving power of sin, for we are *set free* from it *when we believe* in Jesus Christ. Even though that sinful nature *still remains physically within us*, in our blood and flesh, when we believe in Jesus Christ we claim what he accomplished upon the cross as our own—we claim his breaking of the power of that sin. As a result, when we believe in Jesus Christ, even though the sinful nature still resides within us, its *power* of death, fear, and deception *has been broken* within us, has been made *powerless* within us, and it no longer enslaves or deceives us.

This is why, even though Christians still have sin physically residing within us, in our blood, in our flesh, Christians still call God "Father" even though we sin, for we remain one with him, never again separated from him. For sin's power of death, its power of separation from God, is broken; this is why, when as Christians we sin, we do not run away from God to hide from him; rather, we seek him, we come to him and confess our sin, for sin's power of fear is broken. It is also why, when we as Christians sin, we know God always loves us and will always forgive us, for sin's power of deception is broken. Even after we believe in Jesus Christ, our sinful nature remains within us, still residing in our blood, but its *power* of death (separation from God), fear (running away from God), and deception (thinking God will not love or forgive us) has been broken; though our sinful nature is still within us, it is now *powerless*. Its power was broken by Jesus Christ upon the cross, who brought it to full conclusion and completion in his death. With his death, Jesus *disarmed* sin. When we believe in Jesus Christ we are born of his Spirit, and, by being born of his Spirit, we are *appropriating* what Jesus has accomplished on the cross, appropriating the destruction of the power of sin, and are no longer subject to its power, for Jesus has made it powerless. As a result, even when we as Christians sin, we can know God's love for us, call him Father, and turn to him for comfort, strength, and forgiveness.

As a result, every time a Christian sins and comes to God, calls him "Father," confesses their sin, and asks for forgiveness, it is a living witness and testimony to the fact Jesus Christ broke the power of sin that resides within us, the power of our sinful nature—it is still there, but now its power is broken. And so is affirmed the words of Luke 1:77: "To give his people the knowledge of salvation through the forgiveness of their sins" (NIV). We can now *know* God's salvation, God's love, and God's forgiveness because Jesus broke sin's power of deception, fear, and death. So here is what we see—*God does not need the cross to forgive us our sins*; rather, *it is we who need the cross in order to receive God's forgiveness.*

Jesus Forgives Sin before the Cross

Before he went to the cross, Jesus repeatedly, throughout his life, forgave people their sins:

> Some men brought to him a paralyzed man, lying on a mat. When Jesus saw their faith, he said to the man, 'Take heart, son; your sins are forgiven.' (Matt 9:2 NIV)

> Then Jesus said to her, 'Your sins are forgiven.' (Luke 7:48 NIV)

These examples of Jesus forgiving people their sins occurred well before his crucifixion. But how can this be? Obviously, for any penal substitution idea, this is a major problem. Here, there was no cross, no punishment, no anything, yet Jesus is forgiving people their sins.

For those who believe the teaching of penal substitution, the teaching that God must punish Jesus Christ on the cross as payment for the sins of humanity so as to satisfy his law, some almost outlandish ideas about God need to be created in order to accommodate the fact Jesus himself repeatedly forgave people their sins without having to be crucified to do so.

One such idea is Jesus was able to forgive people their sins without being crucified (i.e., without being punished for those sins) because God operates in different dimensions of space and time, and so Jesus forgiving the people their sin was done in some sort of eternal or timeless timescape from a standpoint of eternity, and as such is a looking forward to, or looking backward from, the cross, or looking back and forth across time and eternity or across multiple dimensions. Ultimately, this requires notions that verge into the realm of fantasy. The simple truth is when Jesus forgave people their sin, he actually forgave them their sin, right then and there, for the simple reason that God does not need the cross to forgive sins. He can forgive sins whenever he wants, and he is neither bound nor constrained by the law to do otherwise. The cross has nothing to do with punishment, meaning God does not need the cross to forgive sins, so when Jesus forgave these people their sins, they were fully, truly, and freely forgiven because God is free to forgive sins.

Parable of the Rich King and Forgiveness

Jesus himself gives us a parable to clearly illustrate exactly what he means by forgiveness. It is the parable of a man who owed an enormous amount of money to a king, an amount he was unable to pay:

> Therefore the kingdom of heaven is like a certain king who wanted to settle accounts with his servants. And when he had begun to settle accounts, one was brought to him who owed him ten thousand talents. But as he was not able to pay, his master commanded that he be sold, with his wife and children and all that he had, and that payment be made. The servant therefore fell down before him, saying, 'Master, have patience with me, and I will pay you all.' Then the master of that servant was moved with compassion, released him, and forgave him the debt. (Matt 18:23-27 NKJV)

In this parable, the man who owes an enormous amount of money begs the king for more time to allow him to try and pay back the loan. But the king, upon seeing and hearing the man beg for more time, is moved by compassion and tells the man his debt is forgiven, which is to say his debt is *canceled* and does not need to be paid back. The king does *not* say "Don't worry, I will get someone else to pay me back your loan on your behalf," for if the king did that, then the man's debt would have never been forgiven or canceled—the debt itself would remain outstanding, requiring payment, only to be paid by someone else. But this is *not* what Jesus teaches in this parable. Jesus here makes it very clear what forgiveness is—forgiveness is *canceling* a debt, which means that the debt *never* needs to be paid, remaining forever *unpaid*. *That* is how God views forgiveness.

The Bible constantly tells us our sins are forgiven—it never says our sins have been *paid* for. Throughout the entire New Testament we are repeatedly told our sins are forgiven and we have forgiveness of our sins because of what Jesus Christ has done on the cross.

> In him we have redemption through his blood, the forgiveness of sins, according to the riches of his grace. (Eph 1:7 NKJV)

> And you, being dead in your trespasses and the uncircumcision of your flesh, he has made alive together with him, having forgiven you all trespasses. (Col 2:13 NKJV)

Forgiveness and Payment Cannot Coexist

If our sins have been *paid* for, then they have never been *forgiven*—it cannot be both ways. If Jesus Christ *paid* for our sins upon the cross, then there has never been any *forgiveness* of those sins, there has been only *payment* for those sins.

But the Bible is very clear—our sins have been *forgiven*, therefore they have never been punished, and Jesus himself has clearly illustrated the meaning of forgiveness, of how we are to understand it, in his own parable about debt and forgiveness. To be forgiven means what we owe has been *canceled*—*never* requiring payment. This is in fact what Jesus accomplished upon the cross—he took upon himself the sin of the world and broke its power by bringing it to completion in his death, thereby enabling us to receive God's forgiveness. He is not the Lamb of God who "pays for the sins of the world," but rather, he is the Lamb of God "who *takes away* the sin of the world" (John 1:29). "And you know that he was manifested to take away our sins, and in him there is no sin" (1 John 3:5 NKJV) .With his work upon the cross, Jesus *canceled* our sin.

Our Sins Have Been Canceled

In the Old Testament, God gave a perfect picture of what it means to have our sins *canceled*. In Deuteronomy 15 we are told:

> At the end of every seven years you must cancel debts. This is how it is to be done: Every creditor shall *cancel* any loan they have made to a fellow Israelite. *They shall not require payment* from anyone among their own people, because the Lord's time for canceling debts has been proclaimed. You may require payment from a foreigner, but you must cancel any debt your fellow Israelite owes you. (Deut 15:1–3 NIV)

God here tells Israel that every seven years, all the financial debts of all their people are to be *canceled*, meaning all of those debts will *not* require payment, they will *never* be paid; rather, they will all be canceled, or *forgiven*, remaining forever *unpaid*. This is an exact illustration of what God means by *canceling* one's debt—those debts are to remain forever *unpaid*. Likewise this exact same concept is applied to Jesus Christ and his work on the cross in regards to our sin: "Having *canceled* the charge of our legal indebtedness, which stood against us and condemned us; he has *taken it away*, nailing it to the cross" (Col 2:14 NIV).

Once again, the Bible is very clear—when Jesus was on the cross, he did not *pay* our legal indebtedness, that is, he did not *pay* any penalty for our sin; rather, he *canceled* it, which means he brought *forgiveness* of that legal indebtedness so it remains *forever unpaid, never requiring payment*, exactly as the debts of Israel were canceled every seven years, remaining forever unpaid. The legal indebtedness of our sin, which is what we owed to the requirement of the law, has been *canceled*—our sins have never been paid for, they have been *canceled*, they have been *forgiven*.

The Justice of God—An Adam for an Adam

The perfect justice of God is demonstrated and fulfilled in the *forgiveness* of sins upon the cross, not in the punishment of sins. This perfect justice is demonstrated in the fact it was one man, Adam, who brought all the sin of the world into the world though his blood, and it was one man, Jesus Christ, the Second Adam, who took away that same sin of the world, breaking its power through his blood.

> Therefore, just as sin entered the world through *one man*, and death through sin, and in this way death came to all people, because all sinned. . . . For if the many died by the trespass of the one man, how much more did God's grace and the gift that came by the grace of the one man, Jesus Christ, overflow to the many! Nor can the gift of God be compared with the result of one man's sin: The judgment followed one sin and brought condemnation, but the gift followed many trespasses and brought justification. For if, by the trespass of the one man, death reigned through that one man, how much more will those who receive God's abundant provision of grace and of the gift of righteousness reign in life through the one man, Jesus Christ! Consequently, just as one trespass resulted in condemnation for all people, so also one righteous act resulted in justification and life for all people. For just as through the disobedience of the one man the many were made sinners, so also through the obedience of the one man the many will be made righteous. (Rom 5:12, 15–19 NIV)

This is how we are to understand the work of the cross: it was Jesus Christ, the Second Adam, reversing, taking away, or *redeeming* what the First Adam did. This entire contrast of the First Adam and the Second Adam is outlined in Romans 5:15–19. As a result, we are not presented with a picture of God as a God of vengeance or punishment; rather, we see the perfect picture of God as a God of love, mercy, and forgiveness. It is his love and grace which allowed for a Second Adam to be born, a Second Adam who would redeem what the First Adam had done—this is the fullness of God's character, his grace, his love, and his perfect justice.

Punishment—The Injustice to Unbelievers

The idea of the punishment of Jesus Christ upon the cross, the teaching of penal substitution, presents itself as a teaching of God's justice, but in fact it is not. Rather, the teaching of penal substitution ultimately depicts God as a monstrosity of *injustice*. Here's how.

On the one hand, when talking about the salvation of Christians, penal substitution says all human beings are sinners, having broken God's law, and God's law, his perfect justice, requires punishment for those sins in order for God's law and justice to be satisfied. It goes on to say Jesus took our place on the cross and took the punishment for our sins we owed to the law (i.e., *paying* our legal indebtedness, *not* canceling it), taking that punishment upon himself and, in so doing, he satisfied the

The Crucifixion

requirement of the law and the requirement of God's justice for our sins. As a result, we can now have salvation and fellowship with God, because our sins have now been punished, and justice, God's law, is satisfied.

This entire teaching of penal substitution is based solely and exclusively on being *justified by the law*. There is *nothing* of grace here, although the proponents of punishment say it is God's grace that allowed for Jesus to take our place, but none of that is at all biblical. It is inescapable the teaching of penal substitution is exclusively a justification by the law, even though the Bible clearly tells us no one can be justified by the law (Gal 2:16; 3:11; Rom 3:28). Yet this is how the teaching of penal substitution is applied to Christians.

However, what about non-Christians? What happens when someone dies who is *not* a Christian? The penal substitution teaching says the following: when someone who is *not* a Christian dies, they will be doomed to hell, where they will be *punished for their sins*, because they *rejected the payment of sins* that *was made* on their behalf by Jesus Christ.

In addition to the fact there is no biblical support whatsoever for the idea of penal substitution, it is here the entire teaching of penal substitution not only completely and totally collapses, but also depicts God as utterly unjust. This is best illustrated by looking at a concrete and graphic example.

If you were to ask someone, "Whom do you think is the most evil person who has ever lived?," most people would probably put Adolf Hitler at or near the top of the list. Hitler was responsible for the deaths of 60 million people, and pursued an insane extermination of the Jewish people. This was a kind of evil that is beyond comprehension and, as such, it serves to illustrate the fallacy of penal substitution.

According to penal substitution, when Jesus Christ was on the cross he was punished by God the Father for the sins of Adolf Hitler—Jesus *paid the price*, or *paid the penalty, owed by Hitler* for his sins. The result of this is Hitler could now have salvation *if* he believed in Jesus Christ.

But what happens when Hitler dies an unbeliever, dies *without* accepting Jesus Christ as his Savior, dies *without* believing in him? Penal substitution says in that case, Hitler would go to hell to *pay the penalty* for his own sins, which is eternal damnation and separation from God.

And here is the massive problem—according to penal substitution, Hitler's sins, *all* of them, and the *penalty* for those sins, have *already been paid for* by Jesus Christ on the cross, paid for *in full* so that *nothing was let unpaid*. If Hitler dies an unbeliever, and now must go to hell to pay for his sins, then that means those *exact same sins* of Adolf Hitler are now being paid for *twice*, since Jesus Christ, according to the penal substitution teaching, has *already paid for them* in totality upon the cross.

Is it justice to have the exact same sins being paid for *twice*? That's the same as saying a man owes another man $10,000, and someone else comes along, a third party, and pays the lender the full $10,000 on behalf of the original borrower. Then later the lender comes back to the original borrower and says "I still want another $10,000 from you." Not only is this not just, it is criminal.

Yet this is the heart of penal substitution—there is no justice in it, it is in fact criminal. It teaches God will require not one but *two* punishments for *exactly* the same sin from unbelievers. This is a monstrosity of injustice and depicts God as utterly unjust. Of course, teachers of penal substitution try and create what at times is an almost fantasy-like construct to try and get around this fact, whose ultimate conclusion is a false gospel (i.e., the teaching Jesus did not in fact die for all people, but died only for some people—this is a false gospel, a wretched and evil teaching), but the constructs are meaningless and have no substance. Penal substitution is ultimately a teaching of injustice. Though it presents itself as just, it is a teaching which depicts God as criminal in his injustice—this is inarguable.

In reality though, the teaching of penal substitution, the idea of Jesus Christ being punished on the cross, is a false and unbiblical teaching, and so God is *not* unjust and God does *not* act in a criminal way. The Bible clearly shows there was *no* punishment visited upon Jesus Christ upon the cross. All the sacrifices of the Bible, and especially the sacrifice of Jesus Christ, the Second Adam, upon the cross, is a *taking away* of sin, the breaking of its power by bringing that sin to completion in his death, resulting in the bringing of forgiveness of sins—*forgiveness,* not punishment; a justification by *grace,* not a justification by the law.

As a result, if a person dies an unbeliever, and they have not believed in Jesus Christ and accepted the forgiveness given to them, they are choosing instead to receive the penalty for their sin, to pay that penalty, a penalty which has *never* yet been paid. This means if someone goes to damnation, it will be to endure a punishment that has *never* yet been given for those sins, and so those sins would be punished only *once,* not *twice,* as in the teaching of penal substitution. And so God is shown as just, loving, and gracious.

It must be made absolutely clear God does not want *anyone* to suffer or enter into damnation; he wants *all* people to come to know him, receive his forgiveness, and live with him in joy, love, and beauty, for his love, grace, and forgiveness extend to *all people*:

> The Lord is not slow in keeping his promise, as some understand slowness. Instead he is patient with you, *not wanting anyone to perish,* but *everyone to come to repentance.* (2 Pet 3:9)

Second Peter 3:9 clearly tells us it is *the will* of God that *no one* should perish, but that *all people* would come to salvation. But he has given us all an inviolable free will, and we each get to choose what we will do with our lives, which includes being free to reject God's forgiveness of our sin. God will honor our free-will choice, even if it breaks his heart to do so.

The Parallel between Eden and the Cross—The Two Trees

There is a striking parallel between Eden and the cross, between the First Adam and the Second Adam. The First Adam brought sin and death into the world by eating the fruit of the forbidden tree—it was by way of a *tree* that sin and death came into the world, and to all humanity. The Second Adam took away the sin of the world, broke its power and brought forgiveness of sin to all humanity, by way of a *tree*, by being crucified on a tree:

> The God of our fathers raised up Jesus whom you murdered by hanging *on a tree.* (Acts 5:30 NKJV)

> And we are witnesses of all things which he did both in the land of the Jews and in Jerusalem, whom they killed by hanging *on a tree.* (Acts 10:39 NKJV)

> Who Himself bore our sins in His own body on the tree, that we, having died to sins, might live for righteousness—by whose stripes you were healed. (1 Pet 2:24 NKJV)

Jesus is described as being crucified on a tree, and in fact the Romans often used actual trees as the vertical posts upon which a person was crucified. The condemned man carried the crossbar of the cross upon his back as he made his way to the place of crucifixion. Upon arriving there, there was usually either a manmade post already secured in the ground, or an actual tree growing there, to which the crossbar would be fastened. In the case where the vertical post was a tree, the man was literally being crucified on a tree. The Bible tells us Jesus was crucified upon a tree, which would mean his method of crucifixion was to have the crossbar be literally nailed to an actual tree acting as the vertical post.

It is no coincidence the First Adam brought sin and death into the world by way of a tree, and the Second Adam took away the sin and death of the world, and brought life into the world, through another tree.

The Parallel between the Forbidden Fruit and Communion

The First Adam brought sin and death into the world by literally eating fruit from a tree. Upon *eating* that forbidden fruit, the physical sinful nature came to inhabit Adam's flesh, taking up residence in his blood. It is important to note all of this happened because Adam physically ate something. In effect, all of us have sin within us because Adam *ate* the forbidden fruit, and we have Adam's blood.

It is no coincidence the Second Adam has also given us something to eat. We are to *eat* his body and *drink* his *blood* at communion. Participating in communion is a graphic demonstration of the reversal of eating of the forbidden fruit, and it is also no coincidence that drinking the "blood" of the Second Adam is a key part of communion.

Confession of Sins

> If we *confess our sins*, he is faithful and just and will forgive us our sins and purify us from all unrighteousness. (1 John 1:9 NIV)

If our sins have been taken away, if the power of sin has been broken, and if we, as a result, have the complete forgiveness of our sins, why then are Christians told to "confess our sins," even after we believe in Jesus Christ and after we are born his children? Isn't this redundant? If our sins are already forgiven, why are we told to "confess our sins?"

> If you do what is right, will you not be accepted? But if you do not do what is right, *sin is crouching at your door; it desires to have you,* but you must rule over it. (Gen 4:7 NIV)

Even though Jesus Christ conquered sin and fully broke its power upon the cross, we still have our physical sinful nature residing within us, within our flesh, within our blood, even after we come to Christ. Our sinful nature is still there, even though its power has been broken. It is the nature of sin to desire destruction, so the sin that remains within us, even though it has been made powerless and we are no longer slaves to that sin, still has a *desire* to want to try and *get a foothold* in our lives, it still wants to try and rear its head to somehow try and enslave us again, so as to destroy us. As Ephesians 4:27 warns us: "and do not give the devil a *foothold*" (NIV).

This is why, even after we come to Christ and are born God's children, we can still sin. When we, as Christians, sin, it is the powerless sin within us trying to get a foothold once again upon us, trying to gain a little bit of ground to operate within our lives, to deceive, enslave, and destroy us. It is sin trying to reassert its broken power within our lives again.

This is why when we, as Christians, sin, we are told to *confess* our sin to God. Even though our sinful nature has already been made powerless, and we have received the full forgiveness of our sins by Jesus' accomplishment upon the cross, our act of confessing our sin to God, our Father, and asking for forgiveness of that sin, is an act of *destroying the foothold* the sin within us is *trying* to make. When we sin and then confess our sin, we are affirming our *appropriation* of Jesus' accomplishment upon the cross, affirming our *appropriation* of the complete breaking of the power of sin. By so doing, we are *applying* Jesus' accomplishment upon the cross to the power of the sin that is trying to reassert itself in our lives. In effect, we are reaffirming the destruction of sin's power within our lives. By confessing our sin, we are making that potential foothold of sin in our lives powerless. And so we see the act of confessing our sin is not a begging for forgiveness for we already have full forgiveness of our sin; rather, it is a complete *disarming* of the power of the sin that still resides within us as it tries to reassert itself and gain a foothold within our lives. Our act of confession disarms that attempted reassertion of sin.

Verses Used to Support the Punishment of Jesus Christ

The notion of Jesus Christ being punished for the sins of the world has no scriptural support, yet various Scriptures are quoted as supporting the teaching of punishment upon the cross.

Galatians 3:13

> Christ has redeemed us from the curse of the law, having become a curse for us (for it is written, "Cursed *is* everyone who hangs on a tree"). (NKJV)

Galatians 3:13 is used to try and support the notion of punishment, however, as a clear reading of the verse indicates, there is neither mention nor hint of punishment for sin in that verse. People take the idea of "curse" and equate it with meaning "punishment," which of course it does not. The meaning of "curse" in that verse is, at its very basic level, explained and defined by the verse itself. If a man is hanging on a tree, that man is considered cursed. So, for example, if you're walking down the street and see a man hanging on a tree, you will look at him and say, "that man is hanging on a tree, so he is cursed." It's nothing more than that, at the very basic level—Jesus Christ, just by virtue of being nailed to a tree, was a cursed man, as were also the two thieves crucified with him—they were also hanging on a tree, so they also were cursed, as were all the many tens of thousands of people the Romans crucified over the centuries. The difference between Jesus and everyone else hanging on a tree is Jesus, while he was hanging on a tree, took the sin of the world upon himself, and this brings us to the other level of meaning of the word "curse."

To say Jesus "became a curse for us" means only that he took the sin of the world upon himself and, with it, the whole curse of that sin—the curse of its full death, its brokenness, its fear, and its deception. In fact, in Galatians 3:13, we are clearly told what this curse actually is: the curse of the law, the curse by which sin is caused to increase, or rather, to be shown and to be exposed, making it impossible for anyone with the sinful nature to fulfill the law. Fulfilling the law can only be done by living a sinless life. "The law was brought in so that the trespass might increase. But where sin increased, grace increased all the more" (Rom 5:20 NIV).

Jesus "became a curse" in the same way he was "made to be sin" (2 Cor 5:21)—he was "made to be sin" by taking the sin of the world upon himself and, in doing so, having sin enter into his sinless blood to inhabit it so that, by shedding his blood and by dying, he broke the power of that sin. This is also exactly what it means to say he "became a curse for us"—he became a curse for us by taking the sin of the world upon himself, sin which then came to inhabit his sinless blood, and by shedding his sinless blood as the sacrifice for sins, and by his death, he took away, or made powerless, the sin of the world. There is nothing about punishment here; the phrase "became a curse" has absolutely nothing to do with punishment, but is a further affirmation of the mechanism of sacrifice.

First Timothy 2:6 and Hebrews 9:15

> Who gave himself as a ransom for all people. This has now been witnessed to at the proper time. (1 Tim 2:6 NIV)

> For this reason Christ is the mediator of a new covenant, that those who are called may receive the promised eternal inheritance—now that he has died as a ransom to set them free from the sins committed under the first covenant. (Heb 9:15 NIV)

In these verses Jesus is described as one who "gave himself as a ransom for all people," and as one who "died as a ransom to set them free from sins." In reading these verses, those who are looking to find scriptural support for the punishment of Jesus Christ upon the cross believe it is found here. However, as with every other verse invoked to support the notion of punishment upon the cross, no such meaning is contained within these verses.

What does the term "ransom" mean? The common way people think of it is the same way as one would see it used in a movie about someone being kidnapped—that one has to pay a price in order to get a loved one back. Here are some meanings of the word "ransom":

1. The redemption of a prisoner, slave, or kidnapped person, of captured goods, etc., for a price;
2. The sum or price paid or demanded;
3. Means of deliverance or rescue from punishment for sin, especially the payment of a redemptive fine;
4. To redeem from captivity, bondage, detention, by paying a demanded price;
5. To release or restore on receipt of a ransom;
6. To deliver or redeem from punishment for sin.[1]

---

1. https://www.dictionary.com/browse/ransom?s=t.

A ransom is something given that sets one free. The something given that sets one free here is that Jesus gave himself to death upon the cross. The ransom given was Jesus' death; it was not him being a recipient of the outpouring of legal wrath but rather it was the giving of himself over to death, the giving of his life, his sacrifice, to take away the sin of the world and to break its power. To be a ransom has nothing to do with divine punishment.

The price of the ransom is simply this: Jesus Christ gave his life, gave himself, over to death, taking the sin of the world upon himself and sacrificing himself and shedding his blood, bringing the sin of the world to full conclusion and completion in his death, so as to take away the sin of the world, to break its power. This is also affirmed in the following verses:

> You were bought at a price. Therefore honor God with your bodies. (1 Cor 6:20 NIV)

> You were bought at a price; do not become slaves of human beings. (1 Cor 7:23 NIV)

The price with which we were purchased was the death of Jesus Christ, not the pouring out of the punishing wrath of the Father upon Jesus. Jesus sacrificed himself for us upon the cross, giving his life so as to take away the sin of the world and as a result breaking the power of that sin, so that we can receive God's forgiveness of our sins.

The additional and incalculable cost is that in doing this, in becoming incarnate, in taking on Adam's created flesh forever, Jesus Christ, God the Son, *permanently* and *forever let go of his equality with the Father*, never to be equal with the Father again (Phil 2:6–8). This above all is the true cost of our salvation and of the taking away of our sin, and it is an incalculable cost—Jesus Christ is *eternally* incarnate and, being so, he let go of his equality with the Father, not temporarily, not for thirty-three years, but *forever*. This is the true and incomprehensible cost of our salvation.

Second Corinthians 5:21

> God made him who had no sin to be sin for us, so that in him we might become the righteousness of God. (NIV)

This was already explained previously—this simply means after Jesus took upon himself the sin of the world, that same sin entered into, and came to inhabit, his sinless blood. When the sin of the world entered into his sinless blood, to inhabit his shedding blood, his blood became sin, expressed here as "God made him who had no sin to *be sin* for us." As he hung on the cross, and as he was shedding his sinless blood, Jesus' blood actually, physically, came to be inhabited by the sin of the world, the sin of Adam. It is in this way Jesus was made to "be" sin. This again has nothing whatsoever to do with punishment.

Romans 8:3–4

> For what the law was powerless to do because it was weakened by the flesh, God did by sending his own Son in the likeness of sinful flesh to be a sin offering. And so he condemned sin in the flesh, in order that the *righteous requirement of the law* might be fully met in us, who do not live according to the flesh but according to the Spirit. (NIV)

Jesus, as the Second Adam, came to redeem what the First Adam did—he came to take away the sin of the world which the First Adam, through his blood, brought into the world. The law could not do this; in fact, the law exposes the sinful nature, causes it to react against it, and so we are told the power of sin, that is, the thing which causes sin to react, is the law: "The sting of death is sin, and the power of sin is the law" (1 Cor 15:56 NIV).

The purpose of the law was to expose our sinful nature by causing our sinful nature to react against the law, and so show itself as sin: "The law was brought in so that the trespass might increase. But where sin increased, grace increased all the more" (Rom 5:20 NIV). It was never the purpose of the law to redeem us; rather, its purpose was to show us we cannot fulfill the requirements of the law. Its fulfillment was impossible, since it is the very nature of the law, its very holiness, which causes our sinful nature to react against it, making our sinful nature show itself, to expose our sin. This is what it means when it says the law was "powerless" and was "weakened by the flesh." The flesh is where our sinful natures reside, in our blood, and it is our sinful nature reacting against the law that makes it impossible for us to fulfill the law.

As a result, the purpose of the law was to show us the impossibility of us keeping or fulfilling the law. The purpose of this was to prepare us for the coming of the Second Adam who, by his sinless blood, would take upon himself the sin of the world, take that sin away and break its power, freeing us from the power of sin—which is what the law of God could never do. He did this by dying on the cross, by shedding his blood, which is described as "condemning sin in the flesh." He condemned sin in his own flesh by taking the sin upon himself, into his own sinless blood, into his own flesh, and breaking its power by shedding his blood, by dying, thereby rendering sin powerless, broken, and condemned.

The "righteous requirement" is a reference to the fact the one who took away the sin, the one who broke its power, never sinned—Jesus fulfilled the righteous requirement of the law by *never sinning*—he did *not* fulfill the law by being *punished* on the cross; rather, he fulfilled the righteous requirement of the law by living a life without sin.

Matthew 5:17

> Do not think that I have come to abolish the law or the Prophets; I have not come to abolish them but to fulfill them. (NIV)

Those who want to promote the notion of punishment upon the cross also refer to Matthew 5:17, and to the fact Jesus says he came to "fulfill" the law. They take that verse, and the idea of fulfilling the law, to mean Jesus, upon the cross, satisfied the "requirement" of the law, also as described in Romans 8:3–4, saying this requirement of the law was the punishment for sins. Therefore Jesus upon the cross must have been punished for the sins of humanity, and this is how he fulfilled the requirement of the law. This of course is false.

Jesus neither fulfilled the law, nor the requirement of the law, by being punished on the cross for anyone's sins. Jesus fulfilled the law, and the requirement of the law, by *living a sinless life*. Jesus never sinned. As a result of never sinning, Jesus *fulfilled* the law and its righteous requirement. That which was impossible for us to do—to fulfill the law and its perfect requirement by leading a sinless life, impossible for us because of the sinful nature residing in our flesh, in our blood—Jesus was able to do, and did do, for he had no sinful nature—his blood was pure. As a result, Jesus lived a completely sinless life. This is why he was resurrected, because he never sinned, and, because he never sinned, death, which is the wage of sin (Rom 6:23), had no power over him and could not hold him (Acts 2:24). Jesus did not fulfill the law and its requirement in his death upon the cross; rather, he fulfilled the law and its requirement by his life, by living a completely sinless life. Again, neither Matthew 5:17 nor Romans 8:3–4 have anything to do with punishment for sins.

Atonement, Propitiation, Expiation

In addition to the various Scripture verses invoked to support penal substitution, the words "atonement," "propitiation," and "expiation" are also sometimes invoked. Those who invoke them say these words mean a payment has been made. In fact, none of these words mean a payment has been made; rather, they mean a reconciliation is being made, it means things are being made right. To make atonement means to make right. To be a propitiation or an expiation means to be a reconciliation.

How is reconciliation made? How are things made right? By punishing Jesus on the cross? No; reconciliation is made by *forgiving* sins, as it is by the *forgiveness* of sins that things are made right between God and man, and God and man are reconciled. Atonement, propitiation, and expiation do not mean payment or punishment, they mean reconciliation by way of forgiveness.

Leviticus 5:6

> As *a penalty for the sin they have committed*, they must bring to the Lord a female lamb or goat from the flock as a sin offering; and the priest shall make atonement for them for their sin. (NIV)

Sometimes Leviticus 5:6 is invoked as a support of penal substitution. The reason for this is only in a very few translations of Leviticus is the word "offering" *translated* as "penalty." This is the case in the NIV translation, as well as the NLT translation. Leviticus 5:6 is an example of such an instance. However, in the great majority of Bible translations, this is *not* how Leviticus 5:6 is translated—the great majority do *not* translate the word as *penalty;* rather, it is translated correctly as *offering*. Here is Leviticus 5:6 across a number of standard translations:

> And he shall bring his *trespass-offering* unto Jehovah for his sin which he hath sinned. (ASV)

And bring his guilt *offering* to Adonai for the sin he committed; it is to be a female from the flock. (CJB)

Therefore shall he bring his trespass *offering* unto the Lord for his sin which he hath committed. (Geneva Bible)

And he shall bring his trespass *offering* unto the Lord for his sin which he hath sinned. (KJV)

And bring his guilt *offering* to the Lord, a female lamb or goat, and the priest shall make atonement for him. (TLB)

He shall also bring his guilt *offering* to the Lord for his sin which he has committed. (NASB)

And he shall bring his trespass *offering* to the Lord for his sin which he has committed. (NKJV)

And he shall bring his guilt *offering* to the Lord for the sin which he has committed. (RSV)

And hath brought in his *guilt-offering* to Jehovah for his sin which he hath sinned. (YLT)

In the great majority of cases, Leviticus 5:6 is translated as "offering," not "penalty," and "offering" is in fact the correct translation. Why then do some translations use the word "penalty?" It is because the translators are viewing the text through their preconception of penal substitution, and as such, they read into the text what is not there. Leviticus 5:6 does *not* refer to a sacrifice as being a *penalty* for sin; rather, it is correctly translated as being an *offering*, or *sacrifice*, for sin, with no punishment involved.

Conclusion

There is no scriptural support whatsoever for the teaching of penal substitution. In fact, there is no scriptural support whatsoever for any sacrifice being the recipient of punishment for sins. No such concept of punishment for sin sacrifices exists anywhere in the Bible.

The Bible is very clear Jesus was completely and fully human, with the exact same humanity as Adam, but because he did not have a human father, Jesus did not inherit Adam's sinful nature. As a result, Jesus' blood was free of the sinful nature and so is described as precious, holy, and pure. In his life, Jesus never sinned, and so Jesus conquered sin in his life and received all authority over sin. Upon being crucified, he took upon himself the sin of the world, which is the sin of Adam, and that same sin then entered into, and came to inhabit, his sinless blood—as a result, Jesus was made to actually *be* sin, having the sin of the world come *in* to his body. Jesus then shed his blood, which carried within it the sin of the world, and he died upon the cross, the sacrifice of the Second Adam. Though he himself was completely sinless, by sacrificing himself upon the cross, by dying on the cross while the sin of the world was upon him and within him, Jesus brought the entirety of that sin of the world to full conclusion, bringing it to completion in his death, satisfying that sin's demand, its hunger, its wage, for death. In so doing, by bringing the sin of humanity to completion in his death, Jesus fully and completely broke the power of that sin and made it powerless. That sin was "finished" in his death, fulfilled in the death he gave it, and so was its power. Jesus, by his death, destroyed the power of sin utterly. The result was humanity was now made free to receive God's total and complete forgiveness of sin, the complete forgiveness of the full sin of all humanity.

In all of this, while Jesus was accomplishing this upon the cross, God the Father never turned his face away from Jesus, and there was no divine punishment for sins whatsoever—there was only the breaking of the power of sin, the completion of sin in death, and the forgiveness of sins. Our sins have never been punished, they have been forgiven. God is not a vengeful ogre demanding vengeance, a slave to his own law; rather, he is a God of love, a God who forgives. He has forgiven us our sins and made it possible for us to receive that forgiveness by breaking the deceptive power of our sinful natures, breaking that power upon the cross by the death of Jesus Christ. Our sins have been forgiven; not punished, but *forgiven*. All of this was accomplished in its entirety by the death of Jesus Christ, the Second Adam, upon the cross.

17

The Realm of the Dead

JESUS CHRIST, THE SECOND Adam, brought the sin of humanity to full conclusion and completion in his death upon the cross, satisfying that sin's demand for death, and thereby breaking its power and redeeming the fall of the First Adam. He himself had conquered sin and had gained all authority over it. Jesus Christ faced death head-on—as a result, even though he died, death would not be able to hold him, and in his resurrection he would demonstrate his victory over death. Yet he remained dead and buried for three days. Where was Jesus for those three days? What was he doing for those three days?

For the three days Jesus was dead, Jesus went where every human being who had ever lived and died had gone—he went to the Realm of the Dead, called in Hebrew Sheol, and in Greek Hades.

Sheol and Hades

The Realm of the Dead/Sheol/Hades, is the place where all human beings who had ever lived and died, from the time of Adam to the time of Jesus Christ, had gone to upon their death to await the judgment. No human being had ever gone to heaven, and no human being had ever gone to hell; rather, all human beings, upon their death, went only to Sheol/Hades/the Realm of the Dead. All dead humanity were there: Adam, Eve, Noah, Abraham, Isaac, Jacob, Moses, David, Solomon, John the Baptist, Elijah, and Enoch (John 3:13; 2 Chr 21:12) among others. Every human being who had ever lived and died before Jesus Christ was in the Realm of the Dead at the time of Jesus' death. Upon his own death, for three days, Jesus Christ himself also went to the Realm of the Dead.

Location of the Realm of the Dead

The Bible has many verses about the Realm of the Dead and tells us very clearly where it is located. The Realm of the Dead is located *inside the earth*:

> For a fire will be kindled by my wrath, one that burns *down to the realm of the dead below*. (Deut 32:22 NIV)

> The wicked go down to the realm of the dead, all the nations that forget God. (Ps 9:17 NIV)

> For great is your love toward me; you have delivered me from *the depths, from the realm of the dead*. (Ps 86:13 NIV)

> The path of life leads upward for the prudent to keep them from *going down to the realm of the dead*. (Prov 15:24 NIV)

> The *realm of the dead below* is all astir to meet you at your coming; it rouses the spirits of the departed to greet you—all those who were leaders in the world; it makes them rise from their thrones— all those who were kings over the nations. (Isa 14:9 NIV)

> You went to Molek with olive oil and increased your perfumes. You sent your ambassadors far away; *you descended to the very realm of the dead*! (Isa 57:9 NIV)

> *They are all destined for death, for the earth below*, among mortals who go down to the realm of the dead. (Ezek 31:14 NIV)

> That at the name of Jesus every knee should bow,
> in heaven and on earth and *under the earth*,
> and every tongue acknowledge that Jesus Christ is Lord,
> to the glory of God the Father. (Phil 2:10-11 NIV)

> Then I heard every creature in heaven and on earth and *under the earth* and on the sea, and all that is in them, saying: 'To him who sits on the throne and to the Lamb be praise and honor and glory and power, for ever and ever!' (Rev 5:13 NIV)

Both Revelation 5:13 and Philippians 2:10–11 make specific reference to those in heaven, on the earth and *under* the earth. What does the phrase "under the earth" refer to? It refers to those who are in the Realm of the Dead. It also refers to the fallen angels who would still be in the pit, which is also inside the earth. The Bible is very clear—the Realm of the Dead is located inside the earth.

The Realm of the Dead beneath the Floors of the Seas

Not only is the Realm of the Dead located inside the earth, more specifically it is located *beneath the floors of the seas and oceans*. "The dead are in deep anguish, those beneath the *waters* and all that live in them" (Job 26:5 NIV). This verse does not say the dead are *in* the waters; rather, we are told the dead are *beneath* the waters, which is to say they are *underneath* the waters, or underneath the floors of the seas and oceans.

The seas and oceans are a curse and judgment of God upon the earth. This is the case in Genesis 1:2, where the entire Earth is cursed by darkness, covered by the curse of the global ocean, and rendered utterly uninhabitable. It is also the case with the flood of Genesis 6 and 7. The curse of seas and oceans will finally be removed when God fully redeems Earth and makes it ready to receive his eternal kingdom (Rev 21:1), and at that same time the curse of darkness will also be finally lifted (Rev 22:5). The fact that the Realm of the Dead/Sheol/Hades, is located beneath the floors of the seas is also further affirmed by Revelation 20:13: "The sea gave up the dead that were in it, and death and Hades gave up the dead that were in them" (NIV).

There are some who interpret the words "the sea gave up the dead that were in it" as meaning that the sea gives up the people who were drowned. This cannot be the case, since the sea is not full of the millennia of drowned human corpses. Rather, in this verse, the sea, Hades and death are all interconnected to one another—the dead that Hades and death give up are the *same dead* the sea gives up, for Hades, the Realm of the Dead, is located *beneath* the floors of the seas, beneath the waters, as is specifically outlined in Job 26:5. To say the sea "gave up its dead" is the same as saying Hades gave up its dead, since Hades is located beneath the floors of the seas.

Together these verses are a further affirmation that the Realm of the Dead/Sheol/Hades, is located inside the earth and, more specifically, beneath the floors of the seas and oceans. Being covered by the seas and oceans is an illustration of death being covered by the judgment of God.

Description of the Realm of the Dead

What is the Realm of the Dead like? Does the Bible give us any description of that place? Jesus himself gives us a description:

> There was a rich man who was dressed in purple and fine linen and lived in luxury every day. At his gate was laid a beggar named Lazarus, covered with sores and longing to eat what fell from the rich man's table. Even the dogs came and licked his sores.
> The time came when the beggar died and the angels carried him to Abraham's side. The rich man also died and was buried. In Hades, where he was in torment, he looked up and saw Abraham far away, with Lazarus by his side. So he called to him, 'Father Abraham, have pity on me and send Lazarus to dip the tip of his finger in water and cool my tongue, because I am in agony in this fire.'
> But Abraham replied, 'Son, remember that in your lifetime you received your good things, while Lazarus received bad things, but now he is comforted here and you are in agony. And besides all this, between us and you a great chasm has been set in place, so that those who want to go from here to you cannot, nor can anyone cross over from there to us.'
> He answered, 'Then I beg you, father, send Lazarus to my family, for I have five brothers. Let him warn them, so that they will not also come to this place of torment.'
> Abraham replied, 'They have Moses and the Prophets; let them listen to them.'
> 'No, father Abraham,' he said, 'but if someone from the dead goes to them, they will repent.'
> He said to him, 'If they do not listen to Moses and the Prophets, they will not be convinced even if someone rises from the dead.' (Luke 16:19–31 NIV)

In this passage, Jesus is describing the Realm of the Dead. But is this not just a parable, a story being told for the purpose of illustration? In order to understand this passage, we must remember when the disciples asked Jesus why he speaks to the people in parables, Jesus answered them as follows:

> The disciples came to him and asked, 'Why do you speak to the people in parables?'
>
> He replied, 'Because the knowledge of the secrets of the kingdom of heaven has been given to you, but not to them. Whoever has will be given more, and they will have an abundance. Whoever does not have, even what they have will be taken from them. This is why I speak to them in parables: Though seeing, they do not see; though hearing, they do not hear or understand.' (Matt 13:10–13 NIV)

Jesus tells his disciples he speaks to the people in parables so the people will not understand the knowledge of the secrets of the kingdom of heaven, but to his disciples Jesus speaks plainly, and *not in parables*, so they *will* understand the knowledge of the secrets of the kingdom of heaven. This is important to understand when considering this passage in Luke 16 about the Realm of the Dead.

The passage in Luke 16 was spoken by Jesus to *his disciples* (though others, such as the Pharisees, were present and could overhear, they were not the audience to whom Jesus was speaking). Since Jesus specifically tells us he does *not* speak to his disciples in parables, and since in Luke 16 he *is* speaking to his disciples, we can conclude this passage in Luke 16 is not a parable; rather, it is an account of an actual event. Also, there are other reasons that support the understanding that this passage in Luke 16 is not a parable but rather is an account of actual events.

The passage in Luke 16 is uniquely different from any other parable Jesus taught. In all of Jesus' parables, the people who are the subject of the parable are *general* people with no name ("There was a man who had two sons" [Luke 15:11], "At that time the kingdom of heaven will be like ten virgins" [Matt 25:1], "There was a rich man" [Luke 16:1]). In all cases, the characters in the parables are general figures, nameless, used to illustrate a point.

This is where Luke 16:19–31 differs markedly. This is the only instance of Jesus giving a parable where a character is given a *specific name*—in this case, Lazarus. The very fact that in this parable Jesus *names* the person in the story makes this account in Luke stand out from all other parables. As a result, this is one of the key reasons why people consider Luke 16:19–31 to be a description of actual events and not a parable.

Also, if Jesus, for whatever unique reason, just decided to make up a name for the character in the Luke 16:19–31 parable, he could have chosen any name under the sun, but he did not; rather, he chose the name

Lazarus. This itself is an indication Luke 16 is a description of actual events and not a parable. Jesus would raise another man named Lazarus from the dead, and as a result if Jesus was using only a made-up name in his story of the beggar and the rich man, then why would he use a name that is the same name as the man whom he would later raise from the dead? Would this not lead to a later confusion of events? Would that mean the Lazarus named in Luke 16 is in fact the same Lazarus Jesus would later raise from the dead? What would be the purpose of such a potential confusion if Luke 16 was only a parable?

The fact Luke 16:19–31 is the only instance where Jesus names the person in his story, the fact the name Jesus uses could easily be confused with another later event involving someone of the same name, and the fact Jesus is addressing his disciples, to whom he speaks plainly and not in parables, all leads to the conclusion the account in Luke 16:19–31 is not a parable but rather is an account of actual events.

Jesus Describes the Realm of the Dead

In Luke 16:19–31, Jesus gives specific details about the Realm of the Dead, here called by the Greek name Hades. First, Jesus describes Hades as being divided into two sections—one section is a place of torment (v. 23), and the other section a place of peace (v. 22, "Abraham's Side" or "Abraham's Bosom"). He also describes Hades as having a great chasm, or canyon, dividing the two sections of Hades, so it was impossible for anyone to get from one side to the other (v. 26). He also describes Hades as a place where people from the two sections could communicate with each other across the chasm (vv. 23–24).

From Jesus' account, we see the Realm of the Dead is divided into two sections: one for people who in life had a sort of propensity toward God, and who are now in a place of peace, or even paradise, while the other is a place of torment for people who in life did not pay any regard to God. This is Jesus' description of the Realm of the Dead, a place located inside the earth, located beneath the judgment waters of the seas and the oceans, beneath the floors of the seas.

Today You Will Be with Me in Paradise

When Jesus was upon the cross, two others were crucified together with him. While on the cross, Jesus turned to the thief beside him and said: "Truly I tell you, today you will be with me in paradise" (Luke 23:43 NIV). Jesus did not ascend to heaven until forty days *after* his resurrection (Acts 1:3–11). How then could Jesus say to the thief that "Today" they would be in paradise? When Jesus said those words to the thief upon the cross, he was *not* referring to heaven; rather, he was referring to the Realm of the Dead, more specifically to the "Abraham's Bosom" section of Hades, the "paradise" section, as described in Luke 16. On the very same day Jesus died, he went to the Realm of the Dead, to Abraham's Bosom, a paradise, as did the thief crucified with him.

Jesus in the Realm of the Dead

When Jesus died, he, like all human beings before him, went to the Realm of the Dead, but he did not stay there, for three days later he was resurrected: "Seeing what was to come, he spoke of the resurrection of the Messiah, that he was not abandoned to the realm of the dead, nor did his body see decay" (Acts 2:31 NIV). What did Jesus do for the three days he was in the Realm of the Dead? The Bible tells us:

> For Christ also suffered once for sins, the just for the unjust, that he might bring us to God, being put to death in the flesh but made alive by the Spirit, by whom also he went and preached to the spirits in prison, who formerly were disobedient, when once the divine longsuffering waited in the days of Noah, while the ark was being prepared, in which a few, that is, eight souls, were saved through water" (1 Pet 3:18–20 NKJV)

Jesus Preached to the Spirits in Prison

We are told here that one of the things Jesus did during the three days he was in the Realm of the Dead, was he preached to the spirits in prison who had sinned during the time of Noah. These are almost certainly the fallen angels of Genesis 6:2, the sons of God, whose sexual union with human women was the reason the flood was sent, and who are elsewhere also described as being in a prison of chains and darkness (Jude 6–7).

Most understand this passage to mean Jesus went and pronounced judgment, or triumph and victory, upon those spirits, which is also outlined in Colossians 2:15: "Having disarmed principalities and powers, he made a public spectacle of them, triumphing over them in it" (NKJV).

The Gospel Preached to the Dead

Even more importantly, while Jesus was in the Realm of the Dead, present there with all the human beings who had ever lived upon the earth from the time of Adam right up to the time of his own death, Jesus preached to all the dead, preaching to them that he was the Messiah, their Savior, telling the dead that whoever believed in him would have eternal life. In other words, Jesus preached the gospel to the dead. The Bible clearly tells us this was the case: "For this reason *the gospel was preached also to those who are dead*, that they might be judged according to men in the flesh, but live according to God in the spirit" (1 Pet 4:6 NKJV).

Peter specifically tells us the gospel was preached to the dead. How was this possible? It was preached by Jesus Christ himself during the three days he was in Sheol/Hades, the Realm of the Dead. John the Baptist of course was there, since he was killed before Jesus was crucified, and John the Baptist himself would testify, in the Realm of the Dead, that Jesus was in fact the Messiah, and would bear witness to him. Abraham would also be a witness to him, for Jesus tells us: "Your father Abraham rejoiced to see My day, and he saw it and was glad" (John 8:56 NIV). Abraham, in the Realm of the Dead, would have recognized Jesus as the Messiah, and would have testified to that truth.

While in the Realm of the Dead, Jesus preached the gospel to all the human beings who had ever lived and died before his coming, before his incarnation. This answers two valid questions that have been raised many times concerning the gospel: "What about all the people who lived before Jesus Christ? They didn't get a chance to believe, so how is that fair?" These are powerful questions that speak directly to the love and justice of God. Indeed it would be neither fair nor just of God if he was to abandon all human beings who had lived before Jesus, and not give them the chance to hear the gospel, to believe and have salvation.

But the Bible clearly tells us God did *not* abandon the people who had lived and died before the coming of Jesus Christ, for *all* of those people were in the Realm of the Dead, they were all in the same place Jesus went to after his own death. While Jesus was there in the Realm of the Dead, with everyone who had ever lived, he preached the gospel to them. He declared to them that he was the Messiah and that whoever believes in him would have eternal life. In this way, every human being who had ever lived before Jesus' incarnation had a chance to both hear the gospel and to believe and be saved.

God abandons no one, loves everyone, and brought the gospel to everyone who has ever lived, including the dead, so everyone would have a chance to hear the gospel of Jesus Christ, believe, and inherit salvation.

What Happened When the Dead Believed?

When Jesus declared himself to be the Messiah in the Realm of the Dead, the dead had a chance to believe. If they chose to believe, then they would be taken out of the Realm of the Dead after Jesus' resurrection, and would be taken to heaven after his ascension. In fact, this is exactly what we see in Matthew 27:52–53:

> And the tombs broke open. The bodies of many holy people who had died were raised to life. They came out of the tombs after Jesus' resurrection and went into the holy city and appeared to many people. (NIV)

We are told here that *after* Jesus was resurrected, *other* dead people were *also* resurrected. These resurrected people were in fact only *some* of the dead from Hades who believed upon hearing the gospel, preached to them by Jesus while he was in the Realm of the Dead. Upon Jesus' resurrection, the ones specifically mentioned in Matthew 27:52–53 also physically rose from the dead—these were resurrected as a demonstration and witness of the resurrection and saving power of Jesus Christ.

Not all of the dead who believed, though, were resurrected. Those who were described in Matthew 27:52–53 were only a very small minority of the dead who believed. The great majority of dead who believed were not resurrected; rather, they would remain in the Realm of the Dead until Jesus himself ascended to heaven. After Jesus ascended to heaven (Acts 1:8–11), then all of those in the Realm of the Dead who did believe the gospel would also ascend to heaven. Only after Jesus ascended to heaven would all those in the Realm of the Dead ascend to heaven, forever leaving the Realm of the Dead.

The dead mentioned in Matthew 27:52–53, the ones who were resurrected after Jesus' own resurrection, would also, like Jesus, later ascend to heaven, ascending only after Jesus himself ascended to heaven. While in the Realm of the Dead, Jesus preached the gospel to *all* the people who had ever lived and died, not just to those in paradise, but also to those in torments—*everyone* had a chance to believe and to enter into salvation. This was the love and mercy of God.

The Realm of the Dead Since the Resurrection

Ever since Jesus' resurrection, the paradise side of Hades has been empty, for all those in the paradise section (i.e., Abraham's Bosom) would have believed and become Christians, and so would have ascended to heaven after Jesus himself ascended. Those in the Realm of the Dead who did not believe in Jesus remained in the Realm of the Dead, remaining in the torments section, and remain there still, awaiting judgment (Rev 20:11–14).

Ever since the resurrection of Jesus Christ, when a believer dies, they go directly to heaven to be with him who ascended to sit at the right hand of the Father, and who is there right now (Acts 2:33; 2 Cor 5:8). Upon their death, believers do *not* go to the Realm of the Dead; rather, they go *directly* to heaven to be with Jesus. Also, ever since the resurrection, those who die without believing in Jesus Christ *will* go to the Realm of the Dead, to Sheol or Hades, to await the judgment.

It is God's will that all people come to him, receive his love, and receive the forgiveness accomplished for them by Jesus Christ, but God has given us all free will, and he will honor the free-will choices we make, even if it breaks his heart to do so. Our free will is inviolate and can never be taken away, and the reason God gave us free will is without free will, there can be no love, and God wants our love, given freely, just as he freely loves us.

This then is the wonderful and breathtaking love of God—he abandons no one, he loves everyone, and *all* get a chance to hear the gospel and to believe and inherit salvation, both the living and the dead, for it is the will of God that *all* believe (2 Pet 3:9). God has given us all an inviolable free will, whereby we can *choose* to love him, to believe in him, and thereby spend eternity with him in joy, love, glory, fulfillment, and wonder—and this is God's will and hope for us all. This love, mercy, and grace God extends to *all* people who have ever lived, including all the people who lived and died before the incarnation. God ensured they all had a chance to hear the gospel and believe, to inherit salvation. This is why the gospel was preached to the dead by Jesus himself in the Realm of the Dead during the three days he was dead, so everyone who had ever lived would hear the gospel and have the chance to believe.

Jesus spent three days in the Realm of the Dead. But in his life, Jesus Christ had conquered sin, and by conquering sin he had also conquered death. As a result of conquering death, death could not hold the Second Adam, and so, after the three days, Jesus Christ was resurrected.

18

The Resurrection

IN HIS LIFE, BY remaining sinless, Jesus Christ conquered sin, and he then broke the power of sin while upon the cross. In breaking the power of sin he also broke the power of death and gained victory over it (Heb 2:14; Rev 1:18). As a result of Jesus Christ's triumph over death, death had no power over him (Acts 2:24; Rom 6:9). Jesus died upon the cross, and in so doing he faced death head-on, and for three days he lay dead, residing for that time in the Realm of the Dead within the earth. But since death had no power over him, and since he conquered death, even though he lay dead, death could not hold him. Since death could not hold him, Jesus Christ arose from the dead after three days. The resurrection of Jesus Christ bears witness to his triumph over death, proving he conquered death.

Without the Resurrection, the Cross is Nothing

The resurrection of Jesus Christ was the single greatest event in human history, for without the resurrection the cross is nothing:

> But if it is preached that Christ has been raised from the dead, how can some of you say that there is no resurrection of the dead? If there is no resurrection of the dead, then not even Christ has been raised. And if Christ has not been raised, our preaching is useless and so is your faith. More than that, we are then found to be false witnesses about God, for we have testified about God that he raised Christ from the dead. But he did not raise him if in fact

> the dead are not raised. For if the dead are not raised, then Christ has not been raised either. And if Christ has not been raised, your faith is futile; you are still in your sins. Then those also who have fallen asleep in Christ are lost. If only for this life we have hope in Christ, we are of all people most to be pitied. But Christ has indeed been raised from the dead, the first fruits of those who have fallen asleep. (1 Cor 15:12–20 NIV)

Paul tells us if there is no resurrection, then Christians are to be pitied above all people. In other words, if there is no resurrection, then Christians are fools to believe what they do. But then he affirms, and makes very clear, that Jesus Christ *was* resurrected, and his resurrection makes all the difference.

What Does it Mean that Jesus Was Resurrected?

To be resurrected means to rise from the dead and come back to life. But what kind of rising does this mean? Lazarus was also raised from the dead (John 11:1–44)—was the raising of Lazarus from the dead the same as the resurrection of Jesus Christ?

Lazarus rising from the dead was *not* the same as the resurrection of Jesus Christ. Lazarus was indeed raised from the dead, but he would later die again, whereas Jesus, in his resurrection, will *never* die again—the resurrection of Jesus Christ is *eternal*, it is *permanent*, for with his resurrection Jesus demonstrated his *permanent conquest* and *triumph* over death. Upon his resurrection, Jesus is never again subject to death; rather, death is forever now subject to him.

> For we know that since Christ was raised from the dead, he cannot die again; death no longer has mastery over him. (Rom 6:9 NIV)

The resurrection of Jesus Christ is eternal, it is permanent, for with his resurrection Jesus Christ has destroyed death.

What Does the Resurrection Prove?

Paul tells us if there was no resurrection, then Christians are to be pitied above all people (1 Cor 15:12–20). Why does he say this? The resurrection of Jesus Christ not only *proves* Jesus had no sin, but more importantly it *proves* what he did on the cross—the taking away of Adam's sin, the breaking of the power of that sin, the bringing of that entire sin to full completion and conclusion in his death—*worked*. It proves Jesus *succeeded* in his work on the cross. The resurrection is the final witness and proof of Jesus' victory over sin and death.

> But now he has reconciled you by Christ's physical body through death to present you holy in his sight, without blemish and free from accusation. (Col 1:22 NIV)

> And through him to reconcile to himself all things, whether things on earth or things in heaven, by making peace through his blood, shed on the cross. (Col 1:20 NIV)

> Having canceled the charge of our legal indebtedness, which stood against us and condemned us; he has taken it away, nailing it to the cross. (Col 2:14 NIV)

> Who being the brightness of *his* glory and the express image of his person, and upholding all things by the word of his power, when he had by himself purged our sins, sat down at the right hand of the Majesty on high. (Heb 1:3 NKJV)

> And you know that he was manifested to take away our sins, and in him there is no sin. (1 John 3:5 NKJV)

> But it has now been revealed through the appearing of our Savior, Christ Jesus, *who has destroyed death* and has brought life and immortality to light through the gospel. (2 Tim 1:10 NIV)

These verses affirm Jesus Christ accomplished his work upon the cross by breaking the power of sin and destroying death by bringing that sin to completion and conclusion in his death, resulting in forgiveness of sin to all. It is his resurrection which *affirms* that victory, which *proves* his accomplishment. This is why Paul tells us if we believe in Jesus Christ but do not believe he was resurrected, then we are to be pitied, we are fools, for if Jesus was not resurrected, then he was a sinner, and if he was a sinner, then he accomplished nothing upon the cross. But Jesus Christ was not a sinner, and the resurrection of Jesus Christ shows his victory over death, the full witness and expression of his triumph.

How Was it Possible to Be Resurrected?

How was the resurrection of Jesus Christ possible? Why was no one else prior to Jesus, or after him, resurrected? The Bible tells us the following:

> For the wages of sin is death, but the gift of God is eternal life in Christ Jesus our Lord. (Rom 6:23 NKJV)

> But God raised him from the dead, freeing him from the agony of death, because it was impossible for death to keep its hold on him. (Acts 2:24 NIV)

The Bible tells us clearly "the wages of sin is death"—death is the natural consequence, the only outcome of sin. Firstly, sin results in our *spiritual* death before God; this spiritual death is the real death which breaks our fellowship with God and leaves us separate from him.

Secondly, sin eventually results in our own *physical* death. The fact we start to physically decay after about age thirty or so is witness to the fact we have sin residing within us, in our flesh, in our blood, and ultimately that slow decay, that slow devouring of our physical selves, culminates in our physical death. Our physical aging and decay, and our eventual physical death, is witness to the fact sin is residing within us. The wages of sin, the inevitable result of sin, is death, both physical and spiritual.

But we are told death had no power over Jesus, that it was *impossible* for death to hold him. Even though Jesus physically died, it was impossible for Jesus to stay dead. Why is that? It is because Jesus *had no sin* residing within him, he had no sinful nature, due to the fact he did not have a human father. Because Jesus did not have a human father, he did not inherit the sinful nature, and so he was born without sin. Also, *Jesus never sinned*:

> God made him who had no sin to be sin for us, so that in him we might become the righteousness of God. (2 Cor 5:21 NIV)

> For we do not have a high priest who is unable to empathize with our weaknesses, but we have one who has been tempted in every way, just as we are—*yet he did not sin*. (Heb 4:15 NIV)

Jesus lived a completely sinless life. He never sinned in word, thought, or action. Because he never sinned, Jesus, in his life, *fulfilled* the righteous requirement of the law (Rom 8:1–4), and as a result of that he gained all power over both sin and death. By living a sinless life, both sin and death became subject to him. By never sinning, Jesus became Lord over death, and death therefore had no power over Jesus, for death is the result of sin, and if there is no sin, then death has no power.

Therefore, since Jesus was sinless in his life, even though he physically died, death could not keep him, it could not hold him. As a result, Jesus rose from the dead. By rising from the dead, Jesus showed he had conquered death, destroyed it, triumphed over it by his sinlessness and made death powerless.

> The last enemy to be destroyed is death. (1 Cor 15:26 NIV).

> When the perishable has been clothed with the imperishable, and the mortal with immortality, then the saying that is written will come true: "Death has been swallowed up in victory.
> Where, O death, is your victory?
> Where, O death, is your sting?"
> The sting of death is sin, and the power of sin is the law. But thanks be to God! he gives us the victory through our Lord Jesus Christ. (1 Cor 15:54–57 NIV)

> But it has now been revealed through the appearing of our Savior, Christ Jesus, who has destroyed death and has brought life and immortality to light through the gospel. (2 Tim 1:10 NIV)

Sin and death were defeated by the Second Adam in his life *and* upon the cross, and his resurrection is witness to that truth.

What Was Resurrected?

When Jesus was resurrected, what exactly was resurrected? Was it only his spirit come alive? Did he receive a new and different body upon his resurrection? The Bible is very clear—to be resurrected means the exact same *physical* flesh-and-bone body that died comes back to life.

Jesus was *not* resurrected as some sort of spirit, nor was he resurrected with a *different* physical body; rather, the body that rose from the dead was the exact same body that was crucified, that came from Mary's womb, that was descended from Adam's flesh and bone, that was made from the dust of this earth:

> The angel said to the women, "Do not be afraid, for I know that you are looking for Jesus, who was crucified. He is not here; he has risen, just as he said. Come and see the place where he lay." (Matt 28:5–6 NIV)

> But they did not believe the women, because their words seemed to them like nonsense. Peter, however, got up and ran to the tomb. Bending over, he saw the strips of linen lying by themselves, and he went away, wondering to himself what had happened. (Luke 24:11–12 NIV)

> Early on the first day of the week, while it was still dark, Mary Magdalene went to the tomb and saw that the stone had been removed from the entrance. So she came running to Simon Peter and the other disciple, the one Jesus loved, and said, "They have taken the Lord out of the tomb, and we don't know where they have put him!" So Peter and the other disciple started for the tomb. Both were running, but the other disciple outran Peter and reached the tomb first. He bent over and looked in at the strips of linen lying there but did not go in. Then Simon Peter came along behind him and went straight into the tomb. He saw the strips of linen lying there, as well as the cloth that had been wrapped around Jesus' head. The cloth was still lying in its place, separate from the linen. (John 20:1–7 NIV)

All of the Scriptures describing Jesus' resurrection are very clear—first Mary, and then the disciples, came to the tomb where Jesus was buried and they found *no body*. In fact, we are told the tomb was not actually empty; rather, what they found in the tomb were the burial cloth and linen Jesus' dead body had been wrapped in—the burial cloth and linen were there, but the body was not. The reason Mary and the disciples found no body upon reaching the tomb is because that same physical, flesh-and-bone, human body of Jesus, the same body that was crucified, that came from Mary's womb, and was buried within the tomb, was the same body that was resurrected.

Resurrected, Not Reincarnated

There are some who teach the resurrection body of Jesus was *not* the same body that was crucified and buried. Not only is this false, but such a teaching is heresy.

Jesus Christ is Incarnate God, God eternally and inseparably joined to Adam's *created* flesh and bone. When Jesus united himself with Adam's created humanity, that is the incarnation. There was only *one* incarnation. If Jesus Christ died and then rose again with a *different* body than the body of his incarnation, a body which was not the same body that was crucified or came from Mary's womb, then that means Jesus was *not* resurrected; rather, it means he was *re*-Incarnated, Incarnated a *second time*. Such a teaching is a teaching of reincarnation.

To say Jesus was *reincarnated* is absolutely unbiblical—it is both a heretical and blasphemous statement, and to teach that Jesus, upon his resurrection, was raised with a different body is to teach reincarnation. Jesus Christ was *not* reincarnated; rather, he was *resurrected*. To be resurrected means the exact same body that was born of Mary, crucified, and buried, the exact same body of the one and only incarnation, is the exact same body that was raised from the dead.

The Physicality of the Resurrection

After his resurrection, when Jesus appeared to the disciples, they were afraid and thought that they were seeing a ghost:

> While they were still talking about this, Jesus himself stood among them and said to them, "Peace be with you." They were startled and frightened, thinking they saw a ghost. He said to them, "Why are you troubled, and why do doubts rise in your minds? Look at my hands and my feet. It is I myself! Touch me and see; a ghost does not have flesh and bones, as you see I have." When he had said this, he showed them his hands and feet. And while they still did not believe it because of joy and amazement, he asked them, "Do you have anything here to eat?" They gave him a piece of broiled fish, and he took it and ate it in their presence. (Luke 24:37–43 NIV)

Jesus here specifically tells his disciples he is *not* a ghost, is *not* a spirit; rather, he is *flesh and bone*, is fully, *physically human*. He tells them to look at the nail scars on his hands and feet from being nailed to the cross. Jesus here specifically affirms his resurrected body is the *exact same physical human body* that was crucified upon the cross, bearing upon his resurrected body the scars of the crucifixion. When Jesus appeared to his disciples, Thomas was not among them, and later, when the disciples told Thomas they had seen the resurrected Jesus Christ, Thomas did not believe them;

> Now Thomas (also known as Didymus), one of the Twelve, was not with the disciples when Jesus came. So the other disciples told him, "We have seen the Lord!" But he said to them, "Unless I see the nail marks in his hands and put my finger where the nails were, and put my hand into his side, I will not believe." A week later his disciples were in the house again, and Thomas was with them. Though the doors were locked, Jesus came and stood among them and said, "Peace be with you!" Then he said to Thomas, "Put your finger here; see my hands. Reach out your hand and put it into my side. Stop doubting and believe." Thomas said to him, "My Lord and my God!" Then Jesus told him, "Because you have seen me, you have believed; blessed are those who have not seen and yet have believed." (John 20:24–29 NIV)

Once again, Jesus tells Thomas to physically put his fingers on the nail scars on his hands and put his hand into the scar on his side, where he was pierced by the spear while he was crucified. Thomas does so and sees this indeed was the same Jesus who was crucified. Thomas believes because, in touching the scars of Jesus, Thomas recognizes Jesus' resurrected body as being *the exact same body* that was crucified upon the cross. Jesus again here affirms his resurrected body is the exact same physical, flesh-and-bone human body that was crucified upon the cross. Jesus Christ is a resurrected *man*, a resurrected *human*, the resurrected *Incarnate* God/man, resurrected with the same flesh-and-bone human body with which he was born.

The Eternal Incarnation

The incarnation of Jesus Christ is eternal. Jesus did not become human for only thirty-three years and then, after his death, go back to being what he was before. Such a teaching is heresy, for it demeans the very person, the very nature, of Jesus Christ. Upon his incarnation, Jesus *remains human forever*—he will never again *not* be human for, as witnessed at his resurrection, he is resurrected and ascends into heaven as a flesh-and-bone *human being*. Jesus Christ is incarnate *forever*; he is *forever* God and man, eternally and inseparably made one.

Jesus consistently affirms his full resurrected humanity when he tells his disciples he is *not* a spirit, or a ghost, telling his disciples to *touch* and *feel* his *flesh*, his nail scars, his wounds suffered upon the cross (Luke 24:36–43). The resurrected Jesus Christ is a fully human *man*. Jesus ascended into heaven to sit at the right hand of God the Father as a resurrected *man*. He is there right now as a *human being*. When he returns at his second coming, he will be coming as a resurrected *man*. He will rule eternally, together with God the Father, as a resurrected *man*.

The humanity and divinity of Jesus Christ are inseparable, indivisible, and in fact are indiscernible from one another. His divinity and humanity have combined to form one completely new nature—an *eternally* incarnate nature that is simultaneously and forever 100 percent human and 100 percent God, a nature that is his alone. Jesus is fully human and fully God forever.

Although Jesus was equal with the Father before his incarnation, by becoming man he let go of his equality with the Father (Phil 2:6–8). He did not let go of that equality temporarily, for thirty-three years; rather, since his incarnation is eternal, he let go of that equality *forever*. Jesus will *never* again be equal with the Father. This is the real cost of our salvation.

Blood and the Resurrected Body

Throughout the Bible, blood is connected to sin, the shedding of blood to the forgiveness of sin. It seems certain that blood is not present in the resurrected body. Consider the following verses:

> Look at my hands and my feet. It is I myself! Touch me and see; a ghost does not have flesh and bones, as you see I have. (Luke 24:39 NIV)

> The man said, "This is now bone of my bones and flesh of my flesh; she shall be called 'woman,' for she was taken out of man." (Gen 2:23 NIV)

> But now stretch out your hand and strike his flesh and bones, and he will surely curse you to your face. (Job 2:5 NIV)

> I declare to you, brothers and sisters, that flesh and blood cannot inherit the kingdom of God, nor does the perishable inherit the imperishable. (1 Cor 15:50 NIV)

Since the children have flesh and blood, he too shared in their humanity so that by his death he might break the power of him who holds the power of death—that is, the devil. (Heb 2:14 NIV)

There are three unequivocal instances in the Bible where a human being is described as flesh and bone—Jesus Christ *after* the resurrection (Luke 24:39), Adam *before* the fall (Gen 2:23), and by Satan when talking with God about man (Job 2:5). Some translations have a few other instances of that phrase applied to a human being, but the above three instances are agreed upon by all translations.

The resurrected Jesus Christ specifically describes himself as being flesh and bone. Why does he not describe himself as being flesh and *blood*? We know he certainly was born of flesh and blood (Heb 2:14), and he shed his blood for the redemption of humanity. We also know his blood was precious (1 Pet 1:19) and it was holy and pure for he was without sin (2 Cor 5:21). Since Jesus certainly was born with blood, why then does he not describe his resurrected self as being flesh and blood; rather, specifically describing himself as being flesh and bone? Is it possible the resurrected Jesus had no blood?

Compare this to Adam's description of Eve (Gen 2:23). Adam here describes Eve, and by extension himself, as being flesh and bone. What is interesting to note is Adam is speaking these words *before* the fall. Why does Adam not describe his unfallen self as flesh and blood, but rather, describes himself as flesh and bone, just as Jesus described himself after his resurrection? We know the sinful nature is a physical thing that resides in our blood and which brings us mortality. Is it possible, before the fall, Adam had no blood? Is it possible blood, which carries within it the sinful nature, is in fact the *result* of the fall? If this is the case, then man, upon his original creation, would be a creature of flesh and bone, not a creature of flesh and blood, and blood would be a foreign element within man that resulted from the fall, the result of the habitation of sin.

Consider the third instance of the phrase "flesh and bone." It occurs in Job 2:5, but what is important to note is the speaker is Satan. Satan is here speaking to God about man, and Satan here describes man as "flesh and bone." Why does he not describe man as "flesh and blood?" Satan would have known the true created nature of man, so in speaking here with God is Satan describing man as man was created by God, created as a creature of flesh and bone, and not created as a creature of flesh and blood? Is he here describing the nature of man before being corrupted by sin and the fall?

Taken together, and especially when considered in conjunction with 1 Corinthians 15:50, we have very good reason to think Jesus *after* his resurrection had no blood, Adam *before* his fall had no blood, and man, in his original creation, was made a creature of flesh and *bone*, not flesh and *blood*. Blood would be a foreign substance introduced to humanity through the fall, carrying within it the sinful nature.

We Will Be Like Jesus

This is made very clear when we consider the resurrection and the inheritance of the kingdom of God. We know, of course, Jesus was resurrected. We also know all Christians, and all human beings, whether Christian or not, will be resurrected (1 Cor 15:12–13; Rev 20:4–5). We also know in our resurrection, we will physically be exactly like Jesus (Rom 6:5; 1 John 3:2). Therefore, if the resurrected Jesus is flesh and bone, and not flesh and blood, then that means that we also, in our resurrection, will be flesh and bone and not flesh and blood. The Bible clearly affirms flesh and blood *cannot* inherit the kingdom of God: "Now this I say, brethren, that flesh and blood cannot inherit the kingdom of God; nor does corruption inherit incorruption" (1 Cor 15:50 NKJV). This verse is clear—flesh and *blood cannot* inherit the kingdom of God. However, the Bible clearly tells us, repeatedly, resurrected Christians *will* inherit the kingdom of God (Eph 1:11; 1:18; 5:5, Col 3:24; Heb 9:15, 1 Pet 1:4, etc.). As a result, if flesh and blood *cannot* inherit the kingdom of God, and if resurrected Christians *will* inherit the kingdom of God, then we can say with certainty the resurrected Christians who inherit the kingdom of God will *not* be flesh and blood since 1 Corinthians 15:50 specifically tells us flesh and *blood* will not inherit the kingdom of God.

If resurrected Christians who inherit the kingdom of God will not be flesh and blood, then what will they be? Since Romans 6:25 and 1 John 3:2 specifically tell us that, in our resurrection, we will be exactly like Jesus, and since we know from Luke 24:39 Jesus describes his resurrected self as flesh and *bone*, we can say with certainty that, in the resurrection, Christians will also be flesh and bone, *not* flesh and *blood*. Therefore, it is certain the resurrected body will have no blood. Why will the resurrected body have no blood?

It seems certain the reason is because blood is where the sinful nature resides, and there is good reason to believe blood itself is in fact the result of the fall and was not part of the original creation of man.

As a result, the resurrection, by raising our bodies to life without blood, is removing from our fallen, corrupted bodies that which should not be there, removing the sinful nature from our bodies, resident in our blood, restoring our bodies to God's original intent for our physicality—a holy, uncorrupted humanity. This would be a perfect and physical fulfillment of the following verse: "Without the shedding of blood there is no forgiveness" (Heb 9:22 NASB). Without the presence of blood, no sin, and no sinful nature, will be present in our physical bodies. Our bodies will once again be pure and fully holy. This is the accomplishment of the resurrection—a total, physical redemption of humanity.

The Tree of Life and the Water of Life

If the resurrected body will have no blood, then does that mean the resurrected body will have no veins, since blood flows through our veins? Not necessarily, for it is very possible, even likely, that though blood will not be flowing through the resurrected body the nectar from the tree of life, or the water of life coming from God, will flow through us, inhabiting our bodies fully, giving us eternal life:

> Then the Lord God said, "Behold, the man has become like one of Us, to know good and evil. And now, lest he put out his hand and take also of the tree of life, and eat, and live forever." (Gen 3:22 NKJV)

> To him who overcomes I will give to eat from the tree of life, which is in the midst of the paradise of God. (Rev 2:7 NKJV)

> Blessed are those who do his commandments, that they may have the right to the tree of life, and may enter through the gates into the city. (Rev 22:14 NKJV)

> And he said to me, "It is done! I am the Alpha and the Omega, the Beginning and the End. I will give of the fountain of the water of life freely to him who thirsts." (Rev 21:16 NKJV)

> And the Spirit and the bride say, "Come!" And let him who hears say, "Come!" And let him who thirsts come. Whoever desires, let him take the water of life freely. (Rev 22:17 NKJV)

It is certain the resurrected body will be without blood. In fact, it seems that could be the very reason why there is a resurrection at all—it is by way of resurrection that God *physically* redeems his creation, fully redeems our physical humanity, by removing from our bodies the physical corruption of sin currently present in our bodies, present in our blood, inherited from Adam, thereby making our bodies to be what they were created to be—holy and uncorrupted. This removal of the sinful nature from our bodies, resident within our blood, is accomplished by way of the resurrection and by the removal of blood from the resurrected body.

The Perishable and the Imperishable

The Bible outlines a contrast between our current body and the coming resurrected body, as follows:

> But someone will say, "How are the dead raised? And with what kind of body do they come?" You fool! That which you sow does not come to life unless it dies; and that which you sow, you do not sow the body which is to be, but a bare grain, perhaps of wheat or of something else. But God gives it a body just as he wished, and to each of the seeds a body of its own. All flesh is not the same flesh, but there is one *flesh* of men, and another flesh of beasts, and another flesh of birds, and another of fish. There are also heavenly bodies and earthly bodies, but the glory of the heavenly is one, and the *glory* of the earthly is another. There is one glory of the sun, and another glory of the moon, and another glory of the stars; for star differs from star in glory. So also is the resurrection of the dead. It is sown a perishable body, it is raised an imperishable body; it is sown in dishonor, it is raised in glory; it is sown in weakness, it is raised in power; it is sown a natural body, it is raised a spiritual body. If there is a natural body, there is also a spiritual body. So also it is written, "The first man, Adam, became a living soul." The last Adam became a life-giving spirit. However, the spiritual is not first, but the natural; then the spiritual. The first man is from the earth, earthy; the second man is from heaven. As is the earthy, so also are those who are earthy; and as is the heavenly, so also are those who are heavenly. Just as we have borne the image of the earthy, we will also bear the image of the heavenly. (1 Cor 15:35-49 NASB)

Paul here contrasts what is called the "heavenly" body with the "earthy" body, telling us that the "earthy" body is our current fallen body, and the "heavenly" body is the resurrected body. He describes our current body as being "perishable," as well as "earthy," being sown (that is, dying) perishable but raised "imperishable." He describes our current body as being sown a "natural" body, but raised, or resurrected, as a "spiritual" body.

In this passage Paul illustrates his point by comparing the current body and the resurrected body with a seed and the grain into which it grows. He describes the body that is sown, the "earthy" body, as being like the seed, and the resurrected body as being like the grain that sprouts from the seed. The grain that sprouts from the seed is not different than the seed that is sown; rather, the grain that sprouts from the seed is in fact that same seed in full flower. He likens this to the natural, or "earthy," body and the resurrected body. In this illustration, just as the seed is sown in the ground, so the natural, "earthy" body is sown in the ground—it dies and is buried. Just as the seed then blooms and becomes the grain it was created to be, that same seed growing into that grain, so the natural earthy body becomes the body it was created to be—that same body becoming a sinless, uncorrupted holy body of flesh and bone. Paul tells us it is necessary for this current earthy body to first die in order to rise again and to become the body it was created to be. To be sown in "dishonor" means to be sown a sinful body, that is, a body with the sinful nature resident within the blood. To be raised in glory means the same body that was buried is now resurrected without sin, raised a holy, uncorrupted body of flesh and bone. He describes the body that dies, that is sown in the earth, as a "natural," or sinful, body, and he describes the body that is raised sinless as a "spiritual" body. It is important to remember this is always the same body—this is resurrection, not reincarnation, the same body that dies, that is sown in the earth, is the same body that rises from the dead—the difference is when the body rises from the dead, it rises without the sinful nature, without blood. Paul then goes on to specifically contrast being born of Adam with being born of Christ. He describes being born of Adam as being "earthy," while being born of Christ he describes as being "heavenly." By being born of Adam, we bear Adam's image, which is the earthy, or fallen, nature, whereas by being born of Christ we will now bear his mage, which is the heavenly, or sinless, nature. In each case, we are physical, flesh-and-bone human beings, the difference is from Adam we inherit the sinful nature, whereas when we are raised in the resurrection we will not have the sinful nature since we inherit Christ and his redemption. Since we will not have the sinful nature in our resurrected selves, we, in our bodies, will be imperishable, raised to sinless glory.

The Resurrection

But does the description of the sinful body as "natural" and "earthy," and the resurrected body as "spiritual" and "heavenly," mean the resurrected body is *not* flesh and bone, but is a *spirit* body? No, it does not, for we are to understand all of this in the context of Luke 24:39, where the resurrected Jesus describes himself specifically as *not* being a spirit, but rather, as being a flesh-and-bone human. We are to understand this in the context of Romans 6:25 and 1 John 3:2, which tell us our resurrected bodies will be just like Jesus' resurrected body—a human body that is *not* spirit but rather is a physical *human* body of flesh and bone. Even in 1 Corinthians 15:35-49, Paul affirms we, in our resurrection, will be like Jesus in his resurrection, for this is what is meant by bearing the image of the heavenly. We are also to understand this in the context of 2 Corinthians 5:2-5:

> We grow weary in our present bodies, and we long to put on our heavenly bodies like new clothing. For we will put on heavenly bodies; we will not be spirits without bodies. While we live in these earthly bodies, we groan and sigh, but it's not that we want to die and get rid of these bodies that clothe us. Rather, we want to put on our new bodies so that these dying bodies will be swallowed up by life. God himself has prepared us for this, and as a guarantee he has given us his Holy Spirit. (NLT)

Paul tells us in 2 Corinthians 5:3 we will *never* be spirits without bodies. Since we will never be spirits without bodies, what then does Paul mean when, in 1 Corinthians 15:44, he tells us the resurrected body will be a *spiritual* body? How are we to understand the contrast of the perishable with the imperishable, or the natural with the spiritual, as outlined in 1 Corinthians 15:42-44? Is this a contradiction?

It is not; in fact all of these verses affirm the same truth. In our resurrection, we will be exactly as was Jesus in his resurrection—physical human beings with human bodies of flesh and bone (Luke 24:39; Rom 6:25; 1 John 3:2), and we will *not* be spirits, as is specifically affirmed in 2 Corinthians 5:3. The perishable is the current human body which is inhabited by the sinful nature, residing in our blood. The imperishable is that same human body resurrected without the sinful nature, a body of flesh and bone rather than flesh and blood. The current body of flesh and blood is described as the natural body, whereas the resurrected body of sinless flesh and bone is what constitutes the spiritual body—spiritual because it is born of the resurrected Second Adam. To be *spiritual* does not mean to be *spirit*, since as 2 Corinthians 5:3-5 and Luke 24:39 clearly tell us, we will never be spirits without physical bodies. To be raised "a spiritual body" means we, in our resurrection, are raised with a *sinless* body, the same body that died and was sown in the earth, now raised sinless, without the sinful nature. This resurrection is possible because we are born of the Second Adam, the life-giving spirit, and by being born of the Second Adam we have our physical bodies redeemed. These redeemed bodies are described as "spiritual" since they are spiritually born, that is, they are born as the result of the life-giving Spirit of the Second Adam: "So also it is written, 'The first man, Adam, became a living soul. The last Adam became a life-giving spirit'" (1 Cor 15:45 NASB).

When we are born of the Second Adam, we are born of his Spirit, and so, our redeemed physical body, the ultimate result of that birth, is described as a spiritual body, since it is the result of a spiritual birth, the result of being born of the life-giving spirit that is the Second Adam, Jesus Christ. It is in this context that we are to understand the term "spiritual"—the "spiritual" body is the physically resurrected human body of flesh and bone, resurrected without blood and therefore without the sinful nature. This resurrection is made possible by the accomplishment of the Second Adam, by being born of his Spirit. The resurrected flesh and bone body is imperishable because it is raised without the sinful nature, and is therefore immortal—it can never again die, for sin no longer inhabits that body. In our resurrection, we will be exactly like Jesus in his resurrection—physical human beings with sinless bodies of flesh and bone.

The Resurrection of Nonbelievers

Human beings will never be spirits without bodies (2 Cor 5:3); we will forever be physical, flesh-and-bone human beings, just as was Jesus Christ upon his resurrection. This is true for *all* humanity, since the Bible clearly tells us *both* believers *and* nonbelievers will be resurrected (Rev 20:5).

The resurrection of nonbelievers is a striking truth. Since *all* human beings will be resurrected, including nonbelievers (Rev 20:5), then that means nonbelievers, who will be resurrected to face judgment and who will be cast into the Lake of Fire (Rev 20:15), will be in the Lake of Fire as *resurrected* human beings, meaning they will be in the Lake of Fire *without* the sinful nature. Even though they will be in the Lake of Fire, as resurrected human beings without the sinful nature they will have nothing to deceive them from the love and truth of God. This has profound implications for the ultimate destiny of nonbelievers as well as for our understanding of the full purpose of the Lake of Fire.

The Dominion of the Earth

In addition to breaking the power of sin upon the cross, Jesus, by the sacrifice of his life, also took back the dominion of the earth. The dominion of the earth was originally given to Adam by God. Adam was truly the lord, the ruler, of all the earth, having authority over all the land and over all of Earth's creatures. He was in every way the king of the earth. Eve, who was made from Adam, shared in this authority since she came from Adam and shared his nature.

However, when Adam sinned, not only did he receive the sinful nature, dying immediately before God and having both sin and death come to inhabit him, but in that act of disobedience he also, at the same time, gave away his dominion over the earth—he gave that dominion and authority over to Satan. Ever since Adam's fall, Satan has been the legal ruler of Earth. This is why in Luke 4:6-7, Satan shows Jesus all the kingdoms of the earth, and says he will give them to Jesus if Jesus will worship him, for those kingdoms have been given to him to do with as he wants: "And he said to him, 'I will give you all their authority and splendor; it has been given to me, and I can give it to anyone I want to. If you worship me, it will all be yours'" (Luke 4:6-7 NIV). Who gave these kingdoms to Satan? Who gave him their authority and dominion? It was given to him by Adam when Adam sinned.

When Jesus rose from the dead, accomplishing his work upon the cross, breaking the power of sin, taking away the sin of the world and bringing that sin to full completion and conclusion in his death, at that same time Jesus also *took back* the dominion over the earth that the First Adam had given away. In this way, the Second Adam *fully* redeemed the ruin brought on by the First Adam.

> And having disarmed the powers and authorities, he made a public spectacle of them, *triumphing over them by the cross.* (Col 2:15 NIV)

> And when he has come, he will convict the world of sin, and of righteousness, and of judgment: of sin, because they do not believe in Me; of righteousness, because I go to My Father and you

see Me no more; of judgment, because *the ruler of this world is judged*. (John 16:8–11 NKJV)

What does Jesus mean when he says the "ruler of this world is judged?" He says this in reference to his ascension to heaven to take his seat at the right hand of the Father. This verse tells us Satan, who became the ruler of the world upon Adam's sin and fall, is now judged by Jesus Christ and by his accomplishment upon the cross. To be judged by Jesus Christ and by his accomplishment upon the cross means, upon Jesus' resurrection, Satan is now no longer the legal ruler of the earth because Jesus took back the dominion over the earth that Adam had given away. Ever since Jesus' resurrection, Satan is on Earth *illegally*, for he has been judged and his authority taken away. Ever since the resurrection, Jesus is now the rightful ruler of the earth.

This is of profound importance, for this relates specifically to the second coming. The reason there is a second coming is Jesus Christ is returning to Earth to take what is now his. He is returning to claim his dominion over the earth. Ever since his resurrection, Earth, its dominion and all authority over it, now belongs to Jesus Christ, and only to him—it no longer belongs to Satan. Ever since the resurrection, Satan is here illegally, for he no longer has any right to this earth. Jesus will return at his second coming to take what is now rightfully his, to exercise his dominion and lordship over the earth. This lordship over the earth was accomplished by Jesus upon the cross and at his resurrection, for it was upon his resurrection, upon his accomplishment of redemption, Jesus took back from Satan the dominion of the earth.

Penal Substitution and the Dominion of the Earth

Penal substitution sees the cross as being only a place of punishment for the sins of humanity. Beyond that, penal substitution does not address the much bigger scope of the cross, of what the cross fully accomplished. Penal substitution does not address Jesus' reclamation of the dominion over the earth, yet this was a profound accomplishment of the cross.

Penal substitution also does not address the fact that, in addition to the salvation of all humanity and taking back the dominion of the earth, the cross also accomplished the full redemption of *all creation:*

> For the earnest expectation of the creation eagerly waits for the revealing of the sons of God. For the creation was subjected to

> futility, not willingly, but because of him who subjected *it* in hope; because the creation itself also will be delivered from the bondage of corruption into the glorious liberty of the children of God. For we know that the whole creation groans and labors with birth pangs together until now. (Rom 8:19–22 NKJV)

Romans 8:19–22 clearly tells us the very creation itself is awaiting the full revealing of humanity's redemption, for until that time, the creation remains subject to futility. This tells us the very redemption of the entire cursed creation is inextricably tied in with the salvation of humanity. As a result, since the very redemption of the entire cursed creation is inextricably tied in with the salvation of humanity, and since we know the salvation of humanity has been accomplished by the cross, therefore we know the redemption of the entire cursed creation is an accomplishment of the cross. Once again, there is nothing within the penal substitution teaching that in any way addresses, even remotely, this full scope of what the cross has accomplished, for in the penal substitution teaching the cross is only a place of punishment for sin, a place where the law is satisfied and where salvation is realized as a justification by the law. From every angle possible, the penal substitution teaching shows itself repeatedly as lacking, unbiblical, and false.

The cross did not just accomplish the forgiveness of sins, the taking away of humanity's sin, and the breaking of the power of sin, but it also accomplished the redemption of all things, the reclamation of the dominion over the earth, and the complete triumph of Jesus Christ over the enemy. All of this was accomplished by Jesus upon the cross and affirmed by his resurrection. The mechanism which made all of that possible, including the reclamation of the dominion of the earth, was the fact Jesus was the Second Adam. In his position as the Second Adam, Jesus fully redeemed every aspect of what the First Adam had caused—not just sin and the fall of humanity, but also the reclamation of dominion over all the earth.

The Father of a New Humanity

> So it is written: "The first man Adam became a living being"; the *last Adam, a life-giving spirit.* (1 Cor 15:45 NIV)

To be an Adam is to be a father of humanity. The First Adam was the physical father of all humanity, we are all his physical children, his physical descendants—he was the first father of us all: "Your *first father* sinned" (Isa 43:27 NKJV).

Just as Adam was the first father of us all, the physical father of all humanity, so the Second Adam, Jesus Christ, would become the Father of a new humanity, a redeemed humanity. As Adam's children, as his physical descendants, we are all born into Adam's sin, for his very blood, with his sinful nature, flows through our veins. We are the children of Adam by virtue of being physically born. But how do we become born of the Second Adam, Jesus Christ? We do this when we *believe* in him, partake of him, partake of his nature, and we are then born his children:

> It is the power of God that brings salvation to everyone who *believes*. (Rom 1:16 NIV)

> This righteousness is given through faith in Jesus Christ to all who *believe*. (Rom 3:22 NIV)

> When you *believed*, you were marked in him with a seal, the promised Holy Spirit. (Eph 1:13 NIV)

> Who is it that overcomes the world? Only the one who *believes* that Jesus is the Son of God. (1 John 5:5 NIV)

> If you declare with your mouth, "Jesus is Lord," and *believe in your heart* that God raised him from the dead, you will be saved. (Rom 10:9 NIV)

> For you have been *born again*, not of perishable seed, but of imperishable, through the living and enduring word of God. (1 Pet 1:23 NIV)

> Yet to all who did receive him, to *those who believed in his name*, he gave the right to *become children of God*. (John 1:12 NIV)

> The Spirit you received brought about your *adoption* to *sonship*. And by him we cry, *"Abba,* Father." (Rom 8:15 NIV)

> God sent his Son, born of a woman, born under the law, to redeem those under the law, that we might receive *adoption to sonship*. (Gal 4:4–5 NIV)

Believing—Our Free-Will Choice

Jesus Christ, God himself, is the way, the truth and the life (John 14:6). God has given us all an inviolable free will. Our free-will choice can either make us dead or make us alive. Lucifer and all the created angels were also given an inviolable free will, and likewise they also could exercise their free-will choice which had the power to make them dead or keep them alive.

When Lucifer chose himself over God, he, by his own free will, chose to separate himself from God. Since God is life, by choosing to separate himself from God, Lucifer was choosing to separate himself from life. As a result of separating himself from life, Lucifer's free-will choice resulted in his immediate death, by way of his immediate separation from God, for to be separated from God is to be separated from life, and to be separated from life is to be dead.

Likewise, when we sin, we choose ourselves over God, for choosing ourselves over God is the heart of all sin. As a result, when we sin, it is by our own free-will choice that we choose to separate ourselves from God. By separating ourselves from God, we are separating ourselves from life, for God is life. As a result, by separating ourselves from life, our free-will choice to sin leaves us dead.

In the same way, it is by our free-will choice we can be made alive. When we choose to believe in Jesus Christ, choosing to do so of our own free will, we are then choosing to *unite* ourselves with life. As a result, when we choose to unite ourselves with life by our free-will choice, the Holy Spirit himself then comes to us, unites us with himself, and in so doing makes us alive to God.

As a result, just as our free-will choice can make us dead, it can make us alive. When we choose to *believe* in Jesus Christ, we are exercising our free-will choice to unite ourselves with God, to unite ourselves with life, and by believing in Jesus Christ we are made alive.

The Truth—Our Free-Will Choice

Just as God is "the life," God is also "the truth." As a result, when we sin, choosing to separate ourselves from God, we then choose, by our own free will, to separate ourselves not only from life, but also from truth, for just as to separate ourselves from God is to separate ourselves from life, likewise we separate ourselves from truth. By separating ourselves from truth, we are left in the bondage of deception. As a result, by choosing to believe in Jesus Christ, the Second Adam, we are therefore choosing, of our own free will, to unite ourselves with truth. In so doing, the Holy Spirit himself then comes to us, unites us with himself and makes us alive to God, who himself is truth, resulting in the destruction of sin's power of deception in our lives. It is sin's power of deception which deceives us to think God does not love us but wants to harm or destroy us—all of which is a lie. By believing in Jesus Christ, by choosing to unite ourselves with truth, that power of deception is broken and truth now rules within us.

Adoption as Sons

Adam was the *created* son of God. Jesus was the *begotten* Son of God. Christians are the *adopted* sons of God. When any human being believes in Jesus Christ, that person is then born a child of God by way of the Holy Spirit coming into them and making them alive. And when this happens, the believer becomes an adopted son of God (the term "son" applies to both men and women, just as the term "bride," as in "bride of Christ," applies to both men and women). When we choose to believe in Jesus Christ, his Holy Spirit comes to take up residence within us, unites us with himself, and thereby makes us alive to God in our spirit. He unites us with life as well as truth, bringing to life that which our sinful nature had previously killed, which is our spirit, which is the means through which we have fellowship with God. The sin within us, within our flesh, within our blood, has killed our spirit, has made us dead to God, but when we believe in Jesus Christ, the Holy Spirit then comes to reside within us and makes our spirit alive to God so we can then have union and fellowship with God.

When we believe in Jesus Christ, we *appropriate* Jesus' accomplishment upon the cross for ourselves, which is the appropriation of his destruction of sin and death. As a result, when we believe and appropriate Jesus' accomplishment upon the cross, we appropriate his destruction of the power of sin and death, appropriating his destruction of sin's power of death, fear, and deception, which power then becomes broken within us, made powerless, and so we are left no longer subject, or slaves, to its power. When the Holy Spirit comes to reside in us after we believe in Jesus Christ, when he makes our spirits alive to God, this is described as being born again. It is at that moment of being born again God becomes our Father and we become his adopted children. The first time we are born is when we are born physically of our human parents, whereas the second time we are born is when we believe in Jesus Christ, when his Holy Spirit comes to dwell within us and makes our spirit alive to God and we are born God's child, it is our second birth from the Second Adam. This is how Jesus Christ becomes the Father of a new humanity—when we believe in him we are born of him, born of his nature, born of his Spirit.

This is why Jesus Christ is described as being a "life-giving spirit" (1 Cor 15:45). Jesus is a "life-giving spirit" because to be born a child of the Second Adam is to have our *spirit* be born of his Holy *Spirit*. The First Adam was our physical first father, the father of a fallen humanity, whereas the Second Adam, Jesus Christ, becomes the Father of a new, redeemed humanity, becoming our Father through his Holy Spirit. This occurs when we believe in him, a choice made of our own free will.

The resurrection of Jesus Christ, the Second Adam, is the proof that what Jesus did on the cross worked. By his accomplishment on the cross, Jesus broke the power of sin by taking upon himself the full sin of humanity, the full sin of the one man Adam, and bringing that sin to full conclusion and completion in his death, thereby making sin and death powerless. In doing so, Jesus conquered death, and by being born sinless and by remaining sinless in his life, Jesus took all authority over sin and death, and sin and death had no power over him. Jesus faced death head-on by dying, and after he died, death could not hold him, for he was without sin, and so, as a result, Jesus rose from the dead, affirming his eternal destruction of the power of death. It is also by the cross that Jesus, the Second Adam, took back the dominion of the earth, a dominion which he will claim at his second coming. The resurrection of Jesus Christ is the testimony and witness to his complete and total victory over sin and death, the testimony and witness to his accomplishment of the redemption of all humanity.

19

It is Finished

GOD IS A GOD of love, mercy, and forgiveness, and it is by the grace of God he allowed for a Second Adam, one who would redeem the fall of the First Adam. It is by the accomplishment of the Second Adam we can *receive* the *forgiveness* of our sins, a forgiveness given to us freely by God. Our sins have *never* been *paid for*, they have *never* been *punished*; rather, they have only been *forgiven*.

Adam was the created son of God, who was given one commandment, which he disobeyed. When Adam, our father, broke that commandment by eating from the fruit of the tree of the knowledge of good and evil, sin entered into him, a *physical* sinful nature took up residence in his blood, imbuing every cell of his human flesh. He passed on his blood to each of us, to every human being who would ever live, for it is Adam's blood which now flows through our veins. As a result, we all have the sinful nature residing in our blood, in our flesh, the sinful nature which we inherited from our human fathers. For this reason Paul describes our sinful nature as "the flesh."

This is why the shedding of blood is always connected with the *forgiveness* of sins, for in the shedding of one's blood there is a shedding of the sinful nature. However, by the shedding of one's blood there is also a physical death.

As a result, God began to unfold his plan of redemption, his plan to destroy the power of sin and death and to bring us to life. God's plan of redemption began by God himself providing and performing the first sacrifice for sin, in Eden, as a covering for sin, which represented forgiveness of sins. God then continued to unfold his plan of redemption with the institution of the office of high priest, as well as with the institution of a system of sacrifice that would allow for the temporary taking away and forgiveness of sins. These sacrifices were animal sacrifices. Animal sacrifices were suitable for the taking away of sin, for since animals are not descended from Adam, they do not have Adam's blood, and as a result of not having Adam's blood, they do not have Adam's sinful nature, so the blood of animals is sinless. However, since animals are not descended from Adam, an animal is not a moral being, and since an animal is not a moral being, an animal could therefore never conquer sin. As a result, the shedding of animal blood could never fully redeem what Adam had brought into the world, an animal sacrifice could never result in *permanent* redemption, *permanent* forgiveness, or the *permanent* breaking of the power of sin, only a temporary one. This entire sacrificial system was instituted by the grace of God to be a *picture* of the one redeeming sacrifice to come, the one sacrifice that *would* result in *permanent* redemption. None of the Old Testament sacrifices ever involved punishment for sin (Rom 3:25); they were always and only about the taking away of sin and the forgiveness of sin. The concept of a sacrifice being the recipient of punishment for sin does not exist in the Bible in any way whatsoever.

Adam was the father of the entire human race, and as such he and he alone passed on his sinful nature to all his children, to all humanity, through his blood. Subsequently, the sinful nature is passed on to human beings *only* by our human *fathers*, not by our human mothers. There has never been a single drop of new human blood added to humanity since Adam. *All* the blood of the *entirety* of humanity is *completely and only* the very same blood of our first father Adam—it is his blood that flows through our veins.

It was by the grace of God that a *Second* Adam would be born, a *Last* Adam, for there would never be another Adam after him. Whereas the First Adam was the created son of God, the Second Adam, Jesus Christ, was the *begotten* Son of God, and so, as a result, the Second Adam is God himself joined forever with Adam's created human flesh. This Second Adam was totally, fully, completely human, having the exact same and full humanity as the First Adam, but because he did not have a human father he did not inherit the sinful nature, for though his mother was human, his Father, the one who begot him, was God. The Second Adam was born without sin, without the sinful nature. As a result, he was in the exact same position before God as was the First Adam before the fall—perfect, sinless man.

Like the First Adam, the Second Adam also faced temptation, being tempted *directly* by the devil, which is something the devil was able to avoid with the First Adam in Eden. Whereas the First Adam was in the paradise of Eden with his wife, and had only one commandment to obey, the Second Adam was alone, in the desert wilderness, starving and physically broken, and could be tempted with *any* temptation, and could be tempted *three* times. It was there, in the desert wilderness, the Second Adam defeated the devil and conquered sin, for he resisted all temptation and did not sin.

After he defeated the devil in the desert, accomplishing victory over sin and gaining authority over it, the Second Adam now had to redeem the sin of the First Adam, which is the entire sin of all humanity. Every sin ever committed is born from the sinful nature residing in Adam's blood which permeates all humanity. The Second Adam had that same blood of Adam flowing in his veins, which he received from his human mother, but he did *not* have the sinful nature within his blood, because he did not have a human father—so the Second Adam's blood was precious, holy, and pure.

The Second Adam was also the High Priest of humanity, the representative of all humanity before God, in regards to sin. As the High Priest of humanity, the Second Adam had the authority to take the sin of the world, the entire sin of the First Adam, and lay it upon the sacrifice for that sin so as to take that sin away, to break its power, and to make possible the receiving of God's forgiveness.

Not only was the Second Adam the High Priest of humanity, but he himself was also the sacrifice for the sin of the world. As a result, he took the sin of the world, the entirety of the sin of the First Adam, and put it upon himself as he was sacrificed upon the cross. While on the cross, that sin of the world was literally and physically upon him, along with everything that came with that sin, which included the full death of the world before God. With the sin and the death of the world upon him (the death of the world being the separation of man from God), Jesus Christ himself fully experienced the pain, fear, deceit, and death of the sin that was upon him. As a result, by fully experiencing the death of the world, Jesus, upon the cross, experienced fully the separation from God that the world itself was experiencing. This is evidenced when Jesus cries out, "My God, My God why have You forsaken Me?," as he hangs upon the cross (Matt 27:46). When Jesus cried this out as he hung upon the cross, Psalm 22:24 specifically tells us God the Father did *not* turn his face away from him; rather, God the Father was fully with him, loving him, holding him, embracing him, hearing his cry and feeling his pain. Jesus' cry from the cross was the living witness that, at exactly that moment in time, the sin and the death of the world were fully upon him, and he was fully experiencing the separation from God that was the result of the death of the world being upon him.

While that sin of the world was upon him, the mechanism of sacrifice occurred. The sin of the world, the sin of the First Adam, which Jesus had taken upon himself as he hung on the cross, physically entered into and came to inhabit his own sinless blood, so Jesus was in fact "made to *be* sin" though he himself "knew no sin." As a result of the sin of the world coming to inhabit his own sinless blood, he came to bear the sin of the world *in* his own body, meaning he bore that sin *in* his own blood (1 Pet 2:24; 2 Cor 5:21; Col 1:20, 22). As that sin entered into his sinless blood, he shed his blood and, in so doing, *he died*. By his death, Jesus brought the entirety of the sin of the world that was within him to full completion and conclusion—he satisfied that sin's demand for *human* death, bringing that sin to fulfillment. By bringing the sin of the world to full conclusion and completion, he broke the power of that sin—breaking its power of deception (Heb 3:13) which deceives us into thinking God does not love us and will not forgive us; breaking its power of death (Rom 6:3) which makes us dead to God and separates us from him; and breaking its power of fear (Rom 8:15) which makes us run away from God, fearing his judgment and condemnation. The entirety of this power of sin was broken by Jesus Christ upon the cross by bringing the sin of humanity to full conclusion, completion, and fulfillment in his own death. Upon dying, and facing death head-on, he also destroyed, or conquered, death itself (2 Tim 1:10; Heb 2:14), as witnessed by his resurrection.

With the breaking of the power of sin and death, and with the breaking of its power of fear and deception, Jesus made it possible for all humanity to now come to the knowledge of God's love, God's forgiveness, and his salvation (Luke 1:77), for that power of sin, death, fear, and deception within us was the obstacle, or impediment, to enabling us to come to the knowledge of God's love for us and of his forgiveness. By Jesus breaking sin's power of death, fear, and deception, he removed the obstacle that was keeping us from knowing God's love and forgiveness, and as a result he made it possible for all humanity to come to *believe* in

Jesus Christ. By believing in him of our own free will, we then appropriate Jesus' accomplishment upon the cross, appropriate his breaking of the power of sin, and so, with that appropriation, the power of sin within us then becomes broken and powerless—all of this happens when we believe in Jesus Christ. By believing in Jesus Christ, choosing of our own free will to unite ourselves with him, with life, we are then born God's child, being born of his Holy Spirit, becoming one with life and truth, receiving his free forgiveness. This was the accomplishment of the cross. God does not need the cross to forgive us our sins; rather, it is *we* who need the cross in order to *receive* God's forgiveness.

In all of this, there was *never* any *punishment* for sin poured out upon Jesus Christ while he was upon the cross. The accomplishment of the Second Adam upon the cross was the complete *forgiveness* of all sins, *not* the *payment* of a *penalty* for sins, but the *forgiveness* of sins.

The teaching that Jesus Christ was punished by the Father for the sins of humanity while he hung upon the cross so as to pay a penalty to satisfy God's law is a false and unbiblical teaching which contradicts every aspect of the Bible. Our sins have *never* been *paid* for, for there was *never* any *penalty* to pay; rather, our sins have been forgiven.

Penal substitution, which states our sins have been punished because they required punishment, teaches we are justified solely by the *law*, that punishment was *necessary* to satisfy God's *law*, yet no such Scripture or teaching exists in the Bible. In fact, such a teaching completely contradicts the clear teaching of the Bible, which tells us *specifically* that no one is justified by the fulfillment of the law (Rom 3:20; Gal 2:16; 3:2; 5:4)—there is *no* justification by the law. Penal substitution is an unbiblical teaching that presents a God who is incapable of forgiveness.

Only Two Possible Conclusions of Penal Substitution

The teaching of penal substitution ultimately leads to only one of two possible conclusions, and both conclusions are a false gospel. One conclusion is *all* human beings will be saved, *regardless* of if they believe in Jesus Christ or not. That is to say it is *not necessary to believe in Jesus Christ* to have salvation. This conclusion is the result of the penal substitution teaching that God the Father punished Jesus for *all* the sins of humanity. If God has already punished *all* the sins of humanity so no sin has been left unpunished, then it would be an impossible injustice on the part of God to require a human being to be punished a *second time* for those same sins for which Jesus has *already been* punished. Yet, this is what penal substitution teaches, that, on the one hand, Jesus was punished for *all* the sins of the *entirety* of humanity, and one must *believe* in Jesus Christ in order to *participate* in that accomplishment.

But when considering those who do die unbelievers, a monstrous injustice arises. If someone does *not* believe in Jesus Christ, then according to the penal substitution teaching that unbeliever must be *punished*, or *pay the penalty*, for their sins since they did not accept Jesus' payment for their sins. This means the sins of unbelievers are punished *twice*. Also, in effect, it means Jesus' accomplishment on the cross was *not sufficient* for them. As a result, this double punishment for the same sins would be a great injustice on the part of God.

It is this inarguable injustice of double punishment, born of the penal substitution teaching, that has led to the teaching that all people will inherit salvation *regardless* of whether or not they believe in Jesus Christ, arguing that since Jesus paid the penalty for *all* sin, that means all sins have in fact been punished and paid for and cannot therefore be punished a second time, for to be punished a second time (i.e., the unbeliever being punished in hell for their own sin) would be a wretched injustice. Since such an injustice cannot be made by God, the conclusion is everyone will therefore automatically inherit salvation, *regardless* of whether they believe in Jesus Christ or not—*believing in Jesus Christ is not necessary for salvation*. Yet the Bible clearly tells us in order to have eternal life, we must *believe* in Jesus Christ: "For God so loved the world that he gave his only begotten Son, that whoever believes in him should not perish but have everlasting life" (John 3:16 NKJV). This teaching that belief is not a requirement for salvation is one of the two ultimate conclusions of the penal substitution teaching.

The second ultimate conclusion of the penal substitution teaching flows from the first. Recognizing that having the same sins punished twice would in fact be a monstrous injustice on the part of God, some proponents of penal substitution try to accommodate this injustice by the following teaching: Jesus Christ did *not* die for *everyone*, did *not* pay the penalty for *all* sin, and was *not* punished for the sins of *all* humanity. Rather, they teach Jesus Christ died only for *some*, was punished only for the sins of *some*, paid the penalty only for the sin of *some*, not all. This teaching states God does *not* love all people, but rather he has selected only *some* people for salvation, thereby damning the rest to eternal destruction.

This is a false gospel, a wretched, evil, and Satanic teaching born of the devil himself. Paul tells us clearly about the fate of those who teach such a false gospel: "But even if we or an angel from heaven should preach a gospel other than the one we preached to you, let them be under God's curse!" (Gal 1:8 NIV). The teaching that God loves only *some* people and not *all* people, that Jesus only died for *some* people, and not for *all* people, that only *some* can have salvation, and that salvation is *not* available for all, is in complete contradiction to both the very nature and character of God as well as to the entire Bible, as is blatantly made clear in 2 Peter 3:9: "The Lord is not slow in keeping his promise, as some understand slowness. Instead he is patient with you, *not wanting anyone to perish, but everyone to come to repentance*" (NIV). Second Peter 3:9 *specifically* tells us God does *not* want *anyone* to perish, but wants *everyone* to come to repentance, that is, he *wants* everyone to come to salvation in Jesus Christ. It is *God's will* that *all* come to salvation. This is inarguable. First Timothy further affirms this truth: "For this is good and acceptable in the sight of God our Savior, who desires all men to be saved and to come to the knowledge of the truth" (1 Tim 2:3–4 NKJV). We are also very clearly told in John 3:16: "For God so loved *the world* that he gave his only begotten Son, that *whoever* believes in him should not perish but have everlasting life" (John 3:16).

In John 3:16 it does *not* say God loved only *some* of the world, but that God loved *the world*. To say God loved *the world* means God loved *all* of the world. Also, John 3:16 does *not* say, "only those few chosen ones who believe in him" shall have eternal life; rather, it says *whoever* believes in him shall have eternal life—*whoever* means *anyone*, and is not restricted to a select few. The Bible is clear—Jesus Christ died for *all* people, and *everyone* has the chance to believe in him and have salvation. Any teaching that states Jesus Christ died only for *some* people, and not for *all* people, is a false gospel.

These then are the two ultimate and inescapable conclusions of the penal substitution teaching—either all people will have salvation without any requirement to believe in Jesus Christ, or Jesus died only for some people, and not for all people. Both teachings are false, yet each is the inescapable conclusion of the penal substitution teaching. But the reason both of these conclusions are false is because the premise upon which they are based is false. That premise is the teaching of penal substitution:

Jesus was punished by God the Father for the sins of humanity while he hung upon the cross.

Penal substitution, the teaching that Jesus Christ was punished by the Father for the sins of humanity while he hung upon the cross as a payment of the penalty all human beings owed to God's law, is a false teaching without any scriptural support that relies on the twisting of some Scriptures and the complete ignoring of others. It is a teaching that both demeans and defames the character of God. God is not a God of violence, death, and vengeance; rather, he is a God of love, mercy, and forgiveness, as is clearly outlined throughout the entire Bible. Salvation is not the result of the law being satisfied, of being justified by the law, but rather, it is the result of bringing the sin of the world to full completion and conclusion in the death of Jesus Christ, the breaking of its power and the resulting ability to be able to receive the forgiveness of sin. Jesus himself gives us a clear description of what he means by forgiveness (Matt 18:21–27), giving us an exact illustration of true forgiveness, just as Deuteronomy 15:1–11 likewise makes absolutely clear what it means to have one's debts canceled. To have one's debts *canceled* means those debts will *never* require payment (Deut 15:1–11); rather, by being *canceled* they are *forgiven* and remain forever *unpaid*. Likewise with our sins being *canceled*, having our sins, and their legal indebtedness, canceled (Col 2:14) means our sins have been forgiven, to remain *forever unpaid*. Both Matthew 18:21–27 and Deuteronomy 15:1–11 are teaching exactly the same thing.

God has *canceled* our sins (Col 2:14). To have our sins *canceled* means not only that our sins have *never* been *paid for* but also that they will *never require payment*. This is the love and mercy of God—he has *forgiven* us our sins; not punished them, but forgiven them. Jesus himself forgave people their sins before ever going to the cross (Mark 2:5; Luke 7:48). Jesus did not need the cross to forgive sins, he forgave people their sins because he can forgive sins, for he is a God of love and forgiveness. Yet the cross was still necessary—not necessary to allow God to forgive us our sins, for God does not need the cross to forgive us our sins, but rather, necessary for us to *receive* God's love and forgiveness, for the stumbling block to us receiving God's love and forgiveness was the power of sin. Jesus Christ, upon the cross, broke that power of sin, the power of the sinful nature within us which deceives us and causes us to fear God, to be dead to him, and to not recognize he loves us. By breaking that power of sin, its power of death, fear, and deception, Jesus removed the stumbling block which prevented us from recognizing God's love and forgiveness, thereby making it possible for us to be able to come to him and to *believe* in him, and, in believing, to *receive* God's love and forgiveness (Luke 1:77). By choosing to believe in Jesus Christ, who himself is the way, the truth, and the life (John 14:6), we are uniting ourselves with Jesus Christ; by uniting ourselves with Jesus Christ, we are uniting ourselves with life; and in doing so we are then born his children, set free from the power of sin and death.

Salvation is for *all* people, God loves *all* people, and it is God's will that *all* come to repentance and to salvation. But he has given us free will so we can choose our own course. Our free will is not a fiction, our free will is not an illusion; rather, our free will is real. Just as our free-will choice can lead to death, so can our free-will choice lead to life.

The grace of God is this, not that someone else received the legal punishment for our sins that the law required, which would make us justified only by the law, but rather, it is the grace of God that allowed for a Second Adam to come and redeem the ruin of the First Adam. This is the grace by which we are justified, the grace that allowed for a Second Adam to be born, the Second Adam who took upon himself the sin of the world, the sin of the First Adam, and brought that sin to full conclusion, completion, and fulfillment in his death. In so doing, he broke the power of sin and death over all humanity and made it possible for all to receive God's love and *forgiveness*, to be received by believing in him.

Our sins have never been punished, they have never been paid for; rather, our sins have been forgiven, they have been canceled, no payment required. It is the accomplishment of the cross that we are now free to come and receive the full forgiveness of our sins, a forgiveness freely given by God, given because he loves us.

www.ingramcontent.com/pod-product-compliance
Lightning Source LLC
Chambersburg PA
CBHW071231230426
43668CB00011B/1382